KU-618-519

CONTENTS

LONDON ✦ MEMPHIS ✦ SAN PEDRO

JUNE 2024   ISSUE 367

"The Yardbirds cast a very long shadow. They felt like a foretaste of the music that was on its way."

THE EDGE ON THE YARDBIRDS, P44

Gered Mankowitz/Iconic Images

Stepping up: Mdou Moctar seek justice, Albums, p90.

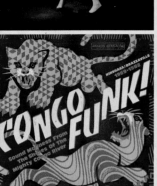

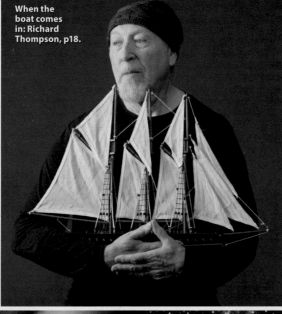

When the boat comes in: Richard Thompson, p18.

Growing pains: Beth Gibbons, Lead Album, p80.

MOJO

REGULARS

9 ALL BACK TO MY PLACE Madeleine Peyroux, J Mascis and Villagers' Conor O'Brien dig for musical treasure.

112 REAL GONE Steve Harley, Karl Wallinger, Eric Carmen and more, we salute you.

120 ASK MOJO What bands used the same name at the same time?

122 HELLO GOODBYE In six short weeks in '77, with his pals Ian McCulloch and Julian Cope, he helped create a Mersey legend. Pete Wylie recalls The Crucial Three.

WHAT GOES ON!

12 ANITA PALLENBERG She's the subject of a new documentary, based on her unpublished memoirs. But what does it tell us about this legendary rock'n'roll woman and her life with The Rolling Stones?

14 LOU REED He's been gone since 2013, but that goldmine canon gleams for ever. Now it gets a new polish with tribute LP *The Power Of The Heart*, and Lucinda Williams and Rufus Wainwright talk about the Lou they knew.

16 BUZZCOCKS Now led by the unsinkable Steve Diggle, the class-of-'76 punk heroes are limbering up for another LP. We get the full skinny on the 'Cocks' new directions.

18 RICHARD THOMPSON It's time to talk of melancholy, out-of-control musical peers and how best to let off steam. It must be the folk rock titan, Confidentially.

22 NIRVANA Charles Peterson took photos of Nirvana in their pomp. Now he collects the best of them, and 30 that have never been seen. Read on for an example, explanation and excitement.

MOJO FILTER

80 NEW ALBUMS Former Portishead singer Beth Gibbons' debut solo LP, plus The Lemon Twigs, St. Vincent, Kamasi Washington, T Bone Burnett, Jessica Pratt and Mdou Moctar.

94 REISSUES AC/DC: back in… gold vinyl, plus Sister Rosetta Tharpe, Air, *Ghana Special 2*, Broadcast, Sun Ra, Laibach and more.

108 BOOKS Bowie's key guitarist Earl Slick's memoir, plus Arthur Russell biography, a history of UK electronic music and more.

MOJO ISSN 1351-0193 (USPS 17424) is published 12 times a year by H Bauer Publishing Ltd, Media House, Peterborough Business Park, Lynch Wood, Peterborough PE2 6EA United Kingdom. Airfreight and mailing in the USA by agent named World Container INC 150-15, 183rd St, Jamaica, NY 11413, USA. Periodicals Postage Paid at Brooklyn, NY 11256. POSTMASTER: Send address changes to MOJO, Air Business Ltd, c/o World Container INC 150-15, 183rd St, Jamaica, NY 11413, USA. Subscription records are maintained at Bauer Media, Subscriptions, CDS Global, Tower House, Sovereign Park, Lathkill Street, Market Harborough, Leicester LE16 9EF, United Kingdom. Air Business Ltd is acting as our mailing agent.

THIS MONTH'S CONTRIBUTORS INCLUDE...

Victoria Segal
Victoria interviews Leyla McCalla (see p40) and reviews the new Beth Gibbons LP. Victoria met Beth on Portishead's 1997 US tour: the singer sweetly dodged interviews but she did lend her roller skates to Victoria, letting her whizz round NYC's Hammerstein Ballroom while the band soundchecked. Best roller-disco ever!

Christoph Dallach
When journalist Christoph decided to explore "Kraut" with his book Neu Klang, Tangerine Dream mastermind Edgar Froese agreed to be interviewed for it – but sadly left this planet before they could meet. Christoph's encounters with other Tangerine Dreamers are extracted from p58.

Brian Aris
Brian, whose photos of Kate Bush and Scott Walker adorn this issue, snapped in war zones from Lebanon to Vietnam before shooting the stars of music, including The Beatles, the Stones, The Clash, Roxy Music, Debbie Harry's *KooKoo* cover and the Iman/Bowie wedding. For his portfolio and prints, go to brianaris.com.

Ben Giles, David Kaptein

4 MOJO

FAT WHITE FAMILY
FORGIVENESS IS YOURS

THE NEW ALBUM   LP / CD / DL   26.04.04

FAT WHITE FAMILY ARE BACK WITH THE MOST SOPHISTICATED,
VITAL AND FLAMBOYANT CREATION OF THEIR CAREER

MOJO WORKING! THE UK R&B EXPLOSION!

THE YARDBIRDS
MANFRED MANN
GENO WASHINGTON
BLUES INCORPORATED
& MORE

MOJO

1 THE BETTERDAYS
DON'T WANT THAT

The West Country's punchy answer to the Stones, The Betterdays' own website notes how they were "banned for playing 'unusual' music from Plymouth's ballrooms". The quintet – originally known as the Saints Beat Combo – chose not to relocate to London, but did release this one superb single in 1965, before re-forming in the 1990s. A garage rock nugget, ripe for rediscovery.

Written by Pitcher. Publisher – Copyright Control ℗1965 The Betterdays ISRC Code – GBBLY2200686 Licensed courtesy of Cherry Red Records Ltd.

2 MANFRED MANN
BRING IT TO JEROME

The sometime Mann-Hugg Blues Brothers were already pop stars by the time their debut album, *The Five Faces Of Manfred Mann*, landed in 1964. No hit singles like 5-4-3-2-1 featured on it, though, with the emphasis on tougher, groovier covers – like this pulsating take on a 1955 Bo Diddley B-side.

Written by Jerome Green and published by Arc Music Corp/Tristan Music Ltd ℗1964 The copyright in this sound recording is owned by East Central One Limited. ISRC: GBAYE6400633. www.eastcentralone.com

3 SCREAMING LORD SUTCH & THE SAVAGES
THE TRAIN KEPT A-ROLLIN'

A standby of British R&B repertoires, this 1965 version of Train Kept A-Rollin' comes from rock'n'roll eccentric Lord Sutch, taking a break from horror-fare such as Jack The Ripper – and from his attempts at a political career leading the Official Monster Raving Loony Party.

Written by Bradshaw/Mann/Kay. Published by Peter Maurice Music Co Ltd ℗1965 Rollercoaster Records Ltd. From *Sutch A Loony – What A Guy!* – RCCD 3067

4 THE GRAHAM BOND ORGANIZATION
GOT MY MOJO WORKING

Another tune in heavy rotation on the scene – and an obvious must for inclusion on this comp – Got My Mojo Working is here given the once-over by Hammond ace Graham Bond and a mighty line-up of his Organization: Dick Heckstall-Smith on sax; and the future Cream rhythm section, already frictional, of Ginger Baker and Jack Bruce.

Written by Morganfield. Jewel Music Pub. Co Ltd 3:08. ISRC: DED466500051

9 GENO WASHINGTON & THE RAM JAM BAND
RIDE YOUR PONY (LIVE)

"From Indiana USA, Britain's own soul brother" Washington was in the USAF stationed in East Anglia when he was spotted in a local club. Within a year The Ram Jam Band were bringing supercharged revue moves to the UK scene; Dexys, among others, were suitably inspired.

Written by Naomi Neville. Burlington Music Co Ltd ℗1966 Sanctuary Records Group Ltd., a BMG company Licensed courtesy of BMG Rights Management (UK) Ltd GBAJE0600392

10 THE MIKE COTTON SOUND
HARLEM SHUFFLE

Another American in East Anglia, Bruce McPherson Lucas fronts this sinuous version of the Bob & Earl classic. Cotton's career began as a trad jazzer trumpeter in the 1950s, before he reoriented his band towards R&B. By the 1970s, Cotton had forged a strong connection with The Kinks, leading their horn section on *Muswell Hillbillies* and beyond.

Written by Relf, Nelson. Publisher – BMG Rights Management (UK) Ltd ℗1966 Mike Cotton ISRC Code – GBBLY1500803 Licensed courtesy of Cherry Red Records Ltd

11 DOWNLINERS SECT
BE A SECT MANIAC

If many mid-'60s R&B upstarts had a proto-punk aggression to their sound, few were quite so raw and snotty as the deerstalker-sporting Downliners Sect. Exhibit A: this relentlessly brutal appropriation of the Bo Diddley beat that closed 1964 debut album *The Sect*. A cult band from the start, both Rod Stewart (who frequently guested with the band) and Steve Marriott were aspiring – though ultimately unsuccessful – candidates to join.

Written by Collier. Ivy Music Ltd. / Campbell Connelly and Co. Ltd. 1.59 ISRC: DED466400071

12 THE ARTWOODS
IF I EVER GET MY HANDS ON YOU

Another Rod connection here, as The Artwoods were led by the titular Arthur 'Art' Wood, brother of Face/Stone Ronnie. Also in the ranks on this flipside to their 1964 debut: keyboardist Jon Lord, some years before he founded Deep Purple; and Keef Hartley, previously employed as Ringo Starr's replacement in Rory Storm & The Hurricanes.

Written by Hawker, Shakespeare. Publisher – Peermusic (UK) Ltd ℗1964 Peer-Southern Productions Ltd ISRC Code – GB7GZ1400052 Licensed courtesy of Cherry Red Records Ltd.

Tony Gale/Alamy, Courtesy of Mike Weston, Mirrorpix/Alamy Stock Photo, Jeremy Fletcher/Getty, Pictorial Press Ltd/Alamy Stock Photo (4), CA/Redferns/Getty, Doug McKenzie/Hulton Archive/Getty image

David Redfern/Getty, GAB Archive/Getty, Getty (2)

"**M**ANIC *ACCELERANDO*," IS WHAT THE YARDBIRDS' FIRST manager, Giorgio Gomelsky, called it; the rave-up, the way his protean band would bend rhythm'n'blues into radical new shapes. As The Yardbirds blazed a trail across London – from Eel Pie Island to the Crawdaddy Club, from Studio 51 to the Marquee – their sound got wilder and more untethered from its roots.

They were not, of course, alone. *MOJO Working!: The UK R&B Explosion!* captures a crucial mid-'60s moment, as a generation of blues scholars, dashing young Mods and garage rock tyros let rip. It's the sound of the British beat boom becoming louder, feistier, crazier, manifesting a proto-punk spirit before psychedelia sent bands off on a very different freak-out. Future legends are here in putative form – not least Eric Clapton, setting Chuck Berry's Too Much Monkey Business on fire. But these 15 tracks also contain scene godfathers like Cyril Davies and Alexis Korner, alongside bands whose careers were much shorter, if no less incendiary. "We really whipped up the audience," remembers Yardbirds drummer Jim McCarty – and now you can bring that frenzy back home.

5 THE SYNDICATS
CRAWDADDY SIMONE

Londoners The Syndicats are mostly remembered as being the first group to feature Yes's first two guitarists, Peter Banks and Steve Howe. On this B-side to their final single, however, the string-bending disruptor is Ray Fenwick, adding avant edge to an underground garage classic – encouraged, no doubt, by producer Joe Meek.

Written by Fenwick/Williams. Publisher – Ivy Music (Music Sales) ISRC Code – GBYDR6600012 ℗ 1965 Ray Fenwick licensed to Another Planet Music. Licensed courtesy of Cherry Red Records Ltd.

6 THE BOYS BLUE
YOU GOT WHAT I WANT

Cavernous drums now, heralding the sole single from Coventry freakbeat pioneers The Boys Blue. When their 1965 breakthrough tour supporting Chuck Berry was cancelled, they had to return all their new gear, and disbanded soon after. Another Coventry band, The Sorrows, released their own very similar, better-known, version of the song a year later.

Written by Dallon. Publisher – Cherry Red Songs ℗1965 Cherry Red Records Ltd ISRC Code – GB23E1100958 Licensed courtesy of Cherry Red Records Ltd

7 THE YARDBIRDS
TOO MUCH MONKEY BUSINESS (LIVE)

Talking of Chuck Berry, here are The Yardbirds in full flight with one of their most uninhibited versions of Berry's 1956 single. Too Much Monkey Business comes live from London's Marquee Club in the summer of 1964, a couple of months after the release of their first single, I Wish You Would. Note the remarkable amount of guitar pyrotechnics Eric Clapton manages to pack into its breathless three-minute duration.

Written by Chuck Berry. Jewel Music Pub Co Ltd 3.02. ISRC: DED462000058

8 THE ALAN BOWN SET
HEADLINE NEWS (LIVE)

A former Hamburg Star-Club attraction and John Barry sideman, Alan Bown formed his Set in 1965, firing up Mod crowds with their energetic takes on the latest US soul hits. This version of an early Edwin Starr single also comes live from the Marquee, via a split 1966 album with Jimmy James & The Vagabonds.

Written by Al Hamilton/Charles Hatcher/Richard Morris. Tro Essex Music Ltd ℗1966 Sanctuary Records Group Ltd., a BMG company Licensed courtesy of BMG Rights Management (UK) Ltd GBAJE0607478

13 BO STREET RUNNERS
SHAME, SHAME, SHAME

This menacing Jimmy Reed cover is from the west London band's first EP (an extension of their debut 7-inch), of which only 99 copies were pressed and sold at gigs. A year after it was released, the band recruited an auspicious new drummer – Mick Fleetwood, en route to The Bluesbreakers and, eventually, Fleetwood Mac.

Written by Reed. Publisher – Tristan Music Ltd ISRC Code – GBBLY1404637 ℗1964 Bo Street Runners under licence to Cherry Red Records Ltd Licensed courtesy of Cherry Red Records Ltd.

14 ALEXIS KORNER'S BLUES INCORPORATED
STORMY MONDAY

Formed in 1961 by Korner and Cyril Davies, Blues Incorporated provided an invaluable R&B finishing school for Charlie Watts, Bruce and Baker, Graham Bond and many more. This 1964 T-Bone Walker cover features Danny Thompson on bass.

Written by T Bone Walker. Concord Copyrights UK/ Copyright Control ℗2006 Alexis Korner Enterprises Ltd under exclusive licence to Sanctuary Records Group Ltd., a BMG company Licensed courtesy of BMG Rights Management (UK) Ltd. GBAJE6400114

15 CYRIL DAVIES AND HIS RHYTHM & BLUES ALL STARS
COUNTRY LINE SPECIAL

Davies left BI in 1962 and formed his R&B All Stars including, very briefly, Jimmy Page. Page was gone by the time they recorded their debut EP in February 1963, but that's Nicky Hopkins on piano, tracking Davies' spectacular harmonica wailing. A year later, Davies was dead.

Written by Cyril Davies. Warner Chappell Music International Ltd. ℗1963 Sanctuary Records Group Ltd., a BMG company. Licensed courtesy of BMG Rights Management (UK) Ltd GBAJE6300036

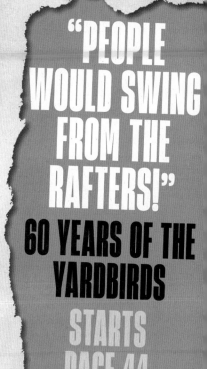

"PEOPLE WOULD SWING FROM THE RAFTERS!"

60 YEARS OF THE YARDBIRDS
STARTS PAGE 44

BLACK DEER

★ FESTIVAL of AMERICANA ★

"One of the most culturally eclectic and rewarding festival experiences in the UK" - The Independent

14TH –16TH JUNE 2024 ERIDGE PARK, KENT

JOE BONAMASSA UK FESTIVAL EXCLUSIVE ★ SHERYL CROW

SEASICK STEVE ★ HERMANOS GUTIÉRREZ ★ THE SHIRES

COURTNEY BARNETT ★ WARD THOMAS ★ THE STAVES ★ VILLAGERS

BC CAMPLIGHT ★ DYLAN GOSSETT ★ JALEN NGONDA ★ DAMIAN LEWIS

BESS ATWELL ★ TURIN BRAKES ★ JJ GREY & MOFRO ★ NICK WATERHOUSE

DALE WATSON & HIS LONESTARS ★ ELI PAPERBOY REED ★ THE DELINES

FERRIS & SYLVESTER ★ KEZIA GILL ★ DYLAN LEBLANC ★ LIZZIE NO ★ TWINNIE

ZANDI HOLUP ★ NAT MYERS ★ MICHELE STODART ★ JARROD DICKENSON

ALYSSA BONAGURA ★ CVC ★ PRIMA QUEEN ★ ÁINE DEANE ★ DIVORCE

HOLLY MACVE ★ MUIREANN BRADLEY ★ BRÒGEAL ★ ARNY MARGRET

LUKE FLEAR ★ HENRY WEBB-JENKINS ★ CLARA MANN ★ SAMUEL NICHOLSON

MORE ARTISTS TO BE ANNOUNCED SOON

BLACKDEERFESTIVAL.COM

CAMPING - YOUNG FOLK ADVENTURES - CUSTOM MOTORCYCLES & TRUCKS - DJS
'LIVE FIRE' - BBQ ARENA - SMOKEHOUSE COOKING - DEMOS & MASTERCLASSES WITH RENOWNED CHEFS

Madeleine Peyroux

JAZZ VOICE (EN ROSE)

What music are you currently grooving to?
Fantastic Negrito's *White Jesus Black Problems*. It's about his own ancestors, a black man who was enslaved from Africa and a white woman from Ireland, who was an indentured servant. The songs are very thoughtful and humanistic.

What, if push comes to shove, is your all-time favourite album?
What would I listen to over and over, and not make me crazy? **John Coltrane**'s *Infinity*.

What was the first record you ever bought? And where did you buy it?
I bought **Tracy Chapman**'s Talkin' 'Bout A Revolution in a record store in downtown Manhattan. It wasn't my first record – when I was a little kid, I had the soundtrack to a '30s cartoon of Gulliver's Travels, I listened to that record over and over again.

Which musician, other than yourself, have you ever wanted to be?

Bob Dylan. I wanted to be the one that wrote Blowin' In The Wind, Idiot Wind, I wanted to have that experience, ha ha! But I gave up. I decided I wasn't gonna be Bob Dylan.

What do you sing in the shower?
The truth is, I do my vocal exercises. I make siren noises – like an ambulance, not like a Greek spirit.

What is your favourite Saturday night record?
Saturday night means it's time for a party with friends, and I want to hear (Night Time Is) The Right Time by **Ray Charles**. Then, you can go anywhere.

And your Sunday morning record?
One of the things that I love to listen to, and it changed my life, is **Marian Anderson**, the contralto, singing spirituals. I don't want to take away from religion, but I think that her music has got all of the information already in it.

Madeleine Peyroux's Let's Walk is out on June 28 via Thirty Tigers.

ALL BACK TO MY PLACE

THE STARS REVEAL THE SONIC DELIGHTS GUARANTEED TO GET THEM GOING...

Conor O'Brien

VILLAGER PERSON

What music are you currently grooving to?
David Hedderman's debut album *Pulling At The Briars* is a real beauty. I'm biased – I produced it – but I keep returning to it. Also, **Dory Previn**'s *Mythical Kings And Iguanas* has been in my ears a lot. I stopped drinking and started going to the gym and I've found that my favourite workout music tends to be narrative-based folk stuff for some reason; the weirder the better usually.

What, if push comes to shove, is your all-time favourite album?
It always changes… I keep returning to *Homogenic* by **Björk**… it's just so

beautiful. Or *Amnesiac* by **Radiohead**. I'm a '90s/noughties kid, but sometimes it feels more like **Nina Simone** …*And Piano!* or *Once Upon A Time In The West (Original Motion Picture Soundtrack)* by **Ennio Morricone**.

What was the first record you ever bought? And where did you buy it?
A cassette tape of *Mellow Gold* by **Beck** with my pocket money from Golden Discs in Stillorgan, County Dublin. The world was never the same again!

Which musician, other than yourself, have you ever wanted to be?
I'm jealous of bass players and drummers. I wish I didn't have the urge to sing but it's unavoidable.

What do you sing in the shower?
I don't because it's usually morning time and I haven't had my coffee. Sometimes I listen to early demos of unfinished songs.

What is your favourite Saturday night record?
Congratulations by **MGMT**. They're a weird hybrid of all my favourite music. They're kind of shallow and deep at the same time; it's kind of trippy, genius stuff, but it's a little bit silly, much like life itself. I like good chords on a Saturday night.

And your Sunday morning record?
A Rainbow In Curved Air by **Terry Riley**. That's a great one. I'm also digging *And In The Darkness, Hearts Aglow* by **Weyes Blood**. It feels like Sunday melancholy bliss.

Villagers' That Golden Time is out on May 10 on Domino.

J Mascis

DINOSAUR JR'S ÉMINENCE GRISE

What music are you currently grooving to?
I'll go with **The Tubs**, **Naima Bock**, **Porridge Radio** and, you know, whatever. There's old stuff too. **Ron Wood**'s first album is always a favourite.

What, if push comes to shove, is your all-time favourite album?
I'll just go generic and say **The Rolling Stones**' *Exile On Main St.* I've been listening to it since I was like 11 years old or something and I'm always finding new things in it that I like. It's magical that way.

What was the first record you ever bought? And where did you buy it?
It was like in a department store, K-Mart or something. I think it was *15 Big Ones* by **The Beach Boys**. Brian Wilson's, like, staring out from the cover… I don't know why I picked it, it said 'hits' I guess. I was probably eight years old.

Which musician, other than yourself, have you ever wanted to be?
I really like **Fred Cole** from Dead Moon. I liked the way he lived – he could build things, you know, like

building guitars, building his house, he made his own records. He was very self-sufficient, and I can't do anything like that, so I've looked up to him. And he had a music store, which I fantasise about, but I don't think I'll ever have one.

What do you sing in the shower?
Guided By Voices' Echos Myron. A good shower melody. It sticks with you, and comes out when the water's flowing.

What is your favourite Saturday night record?
I'd go for *Machine Gun Etiquette* by **The Damned**. The bass at the beginning of Love Song is good for kicking off the evening, when you're hanging with friends.

And your Sunday morning record?
Seed Of Memory by **Terry Reid** is a good Sunday kind of thing. I probably won't do too much. Go for a bike ride, maybe.

J Mascis's What Do We Do Now is out now on Sub Pop.

> "The Damned's Love Song is good for kicking off the evening."
> **J MASCIS**

Ebru Yildiz, Jeffrey Fowler, Andrew Whitton

MOJO

H Bauer Publishing
The Lantern
75 Hampstead Road
London NW1 2PL

Tel: 020 7437 9011
Reader queries: mojoreaders@
bauermedia.co.uk
Subscriber queries: bauer@
subscription.co.uk
General e-mail: mojo@
bauermedia.co.uk
Website: mojo4music.com

Editor
John Mulvey
Senior Editor
Danny Eccleston
Creative Director
Mark Wagstaff
**Production Editor
(Entertainment)**
Simon McEwen
**Associate Editor
(Reviews)**
Jenny Bulley
**Associate Editor
(News)**
Ian Harrison
Deputy Art Editor
Del Gentleman
Picture Editor
Matt Turner
Senior Associate Editor
Andrew Male
Contributing Editors
Phil Alexander,
Keith Cameron,
Sylvie Simmons

**Thanks for their help with
this issue:** Keith Cameron,
Chris Catchpole,
Ian Whent.

This month's contributors:
John Aizlewood, Martin Aston,
Mike Barnes, Mark Blake,
Glyn Brown, John Bungey,
Keith Cameron, Chris Catchpole,
Stevie Chick, Andy Cowan,
Christoph Dallach, Grayson Haver
Currin, Max Décharné, Bill DeMain,
Tom Doyle, David Fricke, Andy Fyfe,
Pat Gilbert, Will Hodgkinson,
David Hutcheon, Jim Irvin,
David Katz, Andrew Male,
Bob Mehr, James McNair, Lucy
O'Brien, Mark Paytress, Andrew
Perry, Clive Prior, Jon Savage,
Victoria Segal, David Sheppard,
Michael Simmons, Sylvie Simmons,
Mat Snow, Irina Shtreis, Ben
Thompson, Kieron Tyler, Charles
Waring, Lois Wilson, Jim Wirth.

This month's photographers:
Cover and inset: Brian Aris,
Jorgen Angel, Clive Arrowsmith,
Gail Butensky, Fin Costello, Steve
Emberton, Koh Hasebe, Gered
Mankowitz, David Markey, Rick
McGinnis, Chris Moorhouse, Abe
Mora, Chris Scheurich, Naomi
Petersen, Charles Peterson, Andrew
Phillips, Barry Plummer, Michael
Putland, Gai Terrell, Rob Verhorst.

MOJO SUBSCRIPTION HOTLINE
0185 8438884
For subscription or back issue queries contact
CDS Global on Bauer@subscription.co.uk
To access from outside the UK
Dial: +44 (0)185 8438884

Theories, rants, etc.

MOJO welcomes correspondence for publication.
Write to us at: MOJO, H Bauer Publishing, The Lantern, 75 Hampstead Road,
London, NW1 2PL. E-mail to: mojoreaders@bauermedia.co.uk

THE HALF MOON PUB IN PUTNEY, SOUTH London, has seen some pretty special musical performances over the years. The summer of 1977, for instance, found it hosting an artist whose theatrical pretensions and grandiose ambition would dominate British music over subsequent decades.

Besides Steve Harris and his early line-up of Iron Maiden, though, the KT Bush band also played the Half Moon that summer, on June 3. It's one of the many strange details of Kate Bush's career that over 47 years she's essentially played three 'tours': 2014's 22-night residency at the Hammersmith Apollo; 1979's two-month Tour Of Life; and roughly a dozen dates around June 1977, taking in various London pubs – The Black Cat, Catford! The White Hart, Tottenham! – as well as a Sunday afternoon out-of-town gig at Tiffany's nightclub in Harlow.

In Tom Doyle's exceptional cover story this month, we uncover these first tentative manoeuvres of Kate Bush: from compulsive pre-teen songwriter, through David Gilmour's mentoring, to Wuthering Heights superstardom and a trio of albums where her vision, authority and self-belief would become ever more prominent. Still, though, this fleeting pub rock phase in the high summer of punk intrigues. What did her version of Honky Tonk Women sound like? Did she shoot the band and audience at the climax of James And The Cold Gun every night? And were you lucky enough to be at any of the shows? Memories, please, to the usual address.

JOHN MULVEY, EDITOR

Darling, it's wonderful. But isn't it very painful?

I was at the Butthole Surfers ULU gig mentioned in issue 365. My first time seeing them and also my first date with a hardcore American woman who had seen them a few times before. They were truly amazing, but after watching the back-projected genital surgery film I flat out fainted, and came round in the foyer with my date fanning my face. Surprisingly I didn't get a second date and I never saw the Butthole Surfers again.
Paul Deighton, Great Malvern

I haven't paid to see anything in years

Loved the Steely Dan article [MOJO 365]. I was fortunate to see them at Leeds University in 1974. I'd just started my first job after leaving school in June, aged 16. My first week's wage was £12 and from that I bought *Countdown To Ecstasy* (£1.99). They kicked off the gig with Bodhisattva and, although it's nearly 50 years ago (that's frightening), I remember thinking this is a bit more grown-up than T.Rex! I recall Skunk Baxter took a bottle of Newcastle Brown from an audience member, took a large swig, handed it back and then threw up at the side of the stage a few minutes later. If memory serves me right, the tour was shortened due to illness. Surely not some dodgy Newky Brown?
Michael Dunham, Leeds

You had me fired! Damn you! Damn you! Damn you!

Thanks for the long overdue and detailed acknowledgement of the career of Steely Dan [MOJO 365]. On the whole, it's hard to disagree with the majority of songs on the list, even if the ranking is somewhat flawed. Nevertheless, exception must be taken with the inclusion of a number of songs. First and foremost Things I Miss The Most. This throwaway ditty suffers from the lack of melody that blighted much of DF's later solo work. Replace it with Jack Of Speed from *Two Against Nature* – The Dan's last GREAT song. Another curious choice is Sign In Stranger; a fine track, but it pales next to the lush jazziness of The Caves Of Altamira or the brooding menace of *The Royal Scam*'s title track. Similarly, the slight Only A Fool Would Say That should be dispensed with in favour of the poignant Brooklyn (Owes The Charmer Under Me) from the same LP, or the elegant Your Gold Teeth II from *Katy Lied*. Finally, there's the mindboggling choice of Barrytown from *Pretzel Logic*. Yes, it's a fine collegiate hipster put-down of a backward pissant burg, but it's patently inferior to the contemplative blues-shuffle of that album's title track.

However, the major objection is why only 30 songs? If I recall correctly, The Beach Boys and Lou Reed both got 50 songs. This injustice is underscored by the recent ruminations in your excellent publication on the longest run of classic LPs by a single artist/band. You suggest Stevie Wonder. His run from *Music Of My Mind* to *Songs In The Key Of Life* makes five brilliant successive releases. Led Zeppelin beat that with their first six LPs. The Dan, meanwhile, produced NINE consecutive masterpieces, if you include the first three 'solo' LPs (*The Nightfly*, *11 Tracks Of Whack* and *Kamakiriad*). Certainly, this ennead of classic LPs featured none of the filler that blighted almost all of the Fab Four's LPs. The only band that comes close to the Dan in terms of sustained excellence is Rush with their octet of tours de force from *2112* to *Power Windows*.

Paul Hunt, Nottingham

If a guy can be enough things in this business, he can make a living

The Liam Gallagher/John Squire interview in MOJO 365 understandably made reference to Oasis and The Stone Roses. However, I would've liked to have heard what John and Liam now think of the 1997 Seahorses LP *Do It Yourself*. Obviously the first Roses LP is iconic, but *DIY* featured a great set of mainly Squire-penned songs, sung by the underrated Chris Helme.

Gordon Barclay, via e-mail

…In the movie Shaun Of The Dead, the two main characters go through a collection of LPs and decide which ones to throw at zombies. Dire Straits, Prince's *Batman* soundtrack and Sade's *Diamond Life* become projectiles, but they spare *Second Coming*. That's right – the second Stone Roses album. The one that everybody seems to hate.

That movie is from 2004. Ten years after the LP's release. In December it'll be 30 years old, and I say it's about time that LP gets a second chance. Yes, I admit it's not nearly as great as the debut. Yes, it came too late. Yes, the title is way too arrogant. Yes, there are songs on it I always skip. But try listening without thinking about its painful creation. Try listening as if it's new and don't compare it to what came before. I think almost any artist would be very proud to release

something that good. It deserves more love – here's hoping that thought spreads.

Dennis Ewald, Heerlen, The Netherlands

I can hear the jingle in the box office

The Blues Brothers movie [MOJO 364] opened in Milwaukee at a drive-in theatre. John Belushi had been in town recently to see Delbert McClinton at Summerfest, when he noticed an unfinished piece of interstate highway that ended abruptly in mid-air. Cut to the final car chase of the film: Elwood and Jake are tearing around downtown Chicago, trying to make their escape. Suddenly the downtown buildings switched from Chicago to Milwaukee, and everyone at the drive-in began joyously blowing their horns. When the car with the neo-Nazi leader flew off the road's end, the laws of physics were blithely ignored and somehow it landed 90 miles to the south, back in Chicago, as we all laughed uproariously. That's entertainment!

Jym Mooney, Milwaukee

He asked of us all forgiveness

I'm stunned Kieron Tyler got so much factual information wrong about Scott 'Top Ten' Kempner in writing his remembrance [MOJO 364]. While Scott was a co-founder of The Dictators, Andy Shernoff was – and still is – the band's principal songwriter. Top Ten's rhythm guitar provided the power and the sparks that fuelled that band's fury, but he didn't blossom as a songwriter until he formed The Del-Lords in the early '80s. Second, Scott's participation in the re-formed Dictators, not the band itself, was curtailed due to the rapid progression of the frontal lobe dementia that eventually took his life. The Dictators are putting the finishing touches on a new LP and are supporting The Damned on several shows across the US this spring. The band was definitely not curtailed by his illness – in fact, it was Scott who championed the band's re-formation. I appreciate MOJO would take the time to remember his contributions, but one expects more from a magazine that does so much to keep rock'n'roll journalism alive. Scott subscribed to MOJO for decades and truly cherished every issue he ever got. He preserved them all in pristine condition – he was that much of a fan.

Rich Nesin, via e-mail

This is one I've never seen before

As a long-time buyer of MOJO, I suppose it had to happen some time. The quotes on the letters page [MOJO 366] are from a film I've watched countless times, Singles, set in Seattle during the time of grunge and featuring the acting talents of Pearl Jam's Eddie Vedder, Stone Gossard and Jeff Ament as (fictitious) local band Citizen Dick. Also notable for Matt Dillon's excellent hair and live performances from the likes of Soundgarden and Alice In Chains. What do I win?

Ian Rankin, Edinburgh

Head of Magazine Media
Clare Chamberlain
MD Bauer Media Advertising
Simon Kilby
Head Of Magazine Brands Anu Short
Brand Director Joel Stephan
Media Planner Ricky Duff
Regional Advertising Katie Kendall
Classified Sales Executive
Imogen Jackaman
Inserts Manager Simon Buckenham
Production Manager Carl Lawrence
**Sales Operations Executive,
BMA Finance** Helen Mear

Co-CEOs of Bauer UK Print Business
Helen Morris, Steve Prentice
EA to CEOs Vicky Meadows
**Chief Financial Officer, Bauer
Magazine Media UK** Lisa Hayden
EA to CFO Stacey Thomas
**Publisher, Premium and
Entertainment** Lauren Holleyoake
Group Production Lead Jenny Croall
PA to Publisher Tayla Todd
Commercial Director - Entertainment
Gemma Dick
Commercial Marketing Director
Liz Martin
Managing Editor Michelle Thorn
Editorial Assistant Whitney Jones
**MOJO CD and Honours Creative
Director** Dave Henderson
Senior Events Producer
Marguerite Peck
Business Analyst Tracey Pickering
Marketing Manager Sarah Norman
Marketing Executive Madeleine
Munro-Hall
Direct Marketing Manager Julie Spires
Direct Marketing Assistant
Holly Aston
Printing: William Gibbons
Subscription queries: To contact us about subscription orders, renewals, missing issues, back issues or any other queries, please email bauer@subscription.co.uk or call our UK number on 01858 438884. To manage your account online visit https://secure.greatmagazines.co.uk/Solo For enquires on overseas newsstand sales e-mail kristina.koshevaya@seymour.co.uk

No part of the magazine may be reproduced in any form in whole or in part, without the prior permission of H Bauer Publishing. All material published remains the copyright of H Bauer Publishing and we reserve the right to copy or edit any material submitted to the magazine without further consent. The submission of material (manuscripts or images etc) to H Bauer Publishing, whether unsolicited or requested, is taken as permission to publish that material in the magazine, on the associated website, any apps or social media pages affiliated to the magazine, and any editions of the magazine published by our licensees elsewhere in the world. By submitting any material to us you are confirming that the material is your own original work or that you have permission from the copyright owner to use the material and to authorise H Bauer Publishing to use it as described in this paragraph. You also promise that you have permission from anyone featured or referred to in the submitted material to it being used by H Bauer Publishing. If H Bauer Publishing receives a claim from a copyright owner or a person featured in any material you have sent us, we will inform that person that you have granted us permission to use the relevant material and you will be responsible for paying any amounts due to the copyright owner or featured person and/or for reimbursing H Bauer Publishing for any losses it has suffered as a result. Please note, we accept no responsibility for unsolicited material which is lost or damaged in the post and we do not promise that we will be able to return any material. Finally, whilst we try to ensure accuracy of your material when we publish it, we cannot promise to do so. We do not accept any responsibility for any loss or damage, however caused, resulting from use of the material. For syndication enquiries go to: syndication@bauermedia.co.uk H Bauer Publishing is authorised and regulated by the FCA (Ref No. 845898). Distributor: Frontline, 1st Floor, Stuart House, St Johns Street, Peterborough PE1 5DD. Tel: 01733 555161. H Bauer Publishing is a company registered in England and Wales with company number LP003328, registered address The Lantern, 75 Hampstead Road, London, NW1 2PL. VAT no 918561701 COMPLAINTS: H Bauer Publishing is a member of the Independent Press Standards Organisation (www.ipso.co.uk) and endeavours to respond to and resolve your concerns quickly. Our Editorial Complaints Policy (including full details of how to contact us about editorial complaints and IPSO's contact details) can be found at www.bauermediacomplaints.co.uk

Bauer Media Group abc

recycle
When you have finished with this magazine please recycle it.

ipso Regulated

SAVE MONEY ON NEWSSTAND PRICES!

AND GET MORE FROM MOJO WITH A SUBSCRIPTION!

BECOME A SUBSCRIBER AND GET EXCLUSIVE REWARDS AND CONTENT

SEE PAGE 26 FOR DETAILS…

MOJO MAKES A GREAT GIFT!!!

SAVE £££ OFF COVER PRICE!

Just A Shot Away

A new **Anita Pallenberg** documentary presents her libertine life and centrality to the Rolling Stones. Plus! **Prince Stash**.

"**I**'VE BEEN CALLED a witch, a slut and a murderer," wrote Anita Pallenberg in the memoir composed during the sober years before her death at 75 in 2017. Now, that unpublished script – titled, with typical defiance, Black Magic – forms the basis of a two-hour documentary, Catching Fire: The Story Of Anita Pallenberg. It hits British cinemas this month.

Inevitably, as First Lady of The Rolling Stones, the doc weaves the personal with the musical. There's her testy 18-month relationship with her doppelganger Stone, Brian Jones. Then the union with Keith Richards from 1967 to 1980. Raw testimony from the pair's children, Marlon and Angela, off-screen contributions from Richards, plus Pallenberg's own observations shed new light on these years.

Given the Richards' family's blessing, the documentary is rich in home movie footage including a cape-wearing Pallenberg dancing freely in a garden and film of the Mick'n'Marianne/Keith'n'Anita getaway to South America at Christmas 1968. But it's Pallenberg's candid recollections, voiced by Scarlett Johansson, that form the spine of the film.

Prince Stanislas Klossowski de Rola – popularly known as Prince Stash – first met her in Paris in 1964 and appears in the film. "Anita could be ruthless and relentless when she wanted something or someone," he tells MOJO. Once 'rescued' from Jones by Richards in spring 1967, Keith recounts that he was initially "bewildered [by] her absolute determination to be… free. Anita just wanted to kick it all over."

During their earliest days together, Pallenberg says, "Keith was so shy." It was her "Italian energy" and eye for Bohemian style that transformed him into "a lion".

"I loved the feeling of culture exploding," Pallenberg says as the film traces her pre-Stones years. She discovers that her great-grandfather was Symbolist painter Arnold Böcklin, who specialised in "bestial satyrs and sleeping nymphs". Stash, a scion of master painter Balthus, tells MOJO that she and he, "shared this whole debauched, libertine lifestyle. The Stones were bourgeois by comparison! Anita brought all that to the Stones."

She also inspired several songs, including Mick Jagger's You Can't Always Get What You Want and Richards' You Got The Silver. As the film reveals, dynamics between Pallenberg and Richards, now parents, changed by the early '70s, when she realised that his music came first. Heroin seemed "like a solution", says the voiceover.

We also learn that, after the sudden death of Jones in 1969, Pallenberg found herself putting pictures of him all around the house. She also disliked the word 'nice' and wasn't big on 'help' either. But after attending AA meetings and rehab in her mid-forties, she graduated from Saint Martins in textiles and fashion, made a return to acting and, feted by superfans like Kate Moss, to the catwalk. "She found her true self," says Moss. Pallenberg even found herself portraying the Queen in Harmony Korine's 2007 movie Mister Lonely, both convincingly and subversively.

"What I loved about Anita," Richards concludes, "was how she operated. [There was] almost an innocence about it even in its most Machiavellian form!"

The final word, of course, is Anita's. "Keith's no angel. But neither am I." *Mark Paytress*

Catching Fire: The Story Of Anita Pallenberg, directed by Alexis Bloom and Svetlana Zill, is released by Dogwoof in UK and Irish cinemas on May 17. anita.film

Honky tonk woman: Anita Pallenberg with the Stones' Keith Richards, Cannes, May 1967; (right) Prince Stash in '67; (left) stills from Catching Fire.

"The Stones were bourgeois by comparison to Anita!"
PRINCE STASH

Reporters Associes/Gamma-Rapho via Getty Images, JRC/The Hollywood Archive/Alamy

Wild sides: (left) Lucinda Williams and (right) Rickie Lee Jones give their hearts to (centre) Lou Reed.

LUCINDA, RICKIE LEE AND MORE SALUTE LOU REED ON *THE POWER OF THE HEART*

THE NUMEROUS album tributes to the late Lou Reed have often taken The Velvet Underground route. Not for Bill Bentley, the Texas-based writer, one-time Sterling Morrison bandmate, Reed's US publicist from 1988 to 2004 and producer of tributes to Roky Erickson, Skip Spence and Doug Sahm. Eleven of the 12 covers he's assembled on *The Power Of The Heart* are devoted to the great man's solo years. "I was missing not having Lou in my life," Bentley explains. "I missed his spirit. So, I started this record."

Those paying tribute include Rickie Lee Jones, Joan Jett, Lucinda Williams, Rosanne Cash, The Afghan Whigs, Bobby Rush, Angel Olsen and – the last to be asked – Keith Richards, who donates a grizzled I'm Waiting For The Man, the sole VU cover. "You don't say no to Keith!" says Bentley. "But it's fitting, because they were contemporaries back in the day."

The first to commit was Jones, turning Walk On The Wild Side into a sensual barfly vamp. "I didn't think anyone could cover Walk On The Wild Side, but Rickie took it to another place," says Bentley. "That's what you want in a cover. Lucinda, too, blew my mind with her originality."

Lucinda Williams, who swings, country-style, through Legendary Hearts, only met Reed once, backstage at one of his LA shows. "I was working up a version of [VU classic] Pale Blue Eyes at the time," she says. "Lou wrote the chords down for me, which was a sweet moment." Williams later invited Reed to join her on-stage in New York. "Lou couldn't make it, but he said we would have sung Legendary Hearts together, and I never forgot that."

Of all the voices paying tribute, Rufus Wainwright – who breathes new life into Perfect Day – knew Reed best. After Reed appeared at 2008's Wainwright-McGarrigle family Christmas shindig, the pair became close. "Lou could be a little cold, and ornery," Wainwright reflects, "but the truth is, if he admired you and wanted you in his life, you were in for life." Perfect Day, he contends, "is Lou's

"Perfect Day... it's Lou's Somewhere Over The Rainbow!"
RUFUS WAINWRIGHT

most lyrical song – it's his Somewhere Over The Rainbow!"

Bentley occasionally offered suggestions, such as pairing soul man Bobby Rush and Sally Can't Dance, "because of its funky rhythm. Lou loved his soul and R&B, and if I hadn't found someone from that world, he would have haunted me!" Bentley thinks Reed "would have been OK" with a tribute album, but wasn't a fan of the format. When Bentley asked Reed to cover a Roky Erickson song, "He said, 'Billy, I won't, but you can have one of my songs to put on it.' He just followed his own light. Even if it meant losing his audience. He'd tell me, 'Don't let anyone tell you what you can't do.'"

Bentley is not finished yet either. He heard that Bob Dylan liked Reed's Doin' The Things That We Want To, but attempts to include him failed; David Byrne was game but ran out of time; and he's desperate to include Reed's wife Laurie Anderson. "That's all for Volume Two," Bentley promises.

Martin Aston

The Power Of The Heart: A Tribute To Lou Reed is released by Light In The Attic on April 20.

GIMME FIVE... UNITS OF MEASUREMENT

T. Rex
One Inch Rock
(FLY, 1970)

Re-recorded electrically from its freak-folk Tyrannosaurus Rex version, Marc Bolan and Mickey Finn play warbling rock'n'roll with scat-singing about what sounds like a Lewis Carroll trip: "I got the horrors 'cos I'm one inch tall."

Dr. Feelgood
Twenty Yards Behind
(UA, 1975)

Jumping New Orleans R&B, via Canvey Island, with a trailing Wilko Johnson recounting how his baby looks so fine she causes car accidents, makes traffic lights turn blue and even sends a steam roller out of control. Sterling Brilleaux gob iron work.

Edwin Starr
Twenty-Five Miles
(GORDY, 1969)

A soulful Romeo has to walk over dale and hill to see his girl, despite tiredness, aching feet, etc. The writers had to give Bert Berns and Jerry Wexler a co-writing credit because it sounded so much like Wilson Pickett's Mojo Mamma.

Stevie Wonder
Heaven Is 10 Zillion Light Years Away
(TAMLA, 1974)

Stevie makes a bold, if mathematically questionable, claim about the whereabouts of the Hereafter, to reflective Moogy funk. Then states that we need God now, and why can't hate be 10 zillion light years away?

Stereolab
Parsec
(DUOPHONIC, 1997)

The 'Lab's homage the astronomical unit (equal to 3.26 light years, or 19.2 trillion miles!) in their tasteful drum and bass phase, with French organ and Swingle voicings. "You were eternity," sings Lætitia, "now you're just the past." Minds blown, twice.

Danny Clinch, Timothy Greenfield-Sanders, Astor Morgan

AEG PRESENTS

DEEP PURPLE

WITH SPECIAL GUESTS
REEF

=1 MORE TIME TOUR

NOVEMBER 2024

MON	4TH	BIRMINGHAM RESORTS WORLD ARENA
WED	6TH	LONDON THE O2
THU	7TH	LEEDS FIRST DIRECT ARENA
SAT	9TH	MANCHESTER AO ARENA
SUN	10TH	GLASGOW OVO HYDRO

AXS.COM | TICKETMASTER.CO.UK | DEEPPURPLE.COM

AEG PRESENTS IN ASSOCIATION WITH UTA

AEG PRESENTS

SEASICK STEVE

A TRIP A STUMBLE
A FALL DOWN ON YOUR KNEES

UK TOUR 2024

SATURDAY 9 NOVEMBER
SOUTHAMPTON O2 GUILDHALL

SUNDAY 10 NOVEMBER
NOTTINGHAM ROYAL CONCERT HALL

TUESDAY 12 NOVEMBER
CAMBRIDGE CORN EXCHANGE

THURSDAY 14 NOVEMBER
BATH FORUM

SATURDAY 16 NOVEMBER
MANCHESTER ALBERT HALL

SUNDAY 17 NOVEMBER
GLASGOW O2 ACADEMY

TUESDAY 19 NOVEMBER
WOLVERHAMPTON THE HALLS

THURSDAY 21 NOVEMBER
LONDON O2 SHEPHERD'S BUSH EMPIRE

AEGPRESENTS.CO.UK AXS.COM
TICKETMASTER.CO.UK SEETICKETS.COM
AEG PRESENTS • FRIENDS BY ARRANGEMENT WITH WME

A TRIP A STUMBLE A FALL SEASICK STEVE DOWN ON YOUR KNEES

NEW ALBUM OUT 07 JUNE

---

elbow
AUDIO VERTIGO
ARENA TOUR 2024

PLUS SPECIAL GUESTS **W AE V E**
(GRAHAM COXON & ROSE ELINOR DOUGALL)

MAY 2024

SOLD OUT	BRIGHTON Centre	11	GLASGOW OVO Hydro
09	LONDON The O2	12	LEEDS First Direct Arena
10	BIRMINGHAM Resorts World Arena	14	MANCHESTER Co-op Live
		15	NOTTINGHAM Motorpoint Arena

ELBOW.CO.UK | AEGPRESENTS.CO.UK | AXS.COM | TICKETMASTER.CO.UK | SEETICKETS.COM   AEG PRESENTS IN ASSOCIATION WITH X-RAY

JOURNEY
50TH ANNIVERSARY

VERY SPECIAL GUEST
Cheap Trick
Cheap Trick

FREEDOM TOUR • UNITED KINGDOM 2024

WED	30 OCT	CARDIFF UTILITA ARENA
THU	31 OCT	NOTTINGHAM MOTORPOINT ARENA
SAT	02 NOV	GLASGOW OVO HYDRO
FRI	08 NOV	MANCHESTER AO ARENA
SAT	09 NOV	LEEDS FIRST DIRECT ARENA
MON	11 NOV	LIVERPOOL M&S BANK ARENA
WED	13 NOV	BIRMINGHAM UTILITA ARENA
SAT	16 NOV	NEWCASTLE UTILITA ARENA
SUN	17 NOV	LONDON THE O2

AEGPRESENTS.CO.UK / AXS.COM / TICKETMASTER.CO.UK / SEETICKETS.COM

AEG PRESENTS BY ARRANGEMENT WITH CAA

ROCK & ROLL HALL OF FAME INDUCTEES

Heart
ROYAL FLUSH TOUR 2024

WITH SPECIAL GUEST
Squeeze

JULY 2024

MON 01 LONDON THE O2
WED 03 BIRMINGHAM UTILITA ARENA
FRI 05 NOTTINGHAM MOTORPOINT ARENA
SAT 06 MANCHESTER AO ARENA
MON 08 LEEDS FIRST DIRECT ARENA
TUE 09 GLASGOW OVO HYDRO

HEART-MUSIC.COM AEGPRESENTS.CO.UK

AEG PRESENTS

> ## "You can't recreate the past, but you can create the future."
> **STEVE DIGGLE**

Close shave: Buzzcocks' Steve Diggle is "in the fast lane now."

industrial estate in Tottenham," says Diggle. "There's a realism to it, you feel like The Velvet Underground in New York!"

The studio also boasts a desk built by German production legend Conny Plank which, says Diggle, was used by Eno, Bowie and Bob Marley. Guitarist Mani Perazzoli may also join for the sessions. "I think [2022 LP] *Sonics In The Soul* was like a bridge album," says Diggle, "where we had all the ingredients you know about Buzzcocks, but it moved on with little twists and turns. Hopefully with his one, we can turn it upside down. You can't recreate the past, but you can create the future."

Songs will include Heavy Street, which Diggle calls "a great heavy funk dub track… about having your phone nicked and being stabbed in the street," while Queen Of The Scene concerns the personality-disordering effects of modern celebrity and media overload. "There's a big power ballad as well," says Diggle, "a story about a girl called The Greatest Of Them All. Imagine if the Small Faces had a stadium anthem." He intends to use a £20 second-hand Bontempi organ. Might Conny Plank's desk lend Deutsche kosmische flavours? "I wouldn't mind metronomic drumming so you can drive along to it, Autobahn-style," says Diggle, "but with guitars, rather than the bleeps.

"I'm in the fast lane now," he continues. "You can see the end of life in some ways. I love being in the studio, so to have *not* doing that hanging over you adds a bit intensity to it."

Is he thinking of Shelley, wonders MOJO? "It breaks my heart and I wish he was still here," he says, "but you cannot live your life just thinking about that. You've got to keep moving, otherwise I'd be in a fucking lunatic asylum. He would have carried on and done what he was doing. Anyway, I'll be seeing him before I know it!"

Something else he's done is a new memoir: co-written with Simon Goddard, Autonomy: Portrait Of A Buzzcock arrives in August. "It's my rock'n'roll journey," says Diggle. "Hopefully it'll be an inspiration for a working-class kid, that things can happen in your life."

Ian Harrison

FACT SHEET
Title: TBC
Due: TBC
Production: TBC
Songs: Heavy Street/Queen Of The Scene/The Greatest Of Them All
The Buzz: "You feel like you're giving it relevance. I know we've got all those classics from the past and so doing the new ones is good and invigorating, you know? It's time to create a new future for the band and take it somewhere else a little bit."
Steve Diggle

STEVE DIGGLE LEADS BUZZCOCKS ONWARDS TO LP ELEVEN

OBSERVERS OF Buzzcocks coiffures took note in February: singer and guitarist Steve Diggle had re-thought his rug with a number one crop. "I had a bit of a scooter accident in Highgate," he tells MOJO, "I scraped my head and I had to have a bit shaved, so I said, Shave it all off!" Aware of the visual metaphor, he goes on: "It symbolises a new start, a new way of looking at things."

The fresh start, he says, will pertain to the as-yet un-recorded eleventh Buzzcocks LP, his second since he took sole charge of the venerable Manc-punk institution after Pete Shelley's death in December 2018. "The record's written and rehearsed," he goes on. "We want to record it for about June or July."

The group – Diggle, bassist Chris Remmington and drummer Danny Farrant – learned the songs at Storm rehearsal rooms on London's Holloway Road. Plans are afoot to decamp to producer Laurence Loveless's studio in the north of the capital. "It's on an

Paul Hartnett, Alamy (2)

ALSO WORKING

…last month **Flavor Flav** (right) told the TMZ site that he's been recording with **PUBLIC ENEMY** partner **Chuck D**. He also revealed, "I'm gonna surprise y'all with an-all instrumental album… it's gonna be all played by myself. Keyboard, bass, guitars" …**SQUEEZE** are recording new music. Reported **Chris Difford** from the studio, "recording two songs from 50 years ago, they sounded like slippers found under the bed… comfy, warm, rewarding" …**DOOBIE BROTHERS'** **Pat Simmons** revealed last month that the band were close to finishing their first LP in 40 years with vocalist **Michael McDonald**: "in my humble opinion it's turning out to be some of the best music we've ever made together," he added …The Sun says

ELTON JOHN will release his new LP before the year is out. "[His] finger is very much still on the pulse," said their source …**THE FOLK IMPLOSION**'s *Walk Thru Me*, their first LP in 20 years, arrives in June. "There are lots of mature themes on this LP," says multi-instrumentalist **John Davis** … **JOHN GRANT**'s *The Art Of The Lie* is out in the summer. Co-produced by **Ivor Guest**, songs include Mother And Son, Father

and Daddy: Grant compares it to "the Carpenters if John Carpenter were also a member" …re-formed '80s hitmakers **FAIRGROUND ATTRACTION** (left) are back in the studio: What's Wrong With The World? is the first released song …footage has emerged of **SAM FENDER** and The War On Drugs' **ADAM GRANDUCIEL** in the studio, accompanied by heartlands rock sounds…

A FESTIVAL OF COUNTRY & AMERICANA
HIGHWAYS
AUDITORIUM

HOSTED BY BAYLEN LEONARD FROM ABSOLUTE RADIO COUNTRY

FRI 17 MAY 2024

THE CADILLAC THREE

SHANE SMITH & THE SAINTS
TANNER USREY
BOWEN * YOUNG

SAT 18 MAY 2024

BRETT YOUNG

THE WAR AND TREATY
JOSH ROSS
WILLIAM PRINCE

ALL TICKETS INCLUDE ENTRY TO THE EXHIBITION:
ALAN MESSER: KEEPING IT COUNTRY

ELGAR ROOM

SAT 18 MORNING	SAT 18 AFTERNOON	SOLD OUT	FRI 17 EVENING	SAT 18 EVENING
COUNTRY FOR KIDS WITH REMEMBER MONDAY	**SONGWRITERS ROUND** BEN EARLE / BOWEN* YOUNG / CATIE OFFERMAN / TANNER USREY		**LATE NIGHT SPECIAL** WITH KEZIA GILL / REMEMBER MONDAY	

EVENTS DIFFER BY SHOW DATE. TICKETS SOLD SEPARATELY

ARENA BARS
FRI 17 & SAT 18
OFFICIAL AFTER SHOW PARTY DJ SET WITH DISKO COWBOY
TICKETS SOLD SEPARATELY

ROYAL ALBERT HALL LONDON
HIGHWAYSFESTIVAL.CO.UK • ROYALALBERTHALL.COM
VENUE DINING, VIP & HOSPITALITY PACKAGES AVAILABLE

LIVE NATION | Absolute Radio COUNTRY | Royal Albert Hall

WITH SPECIAL GUESTS
STEPHEN WILSON JR.
WILY

THE YEARS GO FAST
TOUR 2024

LIVENATION.CO.UK

A LIVE NATION, DF CONCERTS AND MCD
PRESENTATION BY ARRANGEMENT WITH WME

MAY 4	**DUBLIN**	THE ACADEMY
MAY 5	**BELFAST**	LIMELIGHT
MAY 8	**GLASGOW**	O2 ACADEMY
MAY 9	**NEWCASTLE**	NX
MAY 11	**MANCHESTER**	ACADEMY
MAY 12	**LEEDS**	O2 ACADEMY
MAY 14	**NOTTINGHAM**	ROCK CITY
MAY 16	**CARDIFF**	TRAMSHED
MAY 17	**LONDON**	HIGHWAYS AT ROYAL ALBERT HALL

NEW ALBUM
THE YEARS GO FAST
OUT NOW

Join My Live Nation for exclusive benefits. Go to livenation.co.uk/register

Shore thing: Richard Thompson – "I'm fairly optimistic but I know what darkness is."

David Kaptein

BRIGHTEST LIGHTS

Thompson's high five on 33.

1 Bix Beiderbecke
Young Man With A Horn 1924-1930
(NIMBUS, 2010)

2 The Shadows
Greatest Hits
(COLUMBIA, 1963)

3 The Watersons
Frost And Fire: A Calendar Of Ritual And Magical Songs
(TOPIC, 1965)

4 The Left Banke
Walk Away Renée/ Pretty Ballerina
(SMASH, 1967)

5 Brighde Chaimbeul with Colin Stetson
Carry Them With Us
(GLITTERBEAT, 2023)

Richard Thompson

The folk rocker nonpareil talks crime, booze and the bigger picture.

EARPHONES HALOING a head which, from his first photos as a founder member of British folk-rock titans Fairport Convention, seemed borrowed from a mediaeval saint, Richard Thompson speaks to MOJO from his basement. It's close to the infamous New Jersey Turnpike as celebrated in song by Chuck and Bruce and on screen in The Sopranos, which tickles the singer-songwriter/ guitar wizard enormously.

"When they filmed it, they used locations all over New Jersey except for the town of Bloomfield, and that's because that's where the Mafia actually live," he chuckles. "It's just two miles down the road from me; you go to these great mom and pop Italian restaurants and sitting at the bar are these really beefy guys. Oookaaaaay, haha!"

From your terrific new album *Ship To Shore*, The Fear Never Leaves is bleak even by the standards of a songbook suffused with dread. Do you, like your old friend Nick Drake, wrestle with the black dog?

I'm fairly optimistic but I know what darkness is. I wrote this song after watching a documentary about the Falklands and the special units. These guys are tough but suffer from serious PTSD after a brief skirmish, so God knows what they suffer in Ukraine, what my parents suffered after World War Two, my grandfather after World War One. I try to express what those people go through in order to understand the bigger picture – mental health, where we are in the modern world.

Your dad was a Scotland Yard detective who played in a police band. Did you also inherit a sense of our capacity for badness?

On the bookshelves at home were lots of Robert Burns, Walter Scott, Border ballads and criminology. I read some of them so I've always been interested in police procedure. I'd be out with my father and he'd say, "Describe the guy who just walked past," so the next time I was ready. Twenty years ago there was a break-in next door, and I could say exactly what the two guys looked like, their height, what they were wearing.

In 1988 you deplored The Pogues, in particular Shane MacGowan's image of "fall-down drunk Irishman representing the new wave of Irish traditional music." Have you a puritan streak that can't appreciate the cavalier?

I was concerned with the image of Irish music and Ireland generally. People see a land of drinkers and Irish musicians as absolutely legless. We did the Dominion, Tottenham Court Road, back in the '80s and thought it would be great to introduce some young punk-folk bands like The Pogues to an older audience. It was a disaster. Pogues fans came in large numbers and were really disruptive, abusive and obnoxious. I thought I was doing the right thing, and you and your fans turned on an old codger and treated the music I played with zero respect: screw you! People asked me what a great songwriter Shane MacGowan is. I'd just be noncommittal.

Then there was Sinéad O'Connor…

I had really difficult personal relations with her. I know she had mental health issues, but it was above and beyond. People asked, "Are you going to sing at the tribute show?" Sorry, sometimes people's personality gets in the way of their art, and I just can't go there.

Your 2021 song When I Was Drunk tells a tragic tale. Before your 1974 conversion to Sufism you were no exception in a thirsty folk rock milieu, with Fairport's Sandy Denny a tragic victim. Did you need Sufism's discipline if not to slide down that slope yourself?

At the point I encountered Sufism, I felt completely drained and empty, nothing left. To have that spiritual connection was such a relief. I stopped drinking on a sixpence, from healthy consumption to zero. I never missed it and still don't miss it. I was filling the empty space with nutrition, meaning and connection. That's not for everybody. But the way out of addiction has to be spiritual. Otherwise, you're just gonna go back around again.

Tell us something you've never told an interviewer before.

I shouldn't mention masturbation – that would be going too far. But I practise kickboxing on a punch bag here in my basement.

As told to Mat Snow

Ship To Shore is out on May 31 via New West records.

> "I thought I was doing the right thing… screw you!"
> RICHARD THOMPSON

LAST NIGHT A RECORD CHANGED MY LIFE

Aidan Moffat

Arab Strap's merciless observer gawps in awe at Slint's *Spiderland* (Touch And Go, 1991).

SLINT WERE already a favourite band before *Spiderland* came along; I'd ordered their first LP, *Tweez*, at the local record shop after hearing John Peel play their song Darlene in early 1990. The LP took months to arrive, but my mates and I were soon obsessed with its mischievous, jazz-tinted hardcore and cryptic, private-joke lyrics. There was no information about them anywhere, but the sleeve had a contact address, so we wrote them a letter from Falkirk to tell them we loved them.

At that time, only Sounds magazine ever mentioned them, and I remember seeing the news that a second LP was coming – I couldn't wait, and the release was delayed a little, so for two months I'd phone Fopp in Edinburgh every Monday morning from the pay phone at school to ask if it was out, until one day they said they'd just received a promo, so they'd sell me that for £10. I walked straight out of school and got the train to the city, bought it and returned to meet my mate Dave at the school gates. Then we went back to my bedroom, drew the curtains and listened to *Spiderland* in darkness.

It sounded so different – the youthful mischief was gone, and in its place were these tense, emotional songs with slower rhythms and stories of ghosts, vampires and heartbreak, which could all explode in raging noise at any second. But there was a tenderness too, a maturity and vulnerability that took us by surprise. The timing was perfect: I was almost 18, in my last year of school, and it seemed like we were all growing up together. It thrills me the same way now, too, with its balance of beauty and rage, and those howling, cathartic crescendos. The best albums transport you to their own world for a while, and 40 minutes through *Spiderland* is a journey I'll always love taking.

Arab Strap's I'm Totally Fine With It; Don't Give A Fuck Anymore is out May 10 on Rock Action.

AFTER WHITE BICYCLES... JOE BOYD'S 800-PAGE ODYSSEY INTO GLOBAL RHYTHMS

EX-PINK FLOYD and R.E.M. producer Joe Boyd was hoping to make a timely follow-up to his 2006 psychedelic memoir White Bicycles when he embarked on a book about global music. Things got rather out of hand. Some 15 years on, the ex-Witchseason and Hannibal Records boss has finally put the finishing touches to And The Roots Of Rhythm Remain: A Journey Through Global Music. As he tells MOJO with a shrug: "Once you get in, you can't stop."

An inter-continental meander that takes in Africa, the Indian subcontinent, Latin America, the Caribbean and plenty more places besides, the book's 800-plus pages sparkle with gossip, political intrigue and unlikely connections. Reflecting on how paradigm shifts can come from existing sounds being copied badly, Boyd posits that modern Latin music may be rooted in the 18th century, when musicians of African origin in Haiti were compelled to play fashionable English country dances to entertain French settlers.

As he seeks to track the musical crosscurrents that have fed into Western pop, Boyd hits a rich vein of telling anecdotes. "Like George Harrison and John Lennon lying in Zsa Zsa Gabor's bathtub tripping in the summer of '65 while Jim McGuinn and David Crosby explained Indian music to them," he says. "As soon as Harrison got back to London, he went to HMV and bought all the Ravi Shankar albums."

The title of the book is a lyric from Paul Simon's 1986 *Graceland* LP, a voyage into South African sounds Boyd felt was much misunderstood. "Everybody felt so virtuous that by buying Ladysmith Black Mambazo records they were somehow supporting the ANC," he says. "The music of *Graceland* is basically Zulu, and the ANC hated that, because the South African government supported Zulu independence as a way to undermine the anti-Apartheid movement."

As Boyd discovered frequently, traditional music has often come under heavy political manners. Eastern Bloc authorities disdained Bulgarian female harmony groups like the Kate Bush-endorsed Trio Bulgarka, Brazil's military dictatorship exiled the leaders of the Afro-psychedelic Tropicália movement, while Fidel Castro's revolutionaries took a dim view of the Yorùbá-derived rhythms of Cuban music. "Religions and authoritarian governments hate most authentic types of music because it involves women freeing themselves and moving their bodies on the dancefloor," he says.

For Boyd, the kinds of sensuous rhythms despots once loathed are very much in retreat, assailed not by state repression but the relentless march of the drum machine. However, he insists the work of the artists he writes about so lovingly here will stand the test of time.

"When you hear a Congolese rhythm section from the '70s or Tony Allen playing with Fela Kuti or Chano Pozo playing with Dizzy Gillespie, you're hearing a remarkable expression of human civilisation," he says. "Music that's made live in the studio by great musicians looking each other in the eye and picking up the intensity in a nanosecond, and changing the feel just by a nuance of the way somebody plays a bass line. That's going to live for ever."

Jim Wirth

Joe Boyd's And The Roots Of Rhythm Remain: A Journey Through Global Music is published by Faber on July 4.

> "Religions and authoritarian governments hate most authentic types of music."
> **JOE BOYD**

© Andrea Goertler-Boyd, Allan Grant/The LIFE Picture Collection/Shutterstock

Rhythm collision: (above, left) Cuban percussionist Chano Pozo teams up with Dizzy Gillespie, 1948; (inset) globe-travelling author Joe Boyd.

Promised you a miracle: Mark Mulcahy with late-'80s Miracle Legion (from left) Ray Neal, Mulcahy, Steve West and Jeff Wiederschall.

Courtesy Rough Trade

JANGLE POP SAGE MARK MULCAHY REDISCOVERS WHAT WAS LOST

"**H**E CHANGED the way I thought about songs and singing," Thom Yorke remarked of Mark Mulcahy, whilst Nick Hornby devoted a chapter to the man from Connecticut in his 2002 book 31 Songs. But of all those to endorse this compelling, golden-throated storyteller, the most unexpected must be BBC TV's politics weekly The Andrew Marr Show, who flew over the re-formed Mulcahy-fronted Miracle Legion in 2016.

"They cancelled our appearance because of Brexit!" Mulcahy guffaws. "But they said

> ## "There we were, having breakfast with Boris Johnson... a total nutso."
> ### MARK MULCAHY

they'd still film us, and broadcast it later – but there we were, having breakfast with Boris Johnson… a total nutso."

The scenario was another near debacle for the band, whose bristling brand of collegiate jangle had been undermined by line-up shifts, label bankruptcies and comparisons to the more bankable R.E.M. "It wasn't the worst thing," says Mulcahy. "But you know, they say a lot of bands sound like The Beatles, but they mean The Kinks."

Forming in 1983, Miracle Legion hung on for 10 years before guitarist Ray Neal left. Mulcahy and their second rhythm section formed Polaris, ostensibly to write music for the US cable show The Adventures Of Pete & Pete (written by two hardcore

---

MARK THREE

A triple-punch of Mulcahy magic.

Miracle Legion
The Backyard
(INCAS, 1984)

Their mini-album debut is the perfect introduction, the palpable ache in Mulcahy's voice largely informed by the death of his younger brother, over bittersweet reminiscence (the title track), haunted ballad Steven Are You There? and barnstorming Closer To The Wall.

Polaris
Music From The Adventures Of Pete & Pete
(MEZZOTINT, 1999)

Collecting songs from the surrealism-in-the-suburbs Nickelodeon kids' show, the sole album from Muggy, Jersey and Harris Polaris. Not that Miracle Legion couldn't do carefree, but Mulcahy sounded liberated by this head-on excursion into pop.

Mark Mulcahy
In Pursuit Of Your Happiness
(LOOSE, 2005)

The most consistent of his solo albums, with fan favourite Cookie Jar and lengthy elegy He Vanished, plus guests J Mascis and Pixies' Joey Santiago. Includes a board game so you can do what the title advises.

Legion fans), which – of course – was prematurely cancelled.

Starting his own label Mezzotint, Mulcahy then embarked on a string of superb solo LPs in 1997, but when his wife Melissa died in 2008, raising their three-year-old twins took priority. The tribute LP Ciao My Shining Star: The Songs Of Mark Mulcahy (Thom Yorke and Michael Stipe contributed) helped, before he re-emerged in 2012 with a Polaris reunion and 2013 LP Dear Mark J. Mulcahy, I Love You, named after a note left out by his daughter.

Adding Neal to the Polaris trio led to the re-formed Miracle Legion's US and (following the Marr slot) UK tours. "Playing with those guys is like driving a Cadillac," Mulcahy notes. "They were such joyful shows."

Instead of a new Legion album, Mulcahy released two more solo sets. Next up is the Covid-delayed album Woodstock, recorded in 2021 with Connecticut guitarist Chris Harford under the name Birdfeeder ("I love birds," Mulcahy says. "I fed some woodpeckers just before you called!"). Another Miracle Legion US mini-tour is scheduled for June, in time for a remix of their '87 full-length debut Surprise Surprise Surprise. "It sounds now like it should have sounded, free from its '80s cage," Mulcahy says. "But I feel so much better releasing new recordings."

One recent digital EP is The Tinsler, which features covers of Mitski, Faye Webster and Adrianne Lenker songs, inspired by his daughters' road-trip playlists. Of his own music, he says, "I thought I'd lost whatever I once had, but friends have been so wonderful and encouraging. I'm just trying to figure out how to make more."

Martin Aston

Birdfeeder's Woodstock is out via Soul Selects on April 12.

Mulcahy juggles new project Birdfeeder with a resurgent solo career.

THE BLACK KEYS

UK & IRELAND TOUR 2024

IN CONCERT

PLUS GUESTS
CIRCA WAVES

27 APRIL CO-OP LIVE MANCHESTER
30 APRIL UTILITA ARENA CARDIFF
03 MAY 3ARENA DUBLIN
~~05~~ MAY O2 ACADEMY BRIXTON *SOLD OUT*

EXTRA DATE ADDED
09 MAY O2 ACADEMY BRIXTON

TICKETMASTER.CO.UK • GIGSANDTOURS.COM
AN SJM CONCERTS, LIVE NATION AND MCD PRESENTATION BY ARRANGEMENT WITH CAA

KELLY JONES

PLAYING THE NEW ALBUM 'INEVITABLE INCREDIBLE' IN FULL
~ 2 INTIMATE PERFORMANCES EACH NIGHT ~

SUN 05 MAY ~ 7PM & 9PM
BIRMINGHAM TOWN HALL

TUE 07 MAY ~ 7PM & 9PM
GLASGOW CITY HALLS

THU 09 MAY ~ 7PM & 9PM
LONDON ALEXANDRA PALACE THEATRE

MON 13 & TUE 14 MAY ~ 7PM & 9PM
CARDIFF THE GATE

FRI 17 MAY ~ 7PM & 9PM
MANCHESTER AVIVA STUDIOS

THE BRAND NEW STUDIO ALBUM
'INEVITABLE INCREDIBLE'
OUT 3RD MAY
TICKETS ON SALE NOW
WWW.INEVITABLEINCREDIBLE.COM/TOUR

AN SJM CONCERTS, AEG, KILIMANJARO & REGULAR PRESENTATION
BY ARRANGEMENT WITH X-RAY

RUSSELL CROWE'S INDOOR GARDEN PARTY

THE **GENTLEMEN BARBERS**
LORRAINE **O'REILLY**

PLUS SPECIAL GUEST

JULY 2024

MON 01 DUBLIN GAIETY THETARE
THU 04 WARRINGTON PARR HALL
WED 24 LONDON O2 SHEPHERDS BUSH EMPIRE
THU 25 LEEDS BRUDENELL SOCIAL CLUB
FRI 26 INVERNESS EDEN COURT

indoorgardenparty.com
gigsandtours.com / ticketmaster.co.uk

AN SJM CONCERTS, DF CONCERTS & MCD PRESENTATION

KULA SHAKER

APRIL 2024
22 CARDIFF TRAMSHED
23 BEXHILL DE LA WARR PAVILION
25 WOLVERHAMPTON THE WULFRUN
26 LONDON ~~ELECTRIC~~ BALLROOM *SOLD OUT*

EXTRA DATE ADDED
27 LONDON ELECTRIC BALLROOM

29 NEWCASTLE BOILER SHOP
30 GLASGOW SWG3 TV STUDIO
MAY 2024
01 LEEDS O2 ACADEMY
03 MANCHESTER O2 RITZ
04 BRISTOL MARBLE FACTORY
05 BOURNEMOUTH O2 ACADEMY

Gigsandtours.com • Ticketmaster.co.uk • Kulashaker.co.uk
An SJM Concerts presentation by arrangement with 13 Artists

SJM CONCERTS BY ARRANGEMENT WITH WASSERMAN

GARY NUMAN

THE PLEASURE PRINCIPLE / REPLICAS 45TH ANNIVERSARY

MAY 1. *SOLD OUT* ...CH UEA
MAY 20 SHE... *SOLD OUT* ...HE LEADMILL
MAY 21 GLASGOW O2 ACADEMY
MAY 23 NEWCASTLE O2 CITY HALL
MAY 27 BR... *SOLD OUT* ...E ACADEMY
MAY 28 C... *SOLD OUT* ...RAMSHED
MAY 30 BOUR... *SOLD OUT* ...H O2 ACADEMY
MAY 31 BIRM... *SOLD OUT* ...O2 INSTITUTE
JUN 1 NOTT... *SOLD OUT* ...ROCK CITY
JUN 3 LEEDS O2 ACADEMY
JUN 4 LIVE... *SOLD OUT* ...O2 ACADEMY

3RD NIGHT ADDED DUE TO EXCEPTIONAL DEMAND
MANCHESTER O2 RITZ
~~JUN 4~~ *SOLD OUT* / ~~JUN 5~~ *SOLD OUT* / **JUN 6**

3RD NIGHT ADDED – TICKETS ON SALE NOW
LONDON ROUNDHOUSE
~~JUN 5~~ *SOLD OUT* / ~~JUN 8~~ *SOLD OUT* / **JUN 9**

GIGSANDTOURS.COM   TICKETMASTER.CO.UK
GARYNUMAN.COM

Grunge mob blur dance: Nirvana rev up at Seattle's Motorsports International Garage, September 22, 1990.

Kurt So Good

Thirty years on from Cobain's death, photobook **Charles Peterson's Nirvana** remembers the glory that was grunge.

"CHARLES WAS IN the trenches, always right down in front," says Nirvana bassist Krist Novoselic in his foreword to Charles Peterson's Nirvana, which handsomely compiles the photographer's images of the group from 1989 to 1993. Novoselic also reflects on Peterson's black and white, long exposure style, as "the musical technique of dropping a guitar's low E string down to the D note, while sending the signal through a vintage Fuzz box. That's basic Grunge."

There is something raw, immediate and, yes, amplified about Peterson's photographs of Nirvana playing live, between gigs and doing magazine shoots. The book also contains 30 images never before seen, including the wild accompanying shot of the band at the Motorsports International Garage in Seattle on September 22, 1990.

"My informal title for this image is 'the chaos of youth,'" Peterson tells MOJO. "I sometimes forget just how crazy and chaotic these shows could be... our switch was 'on' and for a lot of us we had no idea there was even an 'off' setting. I want the images to evoke that time and energy and passion. It's in the details — the crushed cans on-stage, the duct tape and ripped jeans and flannel shirts, hair and hands emerging from the blur of audience and light, and the youthful faces that are no longer."

He adds that the unseen images were awaiting digital scanning technology to bring them to fruition. "The band was amazingly photogenic and it was really easy, even within a single show, to make a lot of great images of them," he says. "There's still a lot more, but we could only make the books so big!"

It is, unbelievably, three decades since we lost Kurt Cobain. Peterson says what has stayed with him is, "how much of a 'family' the grunge scene was... despite being quite dysfunctional at times, we all had each other's backs. And just how great and powerful Nirvana's music was and still is. There's been a lot of train-spotting and myth-making surrounding this band, but at the end of the day none of it would be important or relevant without the incredible music they made."

Ian Harrison

Charles Peterson's Nirvana is available in Europe through HHV Records in Berlin and TLP in Dublin, and through minormattersbooks.com. An exhibition of Charles Peterson's Nirvana will open on October 5 at the Tacoma Art Museum and will travel thereafter.

© Charles Peterson/Minor Matters Books

"My informal title for this image is 'the chaos of youth.'"
CHARLES PETERSON

> ## "I *had* to be a songwriter. I knew it would do me good."
> **MYRIAM GENDRON**

Mayday alert: Myriam Gendron is caught between catharsis and lullaby on her new LP.

Justine Latour

FROM BUSKING IN PARIS TO DOROTHY PARKER'S ALGONQUIN... THE UNCANNY INTIMACIES OF MYRIAM GENDRON

FACT SHEET
● For fans of: Karen Dalton, Sibylle Baier, Meg Baird, Nathan Salsburg
● Gendron believes the instrumental that opens *Mayday*, There Is No East Or West, is her most autobiographical song. "It's the form of songwriting I most enjoy. Words lock up meaning, whereas I find an instrumental more true to what my real emotions are."
● She lived in Paris from ages 14 to 16, busking in Metro stations. "It was all covers. Pixies. Cranberries. Leonard Cohen. I just wanted to be a bum, a vagabond. I just wanted money to buy marijuana."

KEY TRACKS
● Long Way Home
● Poor Girl Blues
● Threnody

MAYDAY, THE TITLE of Myriam Gendron's new album, is a word with two meanings – one announcing the hopeful start of spring, the other a cry for help. Both ideas unite in this beautiful collection of variegated folk songs, some happy, some deeply sad, some sung in English, others in French, an album caught somewhere between catharsis and lullaby.

"The whole record is about that," says Gendron from a room of guitars, books and music-stands in her Montreal home. "How hard things are in the real world and the safe space you have to find within yourself. My mother died in May 2022, while I was on tour and I'd quit my job as a book dealer. When I came back home I suddenly had nothing except all the grief I hadn't had time to deal with. I *had* to be a songwriter. It's a hard door to open but I need that doorway. I knew it would do me good."

Gendron's initial doorway into songwriting was, she admits, a strange one. "I came

to it through used material, the words of Dorothy Parker. That's how I learned to write." The LP Gendron is referring to is her 2014 debut, *Not So Deep As A Well*, in which she transformed the poems of the Jazz Age satirist into songs of melancholy acoustic wit, brought to life by a voice of doleful yet intimate warmth.

Gendron, who'd had a strong music education through Canada's public school system, and spent her teenage years busking in Paris, was adept at covering the work of others but had never written songs for herself. "I thought they were just demos we'd record professionally later," she says, "but everyone was like, 'No! We're keeping those.'"

Initially released on Feeding Tube Records, *Not So Deep…* gradually accrued a cult following, especially as Gendron seemed to have vanished from the public eye soon after its release. "I was seven months pregnant," she explains. "I went back to my regular life. Then I had another child. I was really into mother-

hood and didn't have a lot of space in my head for being an artist."

A second album, *Ma Délire – Songs Of Love, Lost & Found*, finally arrived in 2021, where she explored French and Québécois traditional songs and made them meaningful for today. It also found Gendron using folk archetypes as footholds by which to create her own magical new songs, which she crafted with the help of experimental guitarist Bill Nace and free/improv drummer Chris Corsano. "When I was opening for more conventional folk artists nothing special was happening with the audience," she says. "But when I was opening for like, Godspeed You! Black Emperor there was something magical there. I felt strong."

It's an idea that's continued on *Mayday*, which Gendron recorded with free folk guitarist Marisa Anderson, Dirty Three drummer Jim White, and Bill Nace, amongst others, all of whom invest the album with a sense of poetic unease. "When I write a song I don't want it to be easy. I want it to be challenging, so you feel like you have to come back to it and there's always something new to discover," says Gendron. "I mean, that's what I like in art."

Andrew Male

Myriam Gendron's Mayday is out May 10 on Thrill Jockey/Feeding Tube.

MOJO PLAYLIST

INTRODUCING CASSIE KINOSHI, BIG BAND TRAILBLAZER FOR THE UK JAZZ RENAISSANCE

C ASSIE KINOSHI relishes her role as part of the UK jazz renaissance, collaborating with Nubya Garcia, Sons Of Kemet and Ezra Collective. But while her own work with big bands and orchestras operates on a grander scale to the smaller ensembles led by contemporaries like Shabaka Hutchings, the composer/saxophonist knows you can have too much of a good thing.

Back in 2020, juggling Afrobeat group Kokoroko, all-star septet Nérija, her own SEED Ensemble – since renamed seed. – and scoring for theatre, Kinoshi found herself suffering "deep burnout". "I needed to rest, to reconnect with my creativity, with myself," she remembers. Respite came with the Covid lockdown, which gave her "space to cook, to read, to think. And then I started writing material for myself again."

From these restorative writing sessions came *Gratitude*, Kinoshi's second LP as leader, a symphonic work in seven movements she describes as "a celebration of nature and the communities that bring me joy. My mum has a 'gratitude book', a notebook where she writes things she feels grateful for, and I found celebrating the small, beautiful things in life really inspiring."

Kinoshi grew up in Welwyn Garden City, with a piano in the front room and music always playing. "My family was into Afrobeat, musicals, jazz. And my dad always played Classic FM on Sundays. I became obsessed with Dvořák's New World Symphony, getting lost in its evocative soundworld."

At 18, she moved to London to study at the Trinity Laban Conservatoire, spending Saturdays at Tomorrow's Warriors, a programme for young musicians interested in jazz and improvisation. "We learned about jazz from incredible British players," she says, "and

> ## "Jazz is no longer centred around elitism. It's about community and dancing and togetherness."
> **CASSIE KINOSHI**

forged really close friendships there." Indeed, SEED Ensemble evolved from the Tomorrow's Warriors Youth Big Band she assembled at Trinity Laban, indulging her obsession with Duke Ellington and Gil Evans. "I love the colours and the layers of big band music – the blending of different harmonies," Kinoshi explains. "But touring and funding a big band like that is pretty difficult."

The 10-piece seed., however, enables Kinoshi's majestic visions on a manageable budget, and serves as "a space to experiment with sound and express my politics". Their debut, 2019's Mercury-nominated *Driftglass*, explored "the othering of black people in British culture as this scary entity" (The Darkies) and the Grenfell tragedy (W A K E), which Kinoshi says is "still buried – it's not resolved at all".

The ensemble's follow-up, *Gratitude*, was recorded live at the Purcell Rooms on the South Bank, accompanied by the London Contemporary Orchestra. And while this ambitious project saw Kinoshi risking further burn-out, the final performance was "cathartic". "I'm an introvert, I often struggle with words, and use music to express my feelings," she says. "For me, music is all about connecting with people. I'd been so isolated writing and preparing this piece, which was about community and shared joy. To finally be able to perform it was incredibly joyful."

Stevie Chick

Cassie Kinoshi's seed.'s Gratitude is out now on International Anthem.

FACT SHEET
● For fans of: Alice Coltrane, Pharoah Sanders, Miguel Atwood-Ferguson
● Kinoshi believes the UK jazz renaissance is long overdue. "Jazz in the UK had become divided by class," she says. "The music now enjoys a better platform, the space to become a social music again. It's no longer centred around elitism and passive listening, it's more about community and dancing and togetherness."
● *Gratitude* welcomes a new guest player to the seed. ensemble: turntablist NikNak, who "brought a lot of texture to the piece, manipulating sounds and improvising with her scratching. She elevated the piece." Kinoshi, meanwhile, returned the favour on NikNak's forthcoming LP, *Ireti*.

KEY TRACKS
● Smoke In The Sun
● i
● iii Sun Through My Window

Thank you for the music: Cassie Kinoshi finds joy through connection.

Keziah Quarcoo, Anders Deros/Aftonbladet/Alamy

Listen up! For the month's blues, dub and Arabic rave.

1 NICK CAVE & THE BAD SEEDS
WILD GOD
Cave gets the old gang – plus Radiohead's Colin Greenwood – together for a rousing return to the environs of Jubilee Street. "HERE WE GO!"
Find it: *streaming services*

2 BOB DYLAN
WHEN I PAINT MY MASTERPIECE
Blue? Don't know where to go? How about Fort Lauderdale, where His Bobness restarted The Rough & Rowdy Ways tour by grafting his 1971 classic onto the tune of Puttin' On The Ritz. Super duper!
Find it: *YouTube*

3 THE SPECIALS FAMILY
WHEN A LIGHT GOES OUT
Lynval Golding's dubby reggae tribute to Terry Hall and John Bradbury, with help from Sir Horace Gentleman.
Find it: *YouTube*

4 JOHN GRANT
THE CHILD CATCHER
Grant goes hyper-Vangelis with a glacial loss-of-self fear-reverie that shifts to anthemic soft-rock.
Find it: *streaming services*

5 SARAH BROWN **AMAZING GRACE**
Supplication in the dark from Simple Minds' gospel division, bringing a shudder of Arthur Russell's deep-vibrato weirdness.
Find it: *streaming services*

6 SLASH FEAT. BRIAN JOHNSON
KILLING FLOOR
AC/DC singer and GN'R guitarist revisit the abattoir to cover Howlin' Wolf's cornerstone.
Find it: *YouTube*

7 USE KNIFE **PTOLEMAIC**
(ZOË McPHERSON REMIX)
Belgian/Iraqi outfit, much dug by MOJO at March's ace Leiden festival Peel Slowly And See, take Arab sounds into the chemical rave.
Find it: *Peace Carnival EP/streaming services*

8 DIRTY THREE
LOVE CHANGES EVERYTHING I
Busy month for Warren Ellis: a Bad Seeds album and his power trio's first in 12 years. Free jazz drums, guitar sputter, frenzied violin; a heroic return.
Find it: *streaming services*

9 STEVE CONTE **WE LIKE IT**
Co-written with XTC's Andy Partridge, the ex-New York Doll glam rocks a lament to sanitised living, with a nod to Ball Of Confusion.
Find it: *streaming services*

10 NIAMH REGAN **MADONNA**
The Irish singer-songwriter picks through memories untethered by loss, with a tremor of psychedelic folk.
Find it: *streaming services*

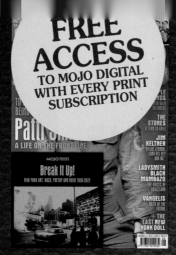

FREE
ACCESS
TO MOJO DIGITAL
WITH EVERY PRINT
SUBSCRIPTION

3 ISSUES OF
MOJO FOR £5*

SUBSCRIBE NOW
WHEREVER YOU ARE IN THE WORLD

greatmagazines.co.uk/mojo
Or call 01858 438884‡ quote SP24

SCAN HERE

Terms & Conditions: *3 issues for £5 is the trial price available on a MOJO subscription. After your first 3 issues, your payment will auto-renew to £32 every 6 months thereafter. UK only. Offer closes 26/05/2024. Your subscription will start with the next available issue. ‡Cost from landlines for 01 numbers per minute are (approximate) 2p to 10p. Cost from mobiles per minute (approximate) 10p to 40p. Costs vary depending on the location. You may get free calls to some numbers as part of your call package – please check with your phone provider. Order lines open 8am-9.30pm (Mon-Fri), 8am-4pm (Sat). Calls may be monitored or recorded. For full T&CS visit greatmagazines.co.uk/terms.

The **Crowded House leader** and tunesmaster on **family politics**, band politics, **Fleetwood Mac politics**, and the advantages of not-quite-stardom. **"There's a certain good fortune in having a moderate amount of success,"** concedes **Neil Finn**, OBE.

Interview by **JOHN AIZLEWOOD** • Portrait by **ABE MORA**

THERE HE IS. IT'S EARLY ONE TUESDAY morning and the lobby of London's sprawling Landmark hotel (if you have to ask the rates, you can't afford it) is teeming with well-heeled tourists, very important business folk and, tucked in a corner, underneath some stairs, hunched over what is clearly not his first coffee of the day – and it won't be his last – Neil Finn. Rather like his music, he's in plain sight, but somehow invisible.

Unlike many 65-year-old pop stars, Finn looks like an older version of himself: sharp, pixie-like features, a wicked grin and a torso that still hasn't spread. The hair might be grey and a little spikey, but it's not thinning. "A full head of hair?" he grins, running his hands through it. "Can't say I'm not pleased."

Hair is not the only thing the New Zealander has to be pleased about. There's a new Crowded House album: the majestic *Gravity Stairs*, their eighth and the latest in a line which began in 1986 with a self-titled album that broke America, before 1991's still-revered *Woodface* did the same for them in Europe. Finn's deep but accessible songwriting carved out an unusual niche for the band, but his decision-making was also unusual, and when they split in 1996, following the departure of drummer Paul Hester, they were on the cusp of next-level success.

Since then, Crowded House has been rebuilt and disassembled at Finn's command. Hester's shocking suicide in 2005 prompted the first reformation, lasting until 2011. Eight years later,

shortly after Finn's unlikely touring stint as part of Fleetwood Mac, Crowded House Mk III emerged with Finn alongside ever-present bassist Nick Seymour, 65; keyboardist (and very first Crowded House producer) Mitchell Froom, 70; and Neil's sons Liam, 40, on guitar, and drummer Elroy, 34.

"Some parenting you get right, some you don't," says Finn, "but Liam and Elroy are good, compassionate, empathetic people, with great values and a huge amount of skill."

It's no real surprise: it's usually been about family for Finn. As a teenager he was drafted into older brother Tim's band, Split Enz. Returning the favour, Tim joined Neil's Crowded House from 1990 to 1991 and the pair have made two Finn Brothers albums since then. Then there's the missus. Neil's wife Sharon shared 2011's Pajama Club project, before Neil and Liam collaborated on 2018's *Lightsleeper*. Completing the circle, Tim appears on a *Gravity Stairs* track, Some Greater Plan (For Claire), based on the World War II diaries of Dick Finn, Neil and Tim's father.

"He sneaked into an officers' dance in Florence," relates Finn. "He met this diplomat's daughter and they had a wonderful two-week affair. When he came home, he met my mum. They had a beautiful, happy marriage, but he always had a wistful look when he talked about Italy. It became a family joke."

The Landmark is getting busier. There's an endless piano loop playing in the too-near distance. Neil Finn orders another coffee.

"Let's go. Have your way…" ➤

WE'RE NOT WORTHY

Johnny Marr on a peer-awing talent.

"I was at the Concert For Linda in 1999, watching Neil soundcheck Don't Dream It's Over when Elvis Costello leant over and said, 'Imagine being *that* good.' That's Neil. His songs are so seamless you don't notice at first how clever they are, and he has this God-given gift for melody."

Abe Mora, Andy Cotterill

What was your first musical memory?

Love Me Do when I was four. It was one of our few singles. There was Pat Boone's Love Letters In The Sand, then Get Off Of My Cloud and Green, Green by The New Christy Minstrels, which still pops into my head all the time.

The Finns were always musical, weren't they?

Dad hated being an accountant but he'd come home, sit with a glass of whiskey and listen to Count Basie and Benny Goodman. At the time I thought it was old-fashioned, but it's ingrained in me. I listen to it often now.

Mum played our piano, but she didn't bother changing chords. Sing-songs were the order of the day. Me and Tim would do Harry Belafonte's Jamaica Farewell in harmony, and at Christmas the two Catholic priests staying with us would do Rolf Harris's Two Little Boys, which may sound sinister now. But my real training ground was washing the dishes with mum, where we'd sing You Are My Sunshine in two-part harmony.

Were the Finns free spirits?

We were very sexually repressed in our family. My mother couldn't stand watching people kissing on television and she'd send us to bed if there was anything remotely racy. The sum of my father's talk about sex came when I walked around the house singing I've Got A Feeling and him asking if I knew what "everybody had a wet dream" meant. I'd no idea. He told me and that was that.

Did you feel obligated to follow Tim into music?

Absolutely not. I was on Tim's coat-tails, eager to jump on board with his discoveries. When his band played my sister's birthday party, I was allowed to tap on the snare drum and that was glorious. Tim was a good older brother – he was never mean to me or excluded me.

Had you non-musical options?

Not from the age of 12. I did a drama workshop in Hamilton, but I couldn't have become an actor – I wouldn't have been able to lose that self-consciousness. I was an orderly in Auckland's former National Women's Hospital, but when a body I was wheeling slipped off a gurney, I knew that wasn't a long-term prospect.

The music industry must have felt so far away from New Zealand, so impossible to be part of…

The other side of the world seemed exotic. We imagined the Marquee was an incredibly glamorous place, not some shithole in Soho where your feet stuck to the floor. That explains Split Enz, who Tim formed while I was at school. They had nothing to relate to, no scene to be part of, so they felt they could be wilfully eccentric, obscure and extreme.

Did being summoned to join Split Enz in London in 1977 turn a teenager's head?

I called my parents and, bless them, they let me go. I had my passport in three days, flew over and went straight into rehearsals in Chalk Farm. It was a shot in the dark for them too. I could sing and probably write, but I couldn't play electric guitar. I jumped around on-stage to compensate, but I was pretty hopeless for the first six months.

You were in the centre of things now…

Yes. A fortnight later we were in AIR Studios, Oxford Street. Kate Bush was recording Wuthering Heights. Paul McCartney and Jimmy McCulloch were mixing live Wings tracks. Later, we recorded I See Red at Startling Studios at Tittenhurst Park which Ringo bought from John Lennon. I took acid as I walked around because it was the appropriate thing to do and I slept in John and Yoko's bed.

Did you take over Split Enz?

No. We were of the same mind to simplify and create more streamlined music because all people were interested in was punk. My songs fit that mode. We had 18-year-old wonderkid producer David Tickle, who'd worked with Mike Chapman on Blondie and Knack records, and was really into creating a buoyant pop record. We didn't want to be like Van Morrison, making similar records all his life.

1980's *True Colours* broke Split Enz internationally and topped the Australian charts…

…for 10 weeks. Being chased down Bourke Street Mall in Melbourne by girls was a hugely transformative experience.

Could that also turn a young man's head?

It's a novelty initially. It's disarming and we enjoyed it with a wry smile, but we were wary of it too. Midnight Oil were peerless live and we admired The Reels' songwriting, but we saw ourselves as separate and we foolishly believed we were.

What did you take from Split Enz into Crowded House?

Following my nose and stumbling on. I'd no idea what I wanted Crowded House to be, but I was ambitious to take it to the world and I wanted to be the leader of a band. The songs that came out decided how we should sound. Myself and Paul Hester, the last Split Enz drummer, gave demos to 34 auditioning bassists to play on. Nick Seymour got the job because he threw out a different style of playing. He put a dance groove underneath That's What I Call Love and he danced while he played. That was enough for me.

You were recording in Los Angeles with producer Mitchell Froom quickly enough…

We were signed by Capitol after A&R man Tom Whalley heard our demos on his first day. Mitchell brought in Jerry Scheff and Jim Keltner, who'd played with John Lennon, to play on Now We're Getting Somewhere because Nick and Paul weren't getting the song's shuffle. That was slightly painful for them but afterwards, Jim and

---

A LIFE IN PICTURES

The Finn crowd: Neil down the years.

1 Harmony in my head: Neil on the New King's Road, London, 1980: "the other side of the world seemed exotic."

2 Beginning of the Enz: Finn on-stage with Split Enz, Rotterdam, June 13, 1981.

3 Splinter group: Split Enz with Tim Finn (far left), Paul Hester (centre, bottom) and Neil (second right).

4 Home-makers: Crowded House (from left) Neil, Nick Seymour, Hester and Tim, Belgium, October 18, 1991.

5 Return of the Mac: Neil (centre) with Fleetwood Mac's (from left) John McVie, Christine McVie, Stevie Nicks, Mick Fleetwood and Mike Campbell, Las Vegas, 2018.

6 On the red carpet: CH MK II (from left) Seymour, Neil, Mark Hart, Matt Sherrod at the 2016 ARIA awards.

7 Split Enz (from left) Eddie Rayner, Neil, Malcolm Green, Noel Crombie, Nigel Griggs and Tim get inducted into the ARIA Hall of Fame, '05.

8 Open-armed: Neil on-stage in NZ, 2021.

9 Finn in 1986: "Brightening people's lives, giving them some comfort and delivering with a light touch would be a nice legacy."

Getty (7), Lynn Goldsmith/Getty, David Corio/Getty

I jammed. When he said, "I felt like I was playing with John," it was one of the greatest things I'd ever heard.

Were you surprised to break in America first?

Yeah, we were outside the times. Some people thought we were too mainstream, others thought we were too alternative, 'hair bands' such as Poison were everywhere. It was appalling to us, awful. We were in a vacuum, so we started doing little acoustic gigs: a seafood restaurant in Seattle; an Indian restaurant in Times Square; Yamashiro in LA. People went nuts. Don't Dream It's Over made its way up the charts and it was all on.

Did you play the game?

We were up for it, although I'm slightly regretful of that caper now. I was troubled by having just left Split Enz and I wished I could share this with Tim. It put a damper on my enjoyment of it, although not too much. Paul and I were reluctant to meet and greet – although Paul was incredibly good when he got into it – but we had a secret weapon: Nick. Nick was a master, so we'd send him into a room 10 minutes before us. Everything would be chilled by the time we got in and people would leave feeling good about us. Looking back, we might have created more mystique by holding back, but Paul used to say we weren't selling out, we were buying in.

You were covertly subversive?

We were subversive in our own way. I just watched Mutiny In Heaven, the Birthday Party documentary. Their trajectory of abandonment, deviant undertones and full commitment to rock'n'roll was admirable, but scary. There was no way that could have been my experience.

Why didn't Crowded House follow through in the US?

Multiple answers. And multiple reasons. Our second album, *Temple Of Low Men*, was easier and more enjoyable to make than the first, but it sounded more low-key, downbeat, reflective and we probably weren't as buoyant. Certainly we were just as good live, but when the first single Better Be Home Soon stalled at 40-something, that was a surprise. A few years ago, I received a letter from someone at Capitol in those days. He said, "We dropped the ball and I still feel really bad. We should have gone all the way, but we fucked it." That was the first I'd heard. I sent a letter back saying "your burden is released".

> ## "We recorded at Tittenhurst Park. I took acid and I slept in John and Yoko's bed."

Was inviting Tim to join for *Woodface* a no-brainer?

I had seven good songs including Fall At Your Feet and Four Seasons In One Day for a Crowded House record, but we didn't have a full album. At the same time, I'd started making songs with Tim. It had been a wonderful development, but I couldn't rationalise that dichotomy. Tim said, "Why don't I join and put our songs on the album." It made such sense. Funnily enough, *Woodface* turned heads in Europe, where the first album had been seen as American MOR. It's a 14-song album. You only need 12 and a couple of songs are shit.

Like what?

Tall Trees is a real low point.

Live, it felt more Crowded House Featuring Tim Finn, less Crowded House…

I know, I know, but it was an easy way to finish the record and get great songs on board. We had good moments on-stage as well, but it was never an easy chemistry because Tim wasn't part of what we'd built. Finn Brothers concerts weren't like that, so Tim and I are capable of that kind of chemistry. He's a frontman, who wasn't a frontman enough in Crowded House, because there was another one.

Did his departure show your ruthless side?

'Ruthless' is a bit strong. It felt totally necessary, but Tim had co-written Weather With You. When it became the flag-bearer for *Woodface*, it was a weird feeling he wasn't there to enjoy it. He recognised it wasn't feeling right too.

After Tim left, were Crowded House better than ever? Or never the same again?

We evolved in a really good way. It was the right thing and I'm glad I did it.

When Crowded House first split in 1996, it seemed like unfinished business for everyone but you…

A lot of people thought it was a shame. Nick was particularly fucked off. At the moment Paul left in 1994, we were poised to become a major band, but things weren't feeling right. Afterwards, we did demos in New Zealand, but nothing bore fruit for me. I was also yearning for a new way of making music and thought it would have been a cheek to keep the name. I was probably stupid and maybe I was a little bit messed up in the head.

Would you have admitted that in '96?

No, but I don't have a huge amount of regret.

Your solo albums seemed relatively unpressurised…

➤

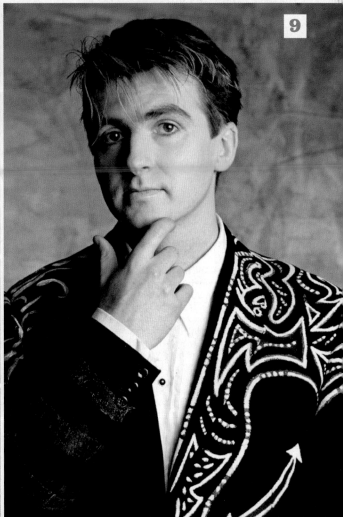

Abe Mora

"Mick Fleetwood spent an hour telling me it wasn't an audition, but it was. I was auditioning them too."

◄ In some ways. They were more exploratory. They didn't hit Crowded House's commercial heights, but there was always belief. I was able to do good shows and I had a young family and was able to watch them develop and grow.

Was *Try Whistling This* [1998] titled passively-aggressively?

People saw that, but I never intended it. I had Marius De Vries, who'd just worked with Nellee Hooper on a Björk record. He had a fridge full of sounds, so he drew on those. I wasn't deliberately being perverse and saying, I'm not going to give you good tunes. They were good tunes, but they were dressed in different clothes.

Could Paul's suicide in 2005 have been prevented?

I just don't know. At the time, I was living in Auckland and Paul was in Melbourne and I had no idea he was so depressed that he would take his life. That was a complete shock to me. The last time I saw him, he was in great form. He got up on-stage with us in Melbourne and we had a wonderful couple of days with him. What I do know is that the moment he left the band might have been handled better.

How?

We were doing an American tour and things weren't firing. *Together Alone* [1993] wasn't performing that well. Paul had just found out he was having a baby, he got really dark and we didn't know how to reach him. Then he left and in a funny kind of way, we were relieved

because we'd been frustrated by Paul not believing any more and there was this weird, awful uneasiness. Capitalism has a survival of the fittest mentality, but there's a lot to be said for protecting the weakest. At that moment, Paul was our weakest and he was unable to cope. Had we the foresight to postpone everything after the last six American shows, we might have found a way to continue with Paul.

Why re-form Crowded House?

The aftermath of losing Paul was a really confronting time. I was making a solo LP and I thought it'd be great to have Nick involved, to hang with him and re-connect after losing Paul. I always had this lingering feeling that bands are the ideal way to face the world. I thought, If Nick's around, maybe it's a band record.

Were you pressured into it?

Oh no, no, no. Circumstances created the idea: it was such a shock to lose Paul and I felt it was the right time to put good feeling into a dark full-stop. I'd been seeing Johnny Marr and ran it by him as a man who understands bands. I thought he might have been, Oh man, don't go there, but he saw it and was very supportive. He's a believer in bands. He's a band man and he played on *Time On Earth* [2007].

What happened to Crowded House Mk II?

To be honest, I'd reached a dead end in my mind. We'd tried to record after *Intriguer* [2010], but I couldn't finish anything with that line-up. It felt like a good time to stop.

Did joining Fleetwood Mac surprise you?

I was gobsmacked. I was 60 and I'd had a wonderfully diverse musical life when Mick called and said, "We've got rid of Lindsey, would you play with us?" I'd just done *Lightsleeper* with Liam so he had a vested interest in my not doing it, but he said, "Give it a shot," so I auditioned.

What? Neil Finn auditioned?

It's the only audition I've ever done. I went to Hawaii and Mick spent an hour telling me it wasn't an audition, but it was. I was auditioning them too: I wasn't sure it was the right thing, I was quite conflicted, but I liked the people and the welcome was universal.

What did you bring?

The naysayers said, "No Lindsey Buckingham, no Fleetwood Mac," but I brought personality and the ability to sing with Stevie and Christine. I could never be capable of sounding like Lindsey but I put a similar intensity into his songs.

Any contact with Lindsey?

No, but I'd really like to have a dinner with him. There's a lot of ill-will, but I don't think he bears any towards me and I do think he had prior appreciation of the music I'd made. Hopefully, once he got over the massive disappointment, he'd have thought, "At least someone with something going for them is singing my songs."

Who's running Fleetwood Mac these days?

It doesn't currently exist, but when I was there

Five's a crowd: the current Crowded House line-up (from left) Nick Seymour, Liam Finn, Neil, Elroy Finn and Mitchell Froom.

Mick carried the flag. He always has and he's the heart and soul. Yet Stevie's the leader in many ways, because Stevie wants it the way Stevie wants it and that's the way it'll be. She couldn't bear to be in a band with Lindsey any more, but she still wanted to do it exactly the way he would have. It was more difficult for Mike Campbell: she was really happy with the way it sounded between me and her, but she put a lot of pressure on Mike to be more like Lindsey. Sometimes Mike's solos would go on and Stevie would get exhausted playing tambourine. She'd be, "Fucking hell, Lindsey only did 12 bars!"

When did you decide to bring Liam and Elroy into Crowded House?

Towards the end of the Fleetwood Mac thing. I'd enjoyed their presence as musicians and it occurred to me that we could do something. It wasn't just them joining dad's band. Liam, Elroy and Mitchell coming in had so much depth, so much connection to the past. And Nick thought it was a great idea.

Do you fear eclipsing your sons?

Who judges that? You can't let the world decide. If it's a case of how much success I've had compared to them, that's the worst measure. I hope it's never, ever an issue. Look, we're a close family, we get on so well. I can't imagine anyone better and it is apparent that we will be eclipsing – sorry, I shouldn't say that – that we will be the equal of any previous line-up.

How does *Gravity Stairs* fit into the canon?

Too early to say. Every time I make a record I feel like it's my best, but later you think, Some of it is, but some maybe not. It's cohesive, though.

Is Crowded House more of a democracy now?

It's never been a democracy. I definitely exert my will over certain aspects, but everyone's approval is important to me. Everyone was involved in the mixing, everybody signed off and everybody had the chance to exert their opinions, but with Nick in Ireland, Elroy in England, Liam and Mitchell in LA and me in New Zealand, that was time-consuming and annoying. If and when we make another record, we have to be in the same place for at least six continuous weeks. Here, we were never together for more than 10 days.

You can't have anything to prove, now. What do you want from *Gravity Stairs*?

Actually, I do have something to prove. There's enormous goodwill for my songs and for the band. I'm always aware of that and grateful. That goodwill gets every record up to a certain level, but it gets you moving forwards too. That's the bottom line.

Apart from Some Greater Plan (For Claire), Thirsty's an obvious standout…

It's Elroy's music and I put a vocal on it. He fell in love when we were on a Mediterranean holiday a couple of years ago, although like many of my songs, the central line – "How come some people never get thirsty?" – is not really related to the story. It's purely factual: many people never drink water, such as Mick Fleetwood's mother.

How do you write a song?

A few lines define a feeling, a character or a sense of time and place. I follow that thread, but I'm very much looking for words that drop into the melody before you know what they mean.

You're a melody-first man?

Essentially, yes. Chords meld atmosphere and sometimes it's a case of not knowing what a song is about until near the end when things start to suddenly tie up. It's a matter of trusting those random subconscious thoughts. This can seem like nonsense, but I believe it. There's skulduggery and bluff involved too, but people sometimes tell me that the line I'm most worried about is the essential one for them. That's why some people use Fall At Your Feet at weddings, others for funerals. I admire narrative songwriters, but that's not me: confessional, diary songwriting feels like over-sharing.

What's it like when it works?

Wow! At the moment I've broken through on a song, there's the thrilling feeling that you have divine power that's unique, important and needed by the world, although that vanity is balanced by feeling you're fighting through cosmic insignificance 90 per cent of the time.

"Important"?

One of the few things the world agrees on is that music is important. It makes things better. In the future there will be different kinds of power harnessed for the good of mankind. One of those is the harmonic power that stems from music's ability to transfer uplift. Look how it triggers Alzheimer's patients' memories. It's miraculous when you think about it. No pharmaceutical product can get there, science can't match what music can do. There's a lot more power in music than we know about.

What's your USP as a songwriter?

Melodic sensibility. The way I put the rhythm of melodies with chords is unique, although it may have echoes in other people's work. And I can generate a unique atmosphere. Beyond that, I can't define it.

Where do you keep your OBE?

In a drawer somewhere. Can't remember which one. I was never sure about accepting it, but I turned down a knighthood, you know…

No 'Arise, Sir Neil'. Why?

Firstly, they wrote a letter describing why I should have it and I kept thinking, That's bullshit. Secondly, most of the people who get those things don't deserve them. And I couldn't stand the idea of people going, "Arise, Sir Neil," like you've just done. So I thought it was better to step aside.

Without being thought of as a goody-goody, you've avoided any kind of scandal: sex, drugs, financial, #MeToo, etc. How come?

Because I'm clever and deceitful. There's a certain good fortune in having a moderate amount of success. It means you don't become interesting to the tabloids. We've probably missed opportunities by not being scandalous, but I'd rather not. Privacy's good.

How would you like to be remembered?

A song being used in 100 years with nobody having any idea who wrote it. That's an immortality which doesn't rely on anything personal. Brightening people's lives, giving them some comfort and delivering with a light touch would be a nice legacy too, but I'm still the guy singing harmony, washing dishes with my mum. Ⓜ

FINN'S FINEST

Three albums in one career, by John Aizlewood.

BROTHERS IN ARMS

Crowded House
★★★★★
Woodface
(CAPITOL, 1991)

A glorious ragbag comprising four Neil songs, a selection of Neil and Tim's efforts, Paul Hester's rather wonderful Italian Plastic and the original trio's How Will You Go. In Neil's Fall At Your Feet and Neil and Tim's Weather With You and Four Seasons In One Day, Crowded House had three songs upon which their reputation would be partly based.

THE LATE WINNER

Neil Finn
★★★★
One Nil
(PARLOPHONE, 2001)

The solo canon's peak merges loops, layers and melody, and features Lisa Germano, Sheryl Crow, Jim Keltner and Midnight Oil's Jim Moginie, but most prominently, Prince consorts Wendy & Lisa. With Wendy Melvoin co-writing five songs, Finn had his most rewarding songwriting partner since Tim, but he's the dominant force and he's never sounded less restrained than on Hole In The Ice.

THE GENERATIONS GAME

Neil & Liam Finn
★★★★
Lightsleeper
(LESTER, 2018)

Subtly merging echoes of Liam's 2014 album *The Nihilist* and Neil's solo work, a delicate mixture of winsome vocals, impish melodies and assorted textures. Mostly written by father and son, but the piano-led Listen, one of two Neil-written tracks, is as gorgeous as anything by Crowded House, while Anger Plays A Part, Liam's only solo write, suggests he's a worthy torch-carrier.

the Thrill *of the* Chase

For diehards, **Scott Walker**'s *Climate Of Hunter* was the comeback of the decade. For insiders, the experience was extraordinary, baffling, often exasperating, as, 40 years ago, the dormant star emerged from the arena of myth to craft his strange, 'Tarkovskian' masterpiece. "When he got into the studio he completely changed," learns **Ian Harrison**. "It was Jekyll and Hyde."

Portrait: **Brian Aris**

IN EARLY 1984, LATE AT night in an underground carpark in Battersea, former '60s pop idol Scott Walker filmed his only music video of the decade. With an alarmed harmony vocal overdubbed by chart hitmaker Billy Ocean, Track Three was muscle-deep, brooding and counter-intuitive, both rock and not-rock, with obtuse lyrics of predestined doom.

The monochrome promo featured a subterranean car chase, anointment by blood and the rolling of mysterious dice. Walker described the clip as "Tarkovskian" to the late Richard Cook of NME, presumably referring to the chamber piled with sand which echoed a famous scene from the Soviet director's 1979 screen classic Stalker. Tarkovsky's movie concerned an illicit trip into the mysterious 'Zone' where unearthly visitors had left various supernatural objects, including a Room where all desires would be granted.

A philosophical, wreckage-strewn work of mindbending science fiction, one of Stalker's themes remains Be Very Careful What You Wish For. Scott would likely sympathise. An American in Britain, in the mid-'60s he'd pursued and enjoyed monstrous pop fame with ersatz siblings The Walker Brothers, before embarking on a stellar solo career in 1967. His life had been complicated by those pin-up years ever since.

With a break for photographer Anton Corbijn to take some portraits, Walker's manager Ed Bicknell recalls the '84 video shoot as "sitting in a caravan for hours while they set everything up and put concrete dust all over the floor. And then, you couldn't write this shit, there was a murder down the street. There were police cars, ambulances… Scott got really rattled and drank and got more and more pissed. It was the only time he ever talked to me about The Walker Brothers."

Walker told Bicknell he'd decided to quit after a car they were in was turned upside-down by a phalanx of ultra-Walkerfans. "They didn't have seatbelts so they were literally up in the roof space," says Bicknell. "Total pandemonium. He'd enjoyed being a pop star for a bit, but as it got bigger and bigger he found the whole thing awful."

Yet here he was, back in the game again. One re-connection with the wider world was an uncomfortable interview on Channel 4 music show The Tube on March 23, 1984, when the non-charting Track Three's video was given its sole broadcast. Speaking to interviewer Muriel Gray in a crowded green room, a polite Walker kept his anorak on as if planning a sudden escape. He spoke evasively of new solo album *Climate Of Hunter*, his first for 10 years. Gray asked reasonable questions: does losing huge fame mess a person up ("It was a relief"), why ➤

Brian Aris

34 MOJO

Night of the Hunter: Scott Walker, back in the game, 1984.

now ("You feel a time for things"), and would he like to achieve his massive success again? A frown, a certain look: "I hope not."

In spring 2006, at the Holland Park home of his managers Charles and Cathy Negus-Fancey, this writer interviewed Scott Walker about his then-new album *The Drift*. The late afternoon lights were low and he kept his baseball cap on, unwilling to be recognised even on friendly ground. At one point, talk turned to *Climate Of Hunter*. "I honestly don't remember it too well," the man born Noel Engel told me, his rich speaking voice a sonorous echo of his singing. "It was sort of a way of… dipping a toe back in the water."

THE DIPPING HAD ACTUALLY BEGUN SIX YEARS earlier. For Walker, the dream had turned bad as the '70s dawned: he'd spent years completing contracts and turning his immaculate croon to MOR covers on palatable-to-mum-and-dad LPs called *We Had It All* and *Any Day Now*, and a Walker Brothers reunion which yielded a UK Top 10 hit with No Regrets in 1975. Yet steeled by the imminent collapse of their GTO label and the impending end of the group, Scott had returned to songwriting for The Walker Brothers' July 1978 farewell *Nite Flights*. His four new songs were a revelation: recorded with an in-studio soundtrack of Bowie's *Low*, these cryptic, ice-packed cries of terror and release warned that something big was stirring. In March 1979, Melody Maker reported that Bowie wanted to produce Walker's next record: the singer declined.

Piqued by Brian Eno's enthusiasm for final Walkers single The Electrician – a Stygian South American love song invaded by a US torture squad – Virgin's Simon Draper duly signed its writer in late '79 for a standard eight-LP deal for £20,000, plus recording costs. "He said he was going to record in May," says Draper, who refutes suggestions made elsewhere that the deal was a bad one for Scott. "The reason was it was spring, which would be conducive to the muse. He always sounded a bit whimsical and disconnected. Then he started making excuses. Come May, nothing happened, and that went on for four years."

There were, though, rumblings that the outside world remembered him. In August 1981, Liverpool's Zoo label released *Fire Escape In The Sky: The Godlike Genius Of Scott Walker*, a compilation of songs from his first five solo records curated by Julian Cope of hit psych-poppers The Teardrop Explodes, who wrote, "I wanted all those post-punk dudes and dudettes to buy Scott in droves." Also that year, *Scott Walker Sings Jacques Brel* collected his majestic '60s covers of the great Belgian chansonnier (with sleevenotes by late MOJO writer Fred Dellar).

Despite excited press attention, Walker resisted the pull of his old self, and an offer to collaborate with Brian Eno was also rebuffed. One celebrated anecdote of these incommunicado years – Virgin staffers recall him driving around London in his orange Volkswagen Beetle listening to Miles Davis on a tape recorder in the glove compartment – involves him complaining that his label was deliberately "getting at him" with noise in his High Street Kensington flat. It transpired that Virgin funded a social charity based downstairs, which was given to therapies of the screaming and shouting kind. "When he said it, I thought, This guy's completely bonkers," says Draper. "But as it turned out, it was actually true."

However tenuously, contact with Virgin was maintained. A&R

"The first time he came into the office, it became obvious to me that he basically had no money."
Ed Bicknell

chief Arnold Frolows played squash with Scott; publicity head Al Clark met him for west London lunches and pub visits to talk cinema. "[His unreadiness] was as frustrating for him as it was for us," says Clark, who later produced the '94 movie The Adventures Of Priscilla, Queen Of The Desert. He adds, "I think Scott found Julian Cope's declared admiration as another fan pressure."

After Walker expressed an interest in production, Clark introduced him to Dire Straits manager Bicknell. "Nobody was interested," says Bicknell, a huge Walker fan who officially took over his affairs in February 1983. "You have to remember, back then Scott Walker was a washed-up former pop star."

He was also a washed-up former pop star who was, unusually, immune to financial inducements. "The first time he came into the office, it became obvious to me that he basically had no money," says Bicknell, who remembers meetings in pitch darkness in the curtained booths at the Kensington Hilton's Hiroko Japanese restaurant after Scott unscrewed the lightbulbs. "And of everybody I've worked with, he was one artist who absolutely was *not* motivated by money. He lived with his then girlfriend, who as far as I could tell pretty much supported him. He lived at night, going to bed around about seven or eight in the morning, like Elvis Presley in Earl's Court."

BY SUMMER 1983, HOWEVER, WALKER WAS ready to work. In August and September he rented a cottage outside Tunbridge Wells and wrote a new set of songs, informing his manager from a payphone that they were complete. "I told Virgin I'd have it ready in two months," he told Richard Cook in March '84, adding that recent musical exposures

Getty (4), Alamy, Arnau Oriol Sanchez

Night flights: (clockwise from top left) Walker signs autographs for fans at London Airport, September 26, 1967; Scott free: Walker solo in 1968; back with 'Brothers' Gary Leeds (centre) and John Maus, 1975; *Climate Of Hunter* co-producer Peter Walsh; Walker with Lulu at the 1968 St Valentine's Day Presentation party; Scott's manager Ed Bicknell.

included Michael Jackson, Elvis Costello and Marc Almond. "I had to run a bluff on myself… I knew I had to find it this time even if I never made another record. C'mon you old bastard, keep moving!"

Virgin paired him with young engineer/producer Peter Walsh, whose recent successes included Simple Minds' *New Gold Dream (81-82-83-84)* and Heaven 17's *Penthouse And Pavement*. "There were no demos, no conversation with the record company," says Walsh. "Nobody knew what we were going to record so I think that there were a lot of fingers crossed. I saw it as, I was working with the best voice, the most powerful emotional voice around that time, but I didn't see it as, We're going to be making another sort of Walker Brothers hit."

It was a good job he didn't. Recorded for £75,000 at Sarm West, EMI studios and The Townhouse from October to December 1983, *Climate Of Hunter* was an off-map psychic seismograph of the deepest kind, transmitting from far into the art-rock beyond with a curiously commercial timestamp of the reverbed-vocals/bass-wanging '80s.

A 31-minute span that could be years, its protagonists all approached it from oblique angles. Keyboardist and arranger Brian Gascoigne recalls Walker giving him hand-drawn piano chords of his own devising which he would then transcribe. "He liked chords that were dissonant but gave you a hint of conventional harmony. My job was to spread them out over the orchestra in a way that produced the chordal effect that he wanted, and then experiment endlessly in the studio with alternative ways of voicing it.

"Then he'd start with the rhythm section," Gascoigne continues. "I'd have written them a part and they'd start with all their standard licks, which Scott immediately ignored, so then they'd go a little bit outside and finally they'd think, Well, I've played him everything I can possibly think of. And they would then go *completely* outside, and Scott would suddenly get terribly happy and say that was exactly what he wanted. Quite an irritating way of working but it achieved the result."

Crucially, the players and Walsh were not privy to the songs' lyrics or melodies. "If there's no vocals, you play less and there's a question mark in how you play it," reflects drummer Peter Van Hooke. "So it was intuitive big blocks, if you know what I mean; you didn't know if that was a chorus, if that was a verse… Scott understood tension in music. You don't get lots of chord changes resolving, I wasn't playing drum fills. He would create landscapes on top of rhythms, and then he was the narrator of that landscape, but in melody. He would deliver this great vocal, and basically pour everything into that moment."

Guitarist Ray Russell, who scrawled into-the-mirror rock solos on Track Three and Track Seven (four of the eight songs have numerical titles) in a single-day session at The Townhouse, compares Walker's Zen studio approach to that of Bill Fay and Gil Evans. Instruction came, he says, via "imagery and words, all very poetical. He told you something that happened to him or a dream, something like that, and we derived the mood of what we should play by the story. He's sitting quietly in the [control room] box listening to what's going on. Approving, nodding, whatever…"

Interviewed on Stephen Kijak's 2006 Walker doc 30 Century Man, free sax improvisor Evan Parker recalled drinking "a very good Chablis" and being told to think about clouds of sound and György Ligeti as preparation for playing on Dealer and Track Six.

"There were a couple of occasions where he would actually bring in a photocopy of a picture of a painting, and say, 'I'm hearing this kind of thing,'" adds Walsh. "At The Townhouse he had a grainy, scrawly black and white abstract pencil drawing sat on the desk."

"You couldn't wish for a more delightful person to be with," notes Gascoigne, "but when he got into the studio he completely changed. It was Jekyll and Hyde. He adopted both a frown and a smile at the same time, as he was listening to stuff. I disagreed with him on the fact that he regarded musicians as having to feel pain in order to convey it." ➤

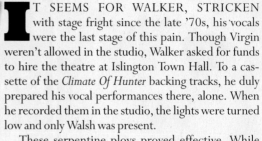

"What we did was great": Walker didn't like producer Daniel Lanois' (above) satin tour jackets; (below) Scott collaborator Brian Eno in 1985.

The Lost '80s Album... Found!

Scott Walker, plus Eno, Lanois and Robert Fripp too. What could possibly have gone wrong, asks Ian Harrison?

IN 2007, late bass session ace Mo Foster told MOJO that he and the *Climate Of Hunter* players entered Phil Manzanera's studio The Gallery in Chertsey on March 6 to 9 and March 11, 1985 to start the follow-up to *Climate Of Hunter*. He recalled "fierce energy" but added, "then it got strange because Virgin brought in Brian Eno and Daniel Lanois [who had recently co-produced U2's *The Unforgettable Fire*], who are really good people, but it killed the mood."

"What we did was great," says drummer Peter Van Hooke today. "But I think Brian Eno was trying to intellectualise it and, of course, Scott can't be bullshitted. And I remember playing a particular track, and Daniel came in and said, 'Can you change it?' And Scott's saying, 'Don't!'"

"It was one of the most unpleasant weeks of my life," recalls Brian Gascoigne. "Absolutely ridiculous, just fucking about in the most ridiculous way."

The sessions were abandoned without vocals being recorded. One legend has it that the singer threw the tapes in the Thames. "One of the reasons Scott gave me for scrapping it was he didn't like the satin tour jackets that Daniel Lanois wore in the studio," says Jeremy Lascelles.

"They had Robert Fripp on the record too," says Simon Draper. "We thought there was the prospect of having a massive album. What happened was demoralising, but you can't force someone to do something."

Courtesy of Draper, and nearly 40 years after they were recorded, MOJO was finally able to hear six unnamed instrumental tracks. Our impressions follow:

TRACK I: Drums crash and a static bass riff repeats. A twang at 45 seconds kicks off a jazz-rock rhythm with a Smiths-esque chord change at 1:04. Twenty-six seconds later the mood becomes more contemplative, while at 2:31 distorted Fripp guitar recalling *Nite Flights'* Shutout grinds into life. At 3:50 it speeds up again and collapses, wailing (4:05).

TRACK II: Bass-driven upside-down rhythms hang suspended. Guitar drones are followed by a blazing sustained note, not unlike *Nite Flights'* Fat Mama Kick. Cue Fripp bending and slashing his guitar. Abrupt, stab-like end (2:13).

TRACK III: Soft '80s ambient pop with gated snares (is that the sound of phantom footsteps?) builds and accelerates with another blinding chordal floodlight. Almost like The Stranglers' La Folie, resolving in a symphonic swell (2:50).

TRACK IV: Exploratory, luminous keys and synth hum, not dissimilar to *Climate Of Hunter's* Rawhide. The lyrics to Scott's Such A Small Love (from 1967's *Scott*) might fit. After another burst of chordal light, "Heroes" guitar directs us into a lush, light-refracting holding pattern with rattling percussion (4:23).

TRACK V: A martial tattoo and synth whistles, recalling Face On Breast from *Tilt*, rocks up at 58 seconds and accelerates, while guitars make like scribbling violas (4:28).

TRACK VI: Aquatic synth washes announce a lurching rhythm *à la* Bowie's Ashes To Ashes. One-note piano is joined by what sounds like a glass harmonica, feedbacking elegantly (4:02).

IT SEEMS FOR WALKER, STRICKEN with stage fright since the late '70s, his vocals were the last stage of this pain. Though Virgin weren't allowed in the studio, Walker asked for funds to hire the theatre at Islington Town Hall. To a cassette of the *Climate Of Hunter* backing tracks, he duly prepared his vocal performances there, alone. When he recorded them in the studio, the lights were turned low and only Walsh was present.

These serpentine ploys proved effective. While Walker's voice was starker than in his velvet heyday, here was a singer in full control, crooning oblique haikus of arrival and departure over static synthesizer lines, ebbing bass and full orchestra. With drip-fed references to late nights, death and darkness, its themes suited the Track Three video's crime scene, but the whole is much more. Serene and unknowable, opener Rawhide brings together the impressions of prehistoric herders, the Palaeolithic cave paintings of Lascaux and gazing upwards at the twinkling constellation of Taurus (possibly). The orchestral Sleepwalkers Woman recalls 1969's perfect Boy Child, and shimmers like Mahler and Van Gogh's The Starry Night as it counts down to "splintering bone ashes," silence and endings. "Everything came together for that," says Walsh, who worked with Walker until his death in March 2019. "It was very difficult to listen to after he passed."

The album fades to black with a Styx-crossing voice-and-guitar cover of the Tennessee Williams/Kenyon Hopkins composition Blanket Roll Blues, as sung by Scott fave Marlon Brando in the 1960 film The Fugitive Kind. With both men in the control room at Sarm West, Mark Knopfler played the National steel guitar that appears on the cover of Dire Straits' *Brothers In Arms*, while Walker sang into a Shure SM58 microphone. The guitar was recorded from two massive speakers out in the studio space. "It was a spontaneous take, with no polishing afterwards," says Walsh. "On the following albums there was always one track that we would put together rather quickly."

"When it was delivered, we all thought, Jesus, is this a stroke of genius?" says then Virgin A&R Jeremy Lascelles. "Or is this so out there it's impenetrable? But then, you listen to his subsequent records and *Climate Of Hunter* sounds like an entry for the Eurovision Song Contest."

Packaging such a work proved, inevitably, another challenge. Snapping the cover portrait at the singer's suggestion was the late Bob Carlos Clarke, who captured Walker as if in the midst of an alarming recollection (according to sleeve designer Chris Morton, the singer kept hold of a "much-loved small stone" throughout the shoot in Fulham). For the inner sleeve, Walker reluctantly provided written lyrics. "It was like pulling teeth," says Bicknell, "almost as if he was ashamed, or very nervous, as to what people's reaction was going to be."

In the event, people's reactions proved mixed. Positive responses included a rapt Biba Kopf concluding in NME that "*Climate Of Hunter* invites the listener to scream into the face of destiny." There was the interview with Cook, the appearance on The Tube, but Walker hardly threw himself into the hurly-burly of promotion. "I think I am a melancholic," the singer told Alan Bangs of the British Forces Broadcasting Service in West Germany, "without any self-pity at all."

Climate Of Hunter charted at UK Number 60 on March 25, slipped to 84 the week after, and then was gone.

WHILE THE SCOTT FAITHFUL HARBOURED hopes that *Climate* might begin a whole new chapter for their hero, such did not prove to be the case. Though Walker began work on an album produced by Brian Eno and Daniel Lanois in March 1985, the project was rapidly aborted (*see sidebar*). Later, the singer made one of his infrequent visits to his manager. "I said, What have you been up to?" recalls Bicknell. "And he said, 'I've been painting.' I said, Oh, oils or watercolours? He said, 'No, man, walls.' He'd been working as a painter and

Getty (2), Alamy, Paul Cox

"There were no demos, no conversation with the record company. Nobody knew what we were going to record."
Peter Walsh

No regrets: (clockwise from top left) Walker checks his specs in 2006; Scott being interviewed by Muriel Gray on The Tube, March 23, 1984; Walker favourite and Blanket Roll Blues singer Marlon Brando with Anna Magnani in 1960's The Fugitive Kind; a poster for Tarkovsky's 1979 film Stalker; 2006 album *The Drift*; Walker's final solo LP, 2012's *Bish Bosch* – "doing it for me alone… how I did my best work."

decorator. He could, at any point, have put The Walker Brothers back together and done the nostalgia circuit, but he would rather, literally, get up a ladder with a pot of Dulux and paint somebody's flat and get a few quid."

Bicknell suggested a conventional album of newly written covers by Knopfler, Boy George, Elvis Costello, Difford and Tilbrook, Chris Rea and other keen collaborators. The singer demurred.

The remainder of the '80s were lean times for Scott fans, with only rumours for sustenance.

One claimed he was working in a fish and chip shop in Stoke-On-Trent; another that he was going to appear alongside Kate Bush, Alvin Stardust and Donovan in radio DJ Mike Read's John Betjeman musical Teddy Bear To The Nation. There was also talk of collaborations with David Sylvian and The Jesus And Mary Chain. The first, gleans MOJO, was mooted only in the vaguest terms. Geoff Travis, co-founder of the Mary Chain's label Blanco Y Negro, says the latter notion was pure moonshine, although he did suggest Kevin Shields when Walker's management eventually came looking for guitarists for 2006's The Drift.

One nutty move that turned out to be real was Walker's appearance in a swinging '60s-themed ad for Britvic 55 orange drink in 1987. Soundtracked by Dusty Springfield's 1963 hit I Only Want To Be With You (produced by Walker's old friend and producer Johnny Franz), the clip starred Springfield, Sandie Shaw and Lulu, with Scott appearing fleetingly as a haunted-looking 'Man In Café'. "I asked him about it and he just kind of laughed," says Bicknell.

Walker's next album would be Tilt in 1995. That year, Hot Press magazine's Joe Jackson floated a theory from 1994 Walker biography A Deep Shade Of Blue, that Climate Of Hunter was some kind of tossed-off con job intended to cock a snook at the record biz, fans and critics. "It's an interesting idea, but it's total crap," said Walker. "Why should I go through this kind of work, often hardship, just to say that… what kind of bitter motherfucker would I have to be?"

While Climate Of Hunter was not the return to contention that many had craved, the singer's associates from the '80s are united in their admiration for him, and it.

"I wouldn't change it for anything," says Bicknell. "He was an absolute delight to work with and to just have in my life. Just a fucking great bloke."

Like others, Gascoigne admits to wishing Walker had used his voice in more easily approached ways. "From Climate Of Hunter on, that gorgeous voice he had was a thing of the past," he reflects. "We had a standing joke, that when Scott Walker sings Cole Porter, I would want to do some of the arrangements. Occasionally, just to wind him up, I'd play a bit of a Cole Porter song in his key, and he would just glare at me. We both knew he was never going to do it."

In 2012, MOJO was back at the Negus-Fancey residence, speaking to Walker about his album Bish Bosch. He was sat in the same room, the same chair, in much the same clothes, speaking with the same mixture of guardedness and candour, as he had in 2006.

"After Climate…, there was another hiatus," he told me, green forage cap pulled down tight. "I was going on to do some painting and just get away from whatever it was. [But] when I think it's gone, I get dragged back…

"Now I just do it for me alone," he declared. "That's how I did my best work, anyway." Ⓜ

After apprenticing in Carolina Chocolate Drops with Rhiannon Giddens, LEYLA McCALLA emerged with a whole new thing – mashing banjo, cello, New York, New Orleans and Haiti into a unique musical gumbo. The history she mines is dark, but as she insists to VICTORIA SEGAL, "I am determined to be joyful."

Photography by CHRIS SCHEURICH

W HEN LEYLA McCALLA WAS TALKING TO HER BAND ABOUT THE GUITAR
freak-out she wanted to close Tree, a track from her newest album *Sun Without The Heat*, she said it should sound "like a woman losing her mind as she's trying to figure out how to get the love she needs."

She wanted it to sound like they were fighting, like they were on the edge of a cliff, that they were making a "catastrophic cacophony" that didn't so much break the tension as smash it on the rocks. "I'm a big proponent of chasing the fun approach to getting to the end of a song," McCalla laughs. "You know, we're on this cliff-hanger – then we just veer in a different direction and turn it into a dance party."

McCalla is used to keeping things in harmonious balance, whether she's moving between cello, banjo and guitar, or writing songs that wear heavy learning with light grace. Her solo debut, *Vari-Colored Songs*, was a tribute to the writer Langston Hughes; her last album, 2022's febrile *Breaking The Thermometer*, explored the archives of Radio Haiti, the country's first Kreyòl-language radio station founded during the brutal Duvalier dictatorship. Born in New York to Haitian parents, raised in New Jersey, "discovered" playing Bach in New Orleans by Tim Duffy, manager of Rhiannon Giddens' string band Carolina Chocolate Drops, McCalla makes music that has stories bursting from every note, a deep, reflective synthesis of Haitian folk and old-time Americana, Afrofuturism and Tropicália, English and Kreyòl.

For Giddens, asking McCalla to join Carolina Chocolate Drops was "a no-brainer"; McCalla's Caribbean styles instantly expanded the group's Northern string-band palette. She played on the 2012 album *Leaving Eden*, but she began as a touring member; Giddens recalls McCalla's audience-delighting performance of Haitian folk song ➤

Chris Scheurich

Here comes the sun: joy-seeker Leyla McCalla feels "like a professional processor of history."

Four strings attached. (clockwise from left) McCalla performing at the New Orleans Jazz And Heritage Festival, April 29, 2022; Leyla in 2024, seeing herself as a "link in some sort of chain"; Our Native Daughters (from left) McCalla, Amythyst Kiah, Allison Russell and Rhiannon Giddens, 2019.

"LEYLA'S ONE OF MY FAVOURITE MUSICIANS AND I WANT THE WHOLE WORLD TO KNOW. SHE SHOULD BE FAMOUS."

Rhiannon Giddens

≺ Rose Marie, which McCalla recorded on *Vari-Colored Songs*.

"It's great when you have an historical, cultural connection, and then it's just a great performance," says Giddens. "There's showbiz you have to think about too! It was all of it together."

McCalla's desire to unfurl her own songwriting skills saw her leave the band in 2014 – "I was so upset, like, Aargh, she's so good!" laughs Giddens – but McCalla reunited with "the big sister I never knew I needed" in 2019 for the Our Native Daughters project, four black female banjo players interrogating slavery, racism and sexism through powerful song.

"She's on speed dial," says Giddens. "I just have nothing but respect and love for what she does. She's one of my favourite musicians and I want the whole world to know. She should be famous."

IT'S BALANCE OF THE WORK-LIFE KIND THAT'S initially the topic of conversation when McCalla, at her home in New Orleans, speaks to MOJO. "Every morning for me is a busy morning," she says, "I have three kids and I'm a single mom." Throughout her own childhood, her father Jocelyn McCalla was Executive Director of the National Coalition For Haitian Rights. Her mother, Regine Dupuy, meanwhile, went to law school the same year her daughter picked up the cello, becoming an immigration lawyer and founder of NGO Dwa Fanm ("Women's Rights").

"Having parents who are doing important things and can explain to you why those things are important to the world, I think that's a gift," McCalla laughs. "I sure hope it is." She tries to involve her nine-year-old daughter and five-year-old twins in her work – not least with cameos in the video for Scaled To Survive, a tender lullaby about motherhood and legacy. "My mother emigrated to the United States in the Jim Crow era in the '60s. My grandmother was a young mother with two small children, emigrating from Haiti. I think about what that might have been like for them and I'm fascinated by it. Fascinated by it. It's not something that I stop thinking about."

Sun Without The Heat was recorded in Maurice, Louisiana in "a deeply collaborative nine-day session" with her band (percussionist Shawn Myers, guitarist Nahum Zdybel, bassist Pete Olynciw) and producer Maryam Qudus. "Leyla and I had put some song ideas together, but besides that, we went into the studio with a blank canvas," recalls Qudus. "Once the song took shape, I'd send Leyla off to sit by the bayou and write lyrics. Words would change in real-time while we'd record the final vocal. The humidity was thick and you'd hear cicadas all day. Leyla's kids and mom visited for a few days."

Freed from the prescriptive frame of *Breaking The Thermometer*, originally commissioned by Duke University, McCalla asked herself "what does it mean to just… make an album?", going back to "the essence of my motivation".

Key among those formative moments were two years spent in Ghana as a teenager while her mother worked with refugees from Sierra Leone and Liberia. There, she discovered highlife music and "kind of recognised myself as a daughter of Africa even though I had never lived there. It broadened my conception of myself and where I come from."

The family made road trips through Togo into Benin, visiting the Dahomey temples – "the origins of Haitian Vodou" – or to Elmina Castle where enslaved people were loaded onto ships through The Door Of No Return. She remembers "feeling the energy in that space, smelling what it smells like to be in hundreds of years of history."

For *Sun Without The Heat* – its title inspired by a speech by black American statesman and writer Frederick Douglass – McCalla partly drew on Adrienne Maree Brown's 2019 book Pleasure Activism. "We can't be activists without centring our pleasure," McCalla explains. "Women in general – but particularly black women – have been programmed with this thought that we are the stability in our families, the ones who need to lift everyone up. Where does that leave us? Oftentimes feeling depleted and neglected. How do I heal that for myself, and my daughters, and their daughters? I think that's where a lot of songs really came from."

The album's first words are "I am trying/To be free."

McCALLA GREW UP IN A HOUSEHOLD WHERE "Paul Simon, Stevie Wonder and [Haitian group] Boukman Eksperyans were the top three sounds of my childhood." Later, her father "got really into the Tropicalismo move-

Chris Scheurich, Getty (3), Alamy (3)

Mac attack: (clockwise from above) Leyla (far right) with Carolina Chocolate Drops, 2012; with cello on-stage in Spain, 2017; (from left) McCalla, Matthew McConaughey, Sam Beam, Lucinda Williams, Willie Nelson and Dom Flemons perform at a Johnny Cash tribute, 2012; Leyla accepts her People's Voice gong during the 2023 International Folk Music Awards.

QUEEN KREYÒL

The best of Leyla McCalla, on record, by **Victoria Segal**.

LEYLA McCALLA
★★★★
Vari-Colored Songs: A Tribute To Langston Hughes
(Music Maker, 2014)

Harlem and Haiti meet on McCalla's solo debut, her spare settings of poems by jazz age figurehead Langston Hughes (Heart Of Gold, Song For A Dark Girl) jostling against Kreyòl folk songs (Mesi Bondye; Rose Marie). A fruitful tangling of roots and branches.

OUR NATIVE DAUGHTERS
★★★★
Songs Of Our Native Daughters
(Smithsonian Folkways, 2019)

Rhiannon Giddens gathered up McCalla, Tennessee's Amythyst Kiah and Canadian singer-songwriter Allison Russell for this black female banjo supergroup. Inspired by guitarist Etta Baker's life and blues, McCalla's I Knew I Could Fly gently amplifies the record's underlying thrum of resilience and self-realisation.

LEYLA McCALLA
★★★★
Breaking The Thermometer
(Anti-, 2022)

Originally commissioned for a theatre piece about Radio Haiti and murdered journalist Jean Dominique, a showcase for McCalla's shaping of complex historical and political narrative into richly emotional music. Highlights include blazing protest song Dodinin, anti-censorship lament Le Bal Est Fini, and a cover of Caetano Veloso's You Don't Know Me.

LEYLA McCALLA
★★★★
Sun Without The Heat
(Anti-, 2024)

"It feels like a personal record," comments McCalla's friend and colleague Giddens, and after Breaking The Thermometer's political weight, there is a marked intimacy to McCalla's fifth album, Tower and Open The Road pushing at the edges of love and freedom.

ment. Then I would discover Haitian music and was just like, Oh my God, why didn't my parents expose me to this stuff?"

It was when her fifth-grade class in Maplewood, New Jersey were told to pick an instrument for orchestra that her musical trajectory shifted. She chose the cello, believing it was "a woodwind instrument, a little piccolo". Once the shock passed, it was love. "The cello really saved my life. It gave me focus." Her cello teacher was "the first person to say, 'Wow, you actually have a talent for this,'" sending McCalla to her own teacher, a Juilliard professor. "That's when I became ambitious about being a musician."

Inspired by a folk-singer aunt, she also taught herself guitar, looking up internet tabs for Karma Police and Blackbird. "It really gave me space to have an identity in music that wasn't about interpreting the notes on the page or going to the next audition and knowing the concerto or sonata."

After graduating from NYU in 2007, McCalla was "bartending, teaching, playing in a church. I've played on so many singer-songwriters' records as a cello player." She started regularly visiting New Orleans, busking to fund trips. "When I decided to move there, it was a conscious decision to figure out if I could be a musician for real. It was the beginning of me thinking of myself more as a composer – but the actual skills that I had were playing Bach on the street."

Shaking off New York's "frigid winters" and financial strains, happily cycling around the French quarter with her cello on her back, she began noticing names from her family tree in the cemeteries, the similarities with Haitian architecture. "I started delving more into New Orleans history and realised how much Haiti is a part of that history. Then I started getting really curious – Why does history disappear? Who makes it disappear? Who does that serve when people don't know the origins of things?" All

the time, she was falling in love with Cajun and Creole music.

"I never thought, I'm going to be a banjo player 'cause the banjo is awesome," she explains. "I thought, I'm going to learn New Orleans traditional songs and I'm going to use the banjo because it has the same strings as the cello. Later, when I discovered Haitian Twoubadou music – which is like banjo music – I was, Oh, that's why I play the banjo, that's what I'm supposed to be learning. I feel it's one of those instruments that calls you."

McCalla has watched in awe as Giddens has amplified that call, playing banjo on Beyoncé's pop-country hit Texas Hold 'Em.

"I think that's super-badass," McCalla says. "There are so many conversations now about the place of blackness in country music – kudos to Beyoncé for capitalising on that. It's challenging the status quo."

CHALLENGING THE STATUS QUO is an impulse that runs deep through McCalla's work, too. Her maternal grandfather, Ben Depuy, founded Socialist newspaper Haïti Progrès – does she sometimes feel like a reporter in her music?

"I feel more like I'm a professional processor of history," she says. "There's still a lot to push up against, but I see how so many generations before me have paved the way for me to be able to do the work that I'm doing now without fear."

That work exists between the cliff-edge and the dance party, never shying away from pain, but holding up this music as testament to survival, to possibility.

"I am very determined to be joyful," says McCalla. "To enjoy my life while I'm alive. Thinking about myself as a link in some sort of chain, I want to be the link that figured out how to be happy."

Ⓜ

GOT LOUD IF YOU WANT IT

INCITING FRENZIES, WITH FANS "SWINGING FROM THE RAFTERS", **THE YARDBIRDS'** FERAL RAVE-UPS PRESAGED GARAGE ROCK, PUNK AND METAL, WHILE STARRING THREE LEAD GUITARISTS FOR THE AGES. SIXTY YEARS SINCE THEIR INCEPTION, THE SURVIVORS REFLECT ON THE BLUES, THE BOOZE AND THE BUST-UPS. "THE REASON WE'RE TALKING ABOUT THE YARDBIRDS NOW IS BECAUSE WE HAD THAT EDGE," THEY TELL **MARK BLAKE**.

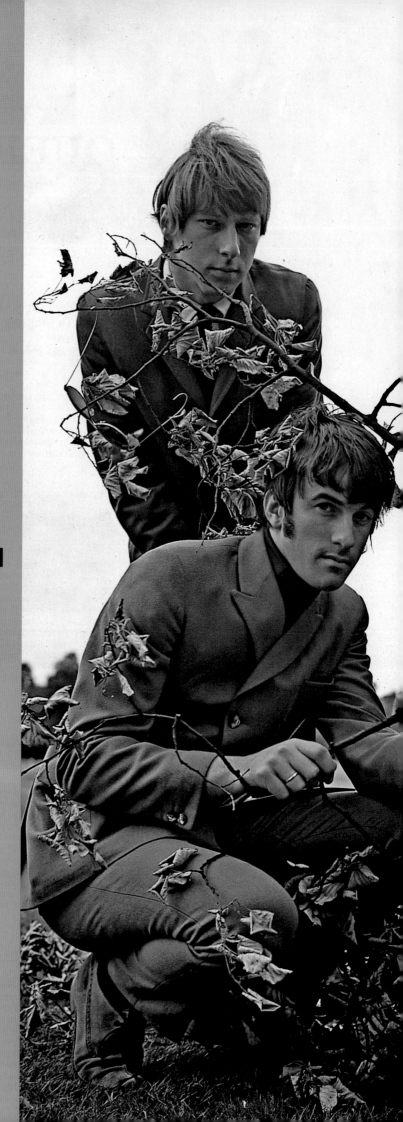

Alamy

Strange things happening:
The Yardbirds in 1966 (from left)
Chris Dreja, Jim McCarty, Jimmy
Page, Keith Relf, Jeff Beck.

"WHERE'S ERIC?" WONDERED THE AUDIENCE, AS THE OTHER YARDBIRDS ARRIVED ON-STAGE to be inducted into the 1992 Rock and Roll Hall of Fame. Eric Clapton had declined the invitation, but his successors, Jeff Beck and Jimmy Page, had joined the rest of the group for the ceremony in Cleveland.

Original bassist Paul Samwell-Smith, drummer Jim McCarty and guitarist-turned-bassist Chris Dreja trooped up to the podium to accept their awards. Then came Jimmy Page, who promised to "keep it short" before introducing vocalist Keith Relf's widow, April, and their son, Jason.

This just left Jeff Beck, who'd missed the memo about wearing a suit and was studiedly casual in jeans and a kaleidoscopic patterned waistcoat.

"Somebody told me I should be proud tonight," he said, with a sly grin and a ruffle of his trademark plumage. "But I'm not, 'cos they kicked me out. They did! Fuck *them*!" Beck stalked off, Page started laughing and the house band burst into The Yardbirds' hit Heart Full Of Soul.

JIM McCARTY, CURRENTLY ENJOYING THE WINTER SUN in his adopted hometown in Provence-Alpes-Côte d'Azur, still ponders their decision to dump Beck in 1966. "Oh it's terrible," he laughs. "I hate saying it, but we fired Jeff Beck. We had to, he kept letting us down."

This year marks the 60th anniversary of The Yardbirds' debut single, I Wish You Would, beginning a run of peerless 45s (including For Your Love, Shapes Of Things and Over Under Sideways Down), during which they morphed from post-war English kids mimicking Chicago blues to pioneers of psychedelia and hard rock, and a vehicle for three of the world's greatest lead guitarists.

"The Yardbirds cast a very long shadow," said U2's Edge in his Hall of Fame induction speech. "They felt like a foretaste of the music on its way – Cream, Led Zeppelin and the Jeff Beck Group."

The surviving Yardbirds are currently revisiting their legacy for a planned film documentary. Relf and Beck are no longer here to contribute, and Dreja suffered a stroke and has retired after a lengthy post-Yardbirds career in commercial photography, so the project is in many ways overdue. The band are more often credited as a breeding-ground for guitar heroes than they are for the music they made, which at its best pioneered the feral British take on R&B that, when exported to the land of its origin, gained revolutionary force, and made the inscrutable Relf a template for the first wave of US garage rock singers.

All of which would have seemed a preposterous fantasy in June 1963, when The Yardbirds formed in south-west London. McCarty and Samwell-Smith were pupils at Hampton Grammar School, while Dreja and Relf were studying at Kingston School Of Art with original Yardbirds guitarist Anthony 'Top' Topham, and his successor Eric Clapton.

Their mutual interests included Chicago blues, American literature and booze. "Keith and I were drinking pals at The Crown in Kingston," explains Samwell-Smith, talking to MOJO from his home studio in Burgundy. "The idea of the happy drop-out was very attractive. I remember Keith and I going camping, like the boys from Steinbeck's [1945 Great Depression novel] Cannery Row. I think we made it as far as Cornwall."

The original five played youth clubs and function halls in various folk and blues groups. "Then we had a jam at a friend's house in Putney and decided to do a new group," says McCarty. "Paul wanted something rockier and I was a rocky drummer."

Their first break came via British bluesman Cyril Davies, whose All-Stars band would include, at times, Beck, Page and Clapton. Relf asked if his group could audition for the interval slot at Davies' Eel Pie Island residency. "Then Cyril asked Keith what we were called and Keith said 'The Yardbirds'," recalls McCarty. "I didn't know anything about Charlie Parker then. I thought it meant a hobo who rode around America on the steam trains."

Davies was impressed enough to offer them another slot at Studio 51, the Soho venue where a nascent Rolling Stones had been regulars. By summer 1963, though, the Stones had outgrown the tiny basement and their Sunday-night residency at Richmond's Crawdaddy club.

The Crawdaddy's owner, Giorgio Gomelsky, had managed the Stones before they flew the coop, and needed a replacement.

Gomelsky was a Georgia-born, Swiss-educated filmmaker and club owner who'd capitalised on the trad jazz and skiffle booms. "He was like the perfect bohemian," says McCarty. "Bit older than us, living in a flat in Earl's Court, smoking Gauloises and being very continental."

Gomelsky filled up The Yardbirds gig sheet and put them into the Stones' old Crawdaddy spot. In October, 16-year-old 'Top' Topham was replaced by Eric Clapton from rival R&B group, The Roosters. "Top's parents told him to leave the band and concentrate on a proper education," says Samwell-Smith. "The others already knew Eric from art school," adds McCarty. "Apparently, he was in the stained-glass club."

THE FIRST TIME GOMELSKY HEARD THE YARDBIRDS HE was impressed by what he called their "manic *accelerando*". Or, in the parlance of the early '60s, their ability to "have a rave-up". On-stage, they cranked up the velocity, extending Bo Diddley's Here 'Tis and I'm A Man into six-minute jams, which inspired their most devout disciples to scale the Crawdaddy's low ceiling beams. "We really whipped up the audience," remembers McCarty. "People would swing from the rafters."

"What I liked about The Yardbirds was that our entire reason for existence was to honour the blues," Clapton would recall. "The covers we chose defined our identity – Good Morning Little Schoolgirl by Sonny Boy Williamson and Smokestack Lightning by Howlin' Wolf."

In winter '63, The Yardbirds backed Williamson on a UK tour. Although Gomelsky was unaware that it was Sonny Boy Williamson II – not the singer of Good Morning Little Schoolgirl (who'd died in 1948) – when he'd arranged the booking.

Performing with a real-life Mississippi bluesman was a culture shock. "Sonny Boy had a briefcase containing his harmonicas and a bottle of Johnnie Walker," says McCarty. "We might have a Scotch now and again but we were usually drinking beer."

After setting his hotel room alight attempting to fry rabbit on a coffee percolator hot plate, Williamson moved in with Gomelsky, and shocked his host by plucking a live chicken in the bath. "But he was a fantastic performer, and we learned a lot," recalls McCarty.

By spring 1964, The Yardbirds had a deal with EMI imprint Columbia. Two singles, Chicago bluesman Billy Boy Arnold's I Wish You Would and the earlier Williamson's Good Morning Little Schoolgirl, showed promise but barely troubled the charts. "I was disappointed," says Samwell-Smith. "It was a bit lo-fi – just stick a microphone in front of the band and get them to play loud."

In contrast, that year's Five Live Yardbirds LP was still lo-fi (Keith Relf's plumber dad Bill dangled a boom mike over the audience at London's Marquee club), but The Yardbirds' take on The Isley Brothers' Respectable sounded like a future instruction manual for the MC5 and The Stooges.

However, Clapton's blues purism quickly ran up against Gomelsky's quest to turn The Yardbirds into a pop act. A few months later, Gomelsky staged a guerilla gig in Labour peer Lord Ted Willis's back garden, after he'd dismissed rock'n'roll as "a cheap, plastic, candyfloss substitute for culture". Willis played along, and was photographed in the Daily Mirror grinning on a sun lounger while ➤

Alamy, Getty (4), Shutterstock

Keeping it rolling: (left) at The Yardbirds' Rock and Roll Hall of Fame induction dinner, Waldorf Astoria Hotel, New York, January 15, 1992 (from right) the late Keith Relf's son Jay, Jimmy Page, Jim McCarty, Paul Samwell-Smith, Chris Dreja and (front) Jeff Beck; (right) Sonny Boy Williamson II in the UK, circa 1964.

THE EALING CLUB
17 March 1962
Alexis Korner & Cyril Davies began British Rhythm & Blues on this site
PLAQUE FUNDED BY EALING'S MUSIC FANS

Hearts full of soul: The Yardbirds Mk II line-up, 1964 (clockwise from left) Chris Dreja, Paul Samwell-Smith, Eric Clapton, Keith Relf, Jim McCarty.

COLUMBIA 45 R.P.M.
MECOLICO
DB 7283
7XGA 26542
SOLD IN U.K. SUBJECT TO RESALE PRICE CONDITIONS SEE PRICE LISTS
Prod. by R & B. Associates
I WISH YOU WOULD
(Billy Boy Arnold)
YARDBIRDS
MADE IN Gt BRITAIN

Emidisc
2.43
GOOD MORNING LITTLE S
30 OCT 1964
YARD BIRDS
KEEP SURFACE CLEAN - USE LIGHTWEIGHT PICK UP

Peer pressure: (above) The Yardbirds with manager Giorgio Gomelsky (front, right) stage a sit-down protest on the lawn of Lord Ted Willis (far left), 1964; (below) Gomelsky, Clapton and Lord Willis share a peace pipe.

Rave on: (below) Keith Relf lays waste to a tambourine as The Yardbirds wow Woolwich Black Cat Club, January 21, 1965 (from left) Dreja, Samwell-Smith, McCarty, Relf and the soon-to-exit Clapton.

"ERIC WAS VERY, VERY HEAVY – SITTING IN THE VAN IN A MOOD ALL DAY. IT'S HARD WHEN YOU'VE GOT TO DEAL WITH THAT."
Jim McCarty

THE BAD, THE GOOD & THE UGLY

The Yardbirds' managers: they were 'colourful characters', writes MARK BLAKE.

THE YARDBIRDS attracted three huge characters as managers, but with variable benefits to the band.

The first, Giorgio Gomelsky, was a keen hustler, who produced their early hits and composed B-sides under the pseudonym, 'Oscar Rasputin'. The group fired him in spring 1966, for working them too hard and not paying them enough. But Gomelsky left with the rights to all their recorded works so far. "To this day, those early recordings are being exploited and we don't see a penny," says original bassist Paul Samwell-Smith.

In the '70s, Gomelsky spent his Yardbirds royalties on a studio in New York, where he worked with artists as diverse as Bill Laswell and Band Of Susans, before his death in 2016.

His successor, dashing man-about-town Simon Napier-Bell, lasted a few months before being replaced by his polar opposite, burly former wrestler and road manager Peter Grant. "Peter knew all the tricks," bassist Chris Dreja told MOJO in 2018. "He came on tour with us, and for the first time ever, The Yardbirds started making money."

Grant (who died in 1995) wasn't easily intimidated. He'd once punched out a drunk Gene Vincent and rolled up a reluctant Little Richard in a hotel carpet, to get him to a date at the Lewisham Odeon. After The Yardbirds were delayed en route to an amusement park gig on Rhode Island, the Mob-connected promoters tried to withhold the balance of the band's fee, even though they'd played the show.

"They came on the bus and told Peter we weren't getting paid," recalled Dreja. When Grant objected, one of them pulled a gun. Grant laughed, walked onto the muzzle, and bounced his would-be assailant down the aisle. "Peter stomach-butted this guy all the way to the front of the bus," Dreja went on, "and we got the cash."

When The Yardbirds split in summer 1968, Grant stuck with guitarist Jimmy Page, helped mastermind Led Zeppelin's career, and stayed by Page's side until the band's demise. Simon Napier-Bell wasn't surprised by their lengthy bromance. "Jimmy was inherently fragile and sensitive, and Peter provided him with some armour," he says. "The pair of them made the perfect team."

> "PETER GRANT STOMACH-BUTTED THIS PROMOTER ALL THE WAY TO THE FRONT OF THE BUS, AND WE GOT THE CASH."
> Chris Dreja

Strictly for the 'birds: The Yardbirds' managers (clockwise from above) Giorgio Gomelsky, 1965, Simon Napier-Bell, 1966, and Peter Grant, 1966.

⊲ The Yardbirds made a racket on his patio. But Clapton, with his fresh military crewcut, looked deadly serious.

"Eric was very conscientious," says McCarty. "If he stayed at your house, he'd be up at nine in the morning practising guitar. He was way more ambitious and profile-conscious too. He had a crewcut and a trench coat to look like Steve McQueen."

However, Clapton was destined for another path. "Giorgio kept us working, working, working," says Samwell-Smith. "Gigs every night, and Eric wasn't happy. But it was For Your Love that finished him off."

FOR YOUR LOVE WAS THE YARDBIRDS' BAROQUE-sounding third single, recorded in spring 1964, and composed by future 10cc man Graham Gouldman. When Samwell-Smith suggested using a harpsichord, the band arrived at IBC Studios to find the instrument waiting. "Giorgio supported the idea, which was extraordinary for a blues band."

However, Clapton was appalled and his sole contribution was a riff in the song's middle-eight. By the end of March 1965, when For Your Love became a UK Number 3 hit and went Top 5 in America, he was gone. "I was starting to take myself far too seriously," he admitted, "and was very critical of anybody who wasn't just playing pure blues. Giorgio didn't exactly fire me, but invited me to resign."

"It was a relief," admits McCarty today. "Because Eric was very, very heavy – sitting in the van in a mood all day. It's hard when you've got to deal with that."

The Yardbirds knew who they wanted as a replacement, but 22-year-old Jimmy Page was reluctant to give up his career as a session musician. Instead, he recommended his friend Jeff Beck. After leaving Wimbledon art school, Beck had bounced between sessions and day jobs, including a stint spraying cars, and was currently playing in another R&B outfit, The Tridents.

"Jeff was the opposite of Eric," recalls McCarty. "He turned up with long greasy hair and scruffy jeans – like a mechanic. Chris had to take him to get his hair cut and down to Carnaby Street for some decent clothes."

Beck made his Yardbirds debut on their next single, Heart Full Of Soul. Samwell-Smith thought the song's riff sounded like a sitar, so Gomelsky booked a sitar player. It would be several months before The Beatles used the same instrument on Norwegian Wood. "But there was a mood at the time of being experimental," says Samwell-Smith. "I was tired of just two guitars, bass and drums."

When the sitar player struggled with the time signature, Beck mimicked the instrument by bending his guitar strings. "Jeff was extraordinary," stresses Samwell-Smith. "He picked up the guitar and the only way I can describe it was he *chewed* it around in his fingers. The guitar just responded to him."

Heart Full Of Soul reached Number 2 in the UK singles chart and empowered The Yardbirds to move further from the blues. "Giorgio also encouraged us to start writing songs, as he saw it as another source of income," suggests McCarty. He and Samwell-Smith co-wrote the group's next B-side, Still I'm Sad, which featured Gomelsky performing a Gregorian monk-style chant.

However supportive he was of these wild ideas, Gomelsky was found wanting as a manager. The Yardbirds played their first US dates in August 1965, but visa problems meant many shows were cancelled. "He fucked us around with money and gigs," says Samwell-Smith. "He was a bit of an arsehole."

The bassist's role in the studio had increased, but Gomelsky insisted on a sole producer's credit: "Giorgio put me down as 'musical arranger', because you don't pay the arranger a percentage. Canny move."

The band returned to the US in January 1966, with the correct visas and a date at Chicago's Chess Studios to record a new single. McCarty's martial drumming cued up Shapes Of Things, a song with lyrics about ecological disaster and a wildly abstract guitar solo. "They wanted a kind of Indian raga psychedelic freak-out," Beck later told MOJO. "Giorgio had steam coming out of his ears when he heard it – 'This is exactly why you're in this band.'"

"Shapes Of Things is still *the* Yardbirds song," states McCarty.

"JEFF WAS *THE* YARDBIRDS GUITARIST. SINCE HIS DEATH, ESPECIALLY, I'VE BEEN FORCED TO REALISE JUST WHAT HE WAS TO US." Paul Samwell-Smith

Acceleration game: performing Over Under Sideways Down on Ready Steady Go!, May 27, 1966 (from left) Samwell-Smith, Relf, (obscured) Dreja, McCarty, Beck; (top) DJ Jeff spins another hit; (below) For Your Love writer Graham Gouldman, 1965.

The public concurred, and it leapfrogged the Small Faces' Sha-La-La-La-Lee into the UK Top 3. The Yardbirds' prototype psychedelia was ahead of the curve, but they had nothing to show for it, and Gomelsky was running them into the ground.

Soon after, Samwell-Smith masterminded what he calls "the Easter uprising". Gomelsky was fired but walked away with the rights to everything The Yardbirds had recorded so far, creating havoc with their back catalogue ever since. The band's friend, Ready Steady Go!'s assistant producer Vicki Wickham, recommended his replacement. Simon Napier-Bell was a jazz musician and film editor, who'd co-written Dusty Springfield's recent hit, You Don't Have To Say You Love Me.

When he first heard The Yardbirds, Napier-Bell was struck by Keith Relf's "sinister voice" and how the bass doubled the guitar solos. "That was unlike anything I'd heard, and that's what became heavy metal," he says. "But I listened to their singles and they were all different. They didn't have an identity."

In the '80s Napier-Bell would steer Wham! to superstardom, but in 1966 his managerial experience was limited. "When you don't know anything, you sometimes do it better," he insists. Napier-Bell renegotiated The Yardbirds' deal with a £25,000 advance ("The Beatles only got £2,000"), and granted EMI the rights to their music for 15 years rather than in perpetuity. "I didn't know you weren't meant to do that. But EMI agreed to it."

The next single, Over Under Sideways Down, followed its predecessor's lead with a simple, snake-charming riff. "In jazz that would have been a five-chord riff, but Jeff's just goes round and round,"

explains Napier-Bell. "I said to them, Won't people get bored? They said, 'Nah.' They were right. It went Top 10."

THE GROUP'S DEBUT STUDIO LP, *Yardbirds* (nicknamed 'Roger The Engineer', after Dreja's sleeve illustration of engineer Roger Cameron), was a mishmash of R&B and flower-power pop, with Samwell-Smith as co-producer. "Thank God for Paul, because although I had good ideas," says Simon Napier-Bell, "I didn't know much about producing records."

'Roger The Engineer' made the UK Top 20 in July. But The Yardbirds' bassist now preferred producing to playing live, and quit after a disastrous May Ball at Queen's College, Oxford. Behind the baleful voice, the shades and the Brian Jones haircut, Keith Relf had struggled with asthma and other health issues since childhood. He was also drinking too much, and was drunk before the show.

"The Hollies were also on the bill, and their lead singer, Allan Clarke, did karate," explains McCarty. "So he dared Keith to karate chop a chair — which he did and he broke his hand."

On-stage, Relf started forgetting lyrics and insulting the audience. Beck had brought Jimmy Page along to watch the show. "And Keith was rolling around the stage blowing his harmonica in all the wrong places," ➤

THE YARDBIRDS
FOR YOUR LOVE   GOT TO HURRY

THE YARDBIRDS
HEART FULL OF SOUL
STEELED BLUES

Getty (4), Alamy (2)

10 LIVE YARDBIRDS

A full-on rave-up, compiled from live albums by MARK BLAKE.

TOO MUCH MONKEY BUSINESS
(from Five Live Yardbirds, Columbia, 1964)

Giorgio Gomelsky's aide, Hamish Grimes, introduces the "most blueswailing Yardbirds" on this frantic Chuck Berry cover from London's Marquee. Eric Clapton's solo shreds, long before that word was in common parlance.

SMOKESTACK LIGHTNING
(from Five Live Yardbirds, Columbia, 1964)

Keith Relf's voice and blues harp dominate this slow-burning take on Howlin' Wolf's signature number. The cue for countless mid-paced heavy rock songs in the years ahead.

I WISH YOU WOULD
(from Live In France, Repertoire, 2020)

From Paris's Palais Des Sports in June 1965, The Yardbirds' debut 45 gets a futuristic makeover from new kid Jeff Beck, with Relf howling during its dissonant mid-song breakdown – like Whole Lotta Love came early.

HEART FULL OF SOUL, VERSION 3
(from Live At The BBC Revisited, Repertoire, 2019)

Beck repeats his sitar-mimicking magic on this livelier version of the hit, recorded for the Beeb's Top Gear in June 1965. (The tablas on the original were played by Denny Piercy, host of the BBC's Parade Of The Pops.)

FOR YOUR LOVE
(from Live In France, Repertoire, 2020)

Clapton baulked at playing on the original single, but Beck has no such qualms here. There's a frenetic looseness to this summer '65

version, with the Palais Des Sports' audience screaming over the chorus.

TRAIN KEPT A-ROLLIN'
(from Live In France, Repertoire, 2020)

US R&B bandleader Tiny Bradshaw's song was passed, like a relay baton, to Johnny Burnette And The Rock'N'Roll Trio and on to The Yardbirds, whose exuberant take here (with Jimmy Page on bass) subsequently inspired Aerosmith.

SHAPES OF THINGS
(from Live At The BBC Revisited, Repertoire, 2019)

The Yardbirds' seventh UK single was still hot off the press before this March 1966 session for Saturday Club, with the Beeb's studio boffins presumably flinching at Beck's barely controlled solo at 1:35.

OVER UNDER SIDEWAYS DOWN
(from 1967, Live In Stockholm & Offenbach, Repertoire, 2018)

With Beck gone and Page playing sole lead guitar, the revamped Yardbirds add extra fire and drive to the previous summer's hit on Sweden's Beat! Beat! Beat! in March 1967.

DRINKING MUDDY WATER
(from Yardbirds '68, Jimmypage.com, 2017)

One of the highlights of the *Little Games* album (basically, Waters' Rollin' And Tumblin'), reimagined with Page's off-the-hook guitar playing during a March 1968 date at New York's Anderson Theatre.

DAZED AND CONFUSED
(Live And Rare, Repertoire, 2022)

Recorded for the French TV show Bouton Rouge in March '68, this take on US folkie Jake Holmes's song is already Led Zeppelin-in-waiting, right down to Page playing his hand-painted 1959 Telecaster with a violin bow.

Psycho mania: Keith Relf kicks out during the testy Dick Clark Caravan Of Stars US tour, October 1966.

recalled Page. "It was fantastically suitable for the occasion."

"I was unhappy already," says Samwell-Smith, "and now our singer was falling over drunk and Jim and I had to take over the singing. But in hindsight, my departure shouldn't have been done in such high dudgeon. It should have been tidier."

Three days after the May Ball, Page made his Yardbirds debut playing bass at London's Marquee club. "But within a week Jimmy and I were talking about doing dual leads," said Beck.

"I said to them, Jimmy Page is never going to stick with playing bass," chuckles Napier-Bell today. "He's coming into The Yardbirds on his way to somewhere else."

In August, the group toured America, but Beck disappeared before a date at San Francisco's Carousel Ballroom. Page took over on lead and Dreja played bass. "It was brave of Chris to do it," says McCarty. "But he worked hard."

The official reason for Beck's absence was tonsillitis. But really he wanted time with his new American girlfriend, Mary Hughes. Beck returned to the tour, and began sharing lead guitar duties permanently. Aspiring US rock musicians, such as Alice Cooper and Aerosmith, saw The Yardbirds at this time and took notes.

"It was fabulous," says Napier-Bell. "Because you'd never had two guitarists playing in stereo on-stage before. But I don't think Jeff liked sharing the applause. Him and Jimmy half-hated and half-admired each other."

"Jeff seemed to be more threatened than Jimmy," adds McCarty. "Jeff could be nervous and Jimmy was super-confident."

The new Yardbirds made their recording debut on Happenings Ten Years Time Ago: a doomy single with another abstract guitar solo. "It sounded like the future," said Page. Too much like the future, it transpired, for the Top Of The Pops audience, and it stalled at Number 43.

BY LATE SUMMER 1966, THE YARDBIRDS WERE unravelling. Keith Relf had recorded a solo single, Mr Zero, and Napier-Bell had overseen a clandestine recording session with Beck, Page, bassist John Paul Jones and The Who's drummer Keith Moon, resulting in the instrumental Beck's Bolero.

However, Napier-Bell shared his predecessor's love of a PR stunt. In October, Italian filmmaker Michelangelo Antonioni was making his Swinging London movie, Blow-Up. The director wanted a rock band cameo but The Yardbirds were not his first choice.

"Antonioni had asked The Who to smash up their equipment in the film," says Napier-Bell. "I was so jealous. Fuck me! I want The Yardbirds to do that." So he advised The Who's co-manager Kit Lambert to ask for £10,000, knowing Antonioni would never agree to it. When the director baulked, Napier-Bell snuck in and offered The Yardbirds for nothing.

Antonioni had recreated Windsor's Ricky Tick Club at Elstree film studios, and filled it with extras (including future broadcaster Janet Street-Porter, seen grooving away in a silver jacket). The Yardbirds played their fuzzed-up take on the old jump blues Train Kept-A Rollin', before Beck jammed his guitar through a Vox amp and threw the remnants into the baying audience.

Life was starting to imitate art. "Jeff wasn't into smashing guitars," says McCarty, "but he would get genuinely wound up and lose his temper on-stage. It was happening more often."

"Jeff was always in a bad mood," sighs Napier-Bell. "Something was always wrong."

It was The Dick Clark Caravan Of Stars in October '66 that finally broke him. The Yardbirds had been booked on the package tour alongside pop acts including Sam The Sham And The Pharoahs. On their previous US dates they'd travelled by private plane. Now they were playing 33 shows in 16 states and sharing a Greyhound bus. "And people were sleeping in the luggage racks," grumbled Page.

Beck bailed out after a gig in a shopping mall and flew to LA to see Mary. The Yardbirds completed the tour without him. "And people started freaking over Page," admitted Beck, who returned to the band but wouldn't commit to an upcoming Australian tour. "So we had a meeting and we fired him," says McCarty. "It sounds crazy, but it was working well as a four-piece."

BLOW-UP

A FILM BY
MICHELANGELO ANTONIONI

VANESSA REDGRAVE DAVID HEMMINGS SARAH MILES
METROCOLOR

Crazy daze: (above) the brief but brilliant Jeff 'n' Jimmy line-up, 1966 (clockwise from left) Beck, Relf, McCarty, Dreja, Page; (left, clockwise) Beck and Relf on-set during Blow-Up's club scene; Page on-stage in Holte, Denmark, April 15, 1967; Relf and Page meet Andy Warhol, 1966; producer Mickie Most with mogul motor, 1966.

"I don't know if they fired Jeff," contradicts Napier-Bell. "I'm sure he got asked once why he left The Yardbirds and replied, 'Because I had a sore cock and a sore brain.'"

Napier-Bell didn't fancy Australia either. "They were a miserable bunch, and I thought, I don't want to be around all this grumbling. I think Jimmy Page was driving the grumbles. When something went wrong, I'd get the stare from Jimmy. I don't blame him. He'd been in the business since he was 15 and he knew more than I did.

"We didn't want each other any more," he continues. "So I asked Mickie Most if he wanted to produce them and Mickie's business partner, Peter Grant, took over as The Yardbirds' manager."

Most had used Jimmy Page's services on numerous hits, and Grant was an ex-bouncer/chauffeur looking for an act to manage. Napier-Bell took on Jeff Beck as a solo client and oversaw his lone hit, Hi Ho Silver Lining: "Jeff could have been a superstar but he hated his voice," he says. "The last time I saw him at the Groucho Club, he was still complaining."

MEANWHILE, THE YARDBIRDS STARTED GOING backwards. April 1967's Mickie Most-produced Little Games was a faux-psychedelic ditty about "Chelsea flats" and "kinky cats". The follow-up, Ha! Ha! Said The Clown, had already been a hit for Manfred Mann before The Yardbirds' version was released in America. "It was a terrible mistake," says McCarty.

More than once, McCarty and Dreja walked into the studio to find session musicians in their place. "Mickie just wanted to run them off quickly and make money."

These singles and a second studio LP, the US-only Little Games, seemed like missed opportunities in the year of Sgt. Pepper, Disraeli Gears and The Who Sell Out. Only a handful of Little Games songs, including the band-composed Drinking Muddy Water, hinted at what The Yardbirds were doing on-stage. "Little pockets of resistance," as Page called them.

On the road in America, Page realised there was a new world of underground clubs and FM radio stations more receptive to his ideas than Mickie Most. On-stage, he played spectral-sounding guitar with a violin bow and sampled the blare of the Staten Island ferry horn. After The Yardbirds shared a bill with The Velvet Underground in Detroit they started including VU's junkie anthem I'm Waiting For The Man in their set.

But The Yardbirds' spring 1968 tour would be their last. Dreja was already planning a new career in photography, and Relf and McCarty were considering forming a folk-pop duo. "I remember telling Jimmy that Keith and I had other ideas," says McCarty, "and Jimmy said, 'OK, I'll go along with it.'"

"Then they told me they loved that song Happy Together by The Turtles, and that was the direction they wanted to go in," recalled Page. "My jaw dropped."

Instead, Page and his Man Friday Peter Grant put together Led Zeppelin, who used The Yardbirds' fusion of rock, blues and folk as a template, but scored the hit albums they never had. "It did feel strange watching how big Zeppelin became," admits McCarty.

The mercurial Keith Relf formed folk rockers Renaissance but only stayed for two albums. Unlike his '60s peers, Jagger and Daltrey, he retreated from the spotlight and spent most of the next decade producing other artists, reappearing as the vocalist in 1975's short-lived 'supergroup' Armageddon before dying in an electrical accident at his home studio a year later. "Keith was an interesting, spiritual man," says McCarty. "It was a tragedy."

Samwell-Smith produced hits for Cat Stevens and many others, and regrouped with McCarty and Dreja as Box Of Frogs in the early '80s. "But it didn't have the edge," he says. "The reason we're talking about The Yardbirds now is because we had that edge."

Jeff Beck shunned pop stardom to become the guitarist's guitarist before succumbing to bacterial meningitis in 2023. Both Page and Clapton were pallbearers at his funeral. "Jeff was The Yardbirds guitarist," says Samwell-Smith. "Since his death, especially, I've been forced to realise just what he was to us."

At the time of writing, lone Yardbird Jim McCarty, aged 80, is about to lead his modern-day version of the group back on the road in America. "It's about the songs," he says finally, "and they are still great songs."

Ⓜ

Getty (4), Shutterstock, Alamy

Holy communion: Tangerine Dream (from left) Edgar Froese, Christopher Franke and Peter Baumann performing at Coventry Cathedral, Warwickshire, October 4, 1975.

Dream On!

Acid, improv, cosmic coincidences and an attempt to assassinate Richard Nixon via telekinesis – all in a *nacht's* work for Tangerine Dream, the biggest band of Germany's '70s sonic revolution. As the prime movers in the group's rise tell Christoph Dallach in his new Krautrock oral history, "Anything could happen at any moment."

Photograph: Michael Putland

N WEST BERLIN'S LATE-'60s SCENE, where left-field musicians gathered to smoke weed and blow minds at Kreuzberg's Zodiak Free Arts Lab, burly, moustachioed guitarist Edgar Froese cut a forbidding figure. Between 1965 and 1967 he had led beat group The Ones, but moved between psych and jazz into free rock as early line-ups of his Tangerine Dream waxed and waned.

The first TD album, 1970's *Electronic Meditation*, featured Froese, drummer Klaus Schulze and multi-instrumentalist Conrad 'Conny' Schnitzler, and alternated meditative balms with intense pile-ups of guitar and organ. As the '70s progressed, Froese's group replaced their more conventional instrumentation – notably, the organ of Steve Schroyder, then Peter Baumann – with electronics, pioneered initially by drummer Christopher Franke. Their albums on the German Ohr label, and then Virgin Records, grew the band

into a surprise fixture in the higher reaches of the UK charts – where their 1974 classic *Phaedra* peaked in the Top 20 – as they became synonymous, along with Kraftwerk and Jean-Michel Jarre, with the cutting edge of electronic music.

What was epic in their sound suited unconventional live music spaces, and some of the band's most talked-about shows in the early to mid-'70s were in places of worship, the cathedrals of Reims, York, Liverpool and Coventry. In the '80s and after (Franke left after 1987's *Tyger* LP), Tangerine Dream retained an avid audience, and continue even now with a line-up (Thorsten Quaeschning, Hoshiko Yamane and Paul Frick) endorsed by Edgar Froese, who passed in 2015.

However, the Tangerine Dream chapter of Christoph Dallach's Neu Klang book, from which the following is extracted, concentrates on the group's 1968-75 phase, when 'the Tangs' were at their most ground-breaking, culturally impactful and, frankly, bananas. ➤

Getty/Michael Putland

Jean-Michel Jarre: I once had a debate with Edgar Froese about which of us had started making electronic music first. I was certain Tangerine Dream came before me but Edgar said it was me, and Tangerine Dream had still been playing prog rock at the time when I was already working electronically. It was a funny argument – neither of us wanted to have come first.

Irmin Schmidt (Can): I went out with a schoolfriend in Berlin one time, the painter Peter Sorge. One night he dragged me along to the Zodiak, said there was a great group there, the musicians all completely barmy, and the guitarist in particular was amazing. So we head over, sit around there for ages, and nothing happens. Someone kept coming and saying they'd be starting any minute now. But then it was a good hour before Edgar Froese came on stage on his own with a guitar and made this grumpy announcement: "My band's left me. I'm gonna play on my ownsome!" And then he played guitar all alone for two hours, the wildest free rock, really getting his anger out. I was incredibly impressed. Afterwards we had a bit of a chat but he was still far too angry for a long conversation. That was at the end of 1967, and then we lost track of each other for a while. Then when I had the idea to start Can and was thinking about guitarists, the first one that came to mind was Edgar. But before I could make contact, Holger [Czukay] suggested Michael Karoli as a guitarist. I met Michael and was really into him right from the first second. But it would have been exciting with Edgar Froese as well. Then there wouldn't have been any Tangerine Dream, and Can would have turned into a very different band.

Klaus Schulze (TD drummer): [Conrad] Schnitzler and I used to have day jobs with the post office, delivering telegrams to pay the rent. Edgar was still painting buses at the time, painting ads on them; he'd studied graphic design. Everyone in Tangerine Dream had day jobs. You'd get DM50 a night for playing in small clubs like the Magic Cave or the Silver Apple, and you couldn't live on that, even in Berlin. We never even thought of being commercial, because then we'd have had to adapt our music and there was no way we wanted to do that.

Manfred Gillig (journalist): I first saw Tangerine Dream in one of their earliest line-ups in February 1969, when they were mainly doing free jazz, at the student bar Litfass in Berlin-Charlottenburg, where [singer-songwriter] Reinhard Mey used to sing as well. Froese was already playing around a bit with electronic stuff but the saxophone was still basically dominant. There were five or six people on a small stage, right up close to the tables where people were sitting, and it was clear that Froese was the man keeping it all together. Like a conductor, he made the music louder and quieter with his gestures and he seemed to be controlling everything but he also allowed long solos. The audience, about 50 people, were fascinated and excited. I was amazed too by what happened there.

Steve Schroyder (TD keyboard player): My first encounter with Tangerine Dream was at the [1968] Essen Song Days [festival]. I didn't know the band that well yet, but their gig was really impressive. The 'politicos', the political students, cut their power cables while they were playing. There was a permanent fight raging between the people who wanted to listen to music and the ones who wanted to debate politics, or about whether music was essentially crap if it wasn't a protest song. So the sounds from Tangerine Dream turned into a kind of contribution to the discussion. When they couldn't play any more, Tangerine Dream went to the front of the stage and just sang. I was bloody impressed.

Winfrid Trenkler (journalist): I was at the Essen Song Days to write up the festival for [German rock magazine] Sounds. I had my first personal encounter with Edgar Froese in the lobby of the Grugahalle, and he said to me in his broad Berlin accent: "Whenever a journalist or someone comes to me and says he can do us a favour, I just wanna punch him straight in the gob." He'd had enough of media people.

> ## "Whenever a journalist comes to me and says he can do us a favour, I just wanna punch him straight in the gob."
> **Edgar Froese**

CATHEDRALE DE REIMS
VENDREDI 13 DÉCEMBRE A 20 H 45
TANGERINE DREAM

Klaus Schulze: Tangerine Dream shows were like rehearsing again – just after the rehearsal and with an audience. The Brits call it an open rehearsal, we called it gigs. We never composed anything in Tangerine Dream, only ever improvised. If you listen to *Electronic Meditation*, you have to say there wasn't any music like that before. Even Pink Floyd had only one long and really crazy track on *A Saucerful Of Secrets*.

Steve Schroyder: I had a life-changing LSD experience in Finland in 1969 and came back that summer a different person. But since the rest of society hadn't changed as much as I thought, I ended up a year later in a mental hospital in Berlin. I'd been picked up in a department store because I wanted to stroll out with Deep Purple's *In Rock* LP without paying, and made no attempt to hide it. I told the staff the record had been made just for me so I didn't need money to pay for it, and anyway money would soon be obsolete in the modern world, since everybody knew it would soon be abolished. So I was promptly arrested and handed over to the police, where a psychologist diagnosed me with depression and I was taken to 'Bonnie's Ranch' – the infamous Karl Bonhoeffer mental institution where terrible things were done in the Third Reich and all Berlin's drug cases were admitted in the early '70s. But I climbed out the window with another guy the next day and split.

Since my Finland trip I'd been hearing voices from outer space, my own cosmic advisers whispering things in my head. I never talked about it publicly but it was a new truth for me. At some point I heard the first Tangerine Dream record, *Electronic Meditation*, and an inner voice told me Tangerine Dream could help me. Someone in a record shop gave me Edgar Froese's address because I wanted to talk to him right then and there. But the address wasn't for Edgar, it was Klaus Schulze's. I went to visit him in Steglitz – I think he was still a postman at the time – but Klaus told me he'd just left Tangerine Dream, and gave me Edgar's address: 7b Schwäbische Strasse. I went right round there and rang the doorbell in the middle of the night. Someone looked out of one of the top windows and said: "Hello?" and I answered: I'm your new organist, appointed by the cosmos! "Fantastic! I'll be right down!" Edgar yelled, and he came down and opened the front door and invited me up to his flat.

After that night, I was in the band. Edgar was in a tight spot at the time, though – Schulze had just left, Schnitzler was gone too, so the band was just him. That's why he'd just got in touch with Christopher Franke as well, who then joined as our drummer. Anyway, he invited me along to a meeting with Christopher the next day. The two of them came over to my place and I played them my organ improvisations, and they liked them.

Klaus Schulze: Everything came about by coincidence, really. We never theorised about our music. We actually hated discussing music. We'd talk more about art, Andy Warhol, David Hockney and that kind of thing. But Stockhausen's avant-garde music wasn't for us; it seemed to be all about avoidance and breaking things, ultimately doing things that aren't nice. Pierre Henry was halfway all right, but even that became less and less appealing – we wanted to have something harmonic in our stuff. Not along the normal scheme, though: chorus, middle eight and then back to the chorus. But just not as structuralist as the new sound people. We wanted neither chart-pop nor avant-garde art, we wanted a third way: underground music.

Steve Schroyder: That love of improvising and experimenting is what marked out Tangerine Dream from the beginning. I still remember our very first session, very clearly. Tangerine Dream had a studio on Ku'damm where we rehearsed. Before we kicked off we turned the lights out. The point was to achieve absolute silence as inspiration. It was pitch black, only the LEDs lit up on the amps. Edgar kept going, "Shhh, shhh." So we sat there motionless in the dark for a few minutes and listened to the silence. After a while someone started making sounds out of that atmosphere, and then the others joined in. That was how we made our tracks back then. Tangerine Dream were much more at home in the art scene than the rock world. And the gigs were a meeting place for the LSD faction.

Klaus Schulze: We were stoned, the crowd was stoned, people did moderate dancing or just lay on the floor. It was all about listening. But it was a peaceful scene. It was music that made a lot of people think – they had to decide for themselves about what. But there could always be surprises at Tangerine Dream gigs, anything could happen at any moment.

Steve Schroyder: The first TD gig I played was in

Courtesy Ute Schreiner, Dalle APRF/IconicPix, GEMA Archive/IconicPix, Alamy, Getty

Dream team: (top, from left) Franke, Baumann, Froese, Klaus Schulze, Steve Schroyder; (above) the Tangs, 1970 (from left) Conrad Schnitzler, Schulze, Schroyder, Froese; (left) a poster for TD's "absolutely grandiose" performance at Reims Cathedral, December 13, 1974.

September 1970, for Austrian TV, a performance with pinball machines. We played in the Austrian studio on a staircase, me on my Farfisa organ and a real Marshall amps stack, Edgar had his Gibson guitar and Christopher Franke his drum kit. And there were four pinball machines as well, hooked up to speakers and operating randomly: the balls got sent up automatically. The sound of the balls in the pinball machines, the rattle of the gaming machines was integrated into our improvised music by contact microphones.

I was looking at the potential of spiritual energies at the time and I thought a lot of improbable things were possible. I even had a telepathic experience with Conny Schnitzler, when we were working in adjacent studios. We were both playing at the same time in our practice rooms without knowing about each other, and after a while I got the feeling someone else was playing along, so I left the room and at the same moment Conny Schnitzler left his room as well; he'd felt the same thing as me. It was pretty phenomenal. And because I was convinced of my telepathic powers, I'd come up

with something special for our Austrian performance: I wanted to send energy to America through my music, to give President Nixon a heart attack. All right, that was intent to kill, it horrifies me to think about it now, but at the time it seemed worth a try. So when we started playing I concentrated really hard to send my deadly beam from the TV studio to Richard Nixon, when suddenly there was a BOOM! What happened? My Marshall amp had burned out. We had to break off the performance and start over. But for me, it was all over from that point because it had really taken it out of me. I'd used up all my energy and shot it off in one moment. Obviously, I was glad the universe had intervened to rescue Nixon from me, because I wouldn't really have wanted an American president on my conscience.

Klaus Schulze: We all developed pretty quickly, but not always in parallel. I was more or less thrown out of Tangerine Dream in those early days; Edgar insisted on me only playing the drums and he wanted to be the guitarist. Thank God, then Schnitzler joined, a student of Joseph Beuys with lots of avant-garde ideas. That made

two of us who had different plans to Edgar. But I was increasingly busy making sounds on the electric guitar myself, and altering sounds. Edgar stuck to his position, though: you either stick to drums or you leave. At some point I really did leave, and set up Ash Ra Tempel with Manuel Göttsching and Hartmut Enke. That only went well for a certain time, again. At the start we were all on the same page, and we recorded our first LP together in 1971, something genuinely new: a 30-minute track on vinyl, using the whole record up to the run-out groove, pure improvisation, recording in the studio but without a concept, the way we played on-stage. No one had ever done that before, not even the Grateful Dead or Pink Floyd. But then Manuel and Hartmut, who'd done blues before, wanted to make more hands-on music rather than experimenting with electronics like before. After that I'd had enough of bands and I worked solo – that way, no one could stick their oar in any more.

Thomas Kessler (musician/studio manager): Tangerine Dream only became an electronic group through Christopher Franke. He was a ➤

Together in electric dreams: TD (from left) Edgar Froese, Christopher Franke and Peter Baumann, 1974.

◄ drummer originally, like Klaus Schulze was, but then he took care of the synthesizers in Tangerine Dream. I played a part in their music a couple of times with tape feeds I'd spliced together, but only at studio sessions, never live on-stage. But ultimately it wasn't my music and I didn't want to intervene, although I thought their concerts were amazing.

Steve Schroyder: When we finished mixing the [second TD album] on the last day, I didn't feel good about it. None of it was my thing any more, somehow. And then there were a few little misunderstandings between us. Working on *Alpha Centauri* [1971] had really exhausted me, partly because of the voices in my head with their constant cosmic inspirations. Driven by them, I went to Köln Cathedral one day to get hold of a choir and an organ for a TD session. I told the people in the cathedral the session would be "the shit!" Of course, I got neither an organ nor a choir, a huge disappointment for me, one of many…

On the last night of the record production I decided it was all getting too much for me and I had to get out of there and do something different. I didn't say goodbye, just packed my things, including the organ, chucked it all in the car and headed for Paris to visit Pierre Henry, which didn't work out either, naturally. Instead, I ended up in jail in France because I'd 'borrowed' a car. I mean, the apartment door had been open and the key was on the table, and anyway I'd left the owner a tarot card in exchange. But since I'd read the guy's tarot cards in a bar beforehand, they picked up on me pretty quick. After 45 days in jail, I hung out in France for a bit, where a pal of mine stole my organ. So making music just faded into the background.

Peter Baumann (TD keyboard player): One day I was at an Emerson, Lake And Palmer gig and they were running late, and I turned around to find someone to talk to. Sitting behind me was Christopher Franke and we ended up in conversation: "What do you do?" he asked me. I said, I make music. But what I'm most interested in is experimental stuff. He said: "That's interesting, where do you live?" Then later I found a note in my letterbox: "Hello from Christopher, we're looking for a new keyboard player."

The first LP I worked on was *Zeit* [1972], which came out on Rolf-Ulrich Kaiser's Ohr label. I got to do what I liked during the sessions, and everything just slotted together. The chemistry worked between the three of us. Edgar only had a guitar at first, then he got a noise generator and Christopher got a couple of oscillators. It was really primitive at the beginning but then we got more devices. Each of us developed our own sounds.

Simon Draper (Virgin Records A&R): Tangerine Dream records were in huge demand via [Virgin's] mail-order [business] and in the shop. And when we decided to start [the Virgin record label] in 1972 and I was on the lookout for artists that suited us, I soon thought of Tangerine Dream. I wasn't all that surprised when they were such a success for us. What made it much easier for them as a German band in the UK was that they didn't have vocals. Back then it was still a massive problem selling anything on the English market with non-native speakers singing on it.

Peter Baumann: The first synthesizer came from England and was called EMS, which stands for Electronic Music Studios. Our version was an AKS1. It was a case with a little synthesizer in it. After that things really kicked off for TD, because we suddenly had a way to shape our very own sound. Christopher Franke was the first one to have a synth; it must have cost about $1,500 at the time, a lot of money for us. Christopher made these brilliant sounds on it, and he lent it to me one weekend. After that I decided: I'm getting one too! It all went pretty fast. Another helpful thing was a visit to the Farfisa company. We went

Orange Is The New Black

The first six Tangerine Dream studio albums, unpeeled by Mike Barnes.

Electronic Meditation
★★★

(Ohr, 1970)

This anomaly in the TD catalogue lands somewhere between psychedelic freak-out and free jazz, with its chaotic collisions of cello, flute, organ, Edgar Froese's spiky guitar, and drum patterns from Klaus Schulze prior to his stint in Ash Ra Tempel. The results are raw, abrasive and uneven, but exciting in places.

Alpha Centauri
★★★★

(Ohr, 1971)

The group's first *kosmische* album, dedicated "to those obliged to space", opens with the stately, organ-based Sunrise In The Third System. Elsewhere Steve Schroyder's "echo machines" and Chris Franke's drum clusters add a *Saucerful Of Secrets* vibe,

and synth and flute lines wander through the dreamy, weightless title track, which concludes with eerie vocal chorales.

Zeit
★★★★

(Ohr, 1972)

A sprawling double album of proto-dark ambience, *Zeit* feels like the space between the sonic details of *Alpha Centauri*. Tracks are rarely as aptly titled as Nebulous Dawn – the sound of aliens signalling through a murky half-light. *Zeit* was Peter Baumann's TD debut but barely feels like it was made by humans.

Atem
★★★★

(Ohr, 1973)

One of John Peel's records of 1973, *Atem* is the band's most adventurous album. The title track's grandiose processional accelerates and ultimately explodes, atomising into abstract drift; Fauni-Gena finds Froese's mellotron conversing

tangerine dream

with avian chatter; and on Wahn the trio yelp like primitive hominoids before embarking on a drum-led space rock groove.

Phaedra
★★★★★

(Virgin, 1974)

Edgar Froese sought "transparency" in music and TD's Virgin debut has great colour, depth and texture and introduced Chris Franke's Moog sequencer, which pulses through these shifting electronic soundscapes. The title track's majestic mellotron and electric piano finale is the group's most affecting moment. Hugely influential, *Phaedra* even charted Top 20 in the UK.

Rubycon
★★★★★

(Virgin, 1975)

More structurally coherent than *Phaedra*; on each part, Franke's sequencer patterns are bookended by impressionistic sections. It's luminously beautiful in places and avant-garde elements are integrated seamlessly. Prepared piano chords punctuate Part 1, and Part 2 begins with a wind-tunnel of mellotron voices, reminiscent of composer György Ligeti, one of TD's acknowledged influences.

Strange fruit: (clockwise from left) Tangerine Dream's Edgar Froese on the grand piano, 1976; Froese performing in Paris, May 22, 2014; the latest TD line-up (from left) Paul Frick, Hoshiko Yamane and Thorsten Quaeschning; US President Richard Nixon, to whom Steve Schroyder sent his "deadly beam".

> ## "I wanted to send energy to America through my music, to give President Nixon a heart attack. It horrifies me to think about it now."
> **Steve Schroyder**

Photofest, Laurens Van Houten/Dalle/IconicPix, Getty, Melanie Reinisch, David Wolff, Patrick/Redferns via Getty Images

by after a gig and they gave us all this equipment as a promo opportunity. That must have been 1972. They were confident we'd make it big.

Manfred Gillig: I saw Tangerine Dream in the Royal Albert Hall in 1974. That was my first big trip for Sounds; I was invited by Virgin Records. I'd missed my flight because I'd been partying too long the night before and got there late, so they let me go in the last car from the Virgin office to the Royal Albert Hall. There was this young beardy guy in the car as well and we talked all the way there. He wanted to know what Sounds was, and asked me about the German music scene. At some point I asked him who he was, and he introduced himself as Richard Branson and told me what he'd done so far. Tangerine Dream were the first big thing for Virgin after Mike Oldfield.

Peter Baumann: People were much more open to us in the UK than in Germany. John Peel played our music intensively on his show, especially *Phaedra*, and that had a great effect.

Simon Draper: John Peel was important for the music. We knew him well and he supported Virgin from the outset. He loved Mike Oldfield's *Tubular Bells* and played it in full, which was a big help, of course. A band like Tangerine Dream would never have got as big in the UK without Peel's help. How else would people have heard music like that on the radio? TD didn't even release singles. But whenever he played something from one of their LPs, sales shot up.

Peter Baumann: We'd recorded *Phaedra*, our first record for Virgin, in Oxford. I was in Italy with my girlfriend when it came out, and I got a telegram from Richard Branson telling me to come straight to England to do interviews because our record was in the Top 10. And I just thought, What Top 10? We'd never really imagined we'd ever have more than a couple of hundred listeners. I called Richard Branson and he said: "It's unbelievable, the record is selling very well – you have to come to London." So we all flew to London and did dozens of interviews.

Simon Draper: Our technicians didn't like working with Tangerine Dream because they did everything themselves. When we sent the recordings for their *Phaedra* LP to the pressing plant, one of our technicians, Phil Becque, went

along to keep an eye on things. Anyway, then the record accidentally got cut backwards and none of the tech guys noticed. It all sounded the same to them! When we finally realised, I said to Edgar: "It's great, now we can bring your records out again backwards. We've got a real treasure trove here." He laughed at that.

Jean-Michel Jarre: I went to the legendary 1974 Tangerine Dream concert in Reims Cathedral. I just happened to be there by chance, working on an installation with tape machines and electronics. I heard a German band would be playing in the cathedral with synthesizers, which obviously interested me. And then it was absolutely grandiose. I'm very happy I was able to talk to Edgar about it before he died.

Harald Grosskopf (drummer/keyboard player, Ash Ra Tempel etc): When Tangerine Dream played in the cathedral in France, people took a crap in the corners. It was a huge scandal that really pushed their sales. Scandals are a good thing. Ash Ra also often performed in special places, like planetariums and churches. The audience

looked as unusual as we did, long-haired hippies in sacred spaces.

Peter Baumann: Money wasn't important, but then *Phaedra* was very successful, and *Rubycon* [1975] as well, the next record, and that does influence you in some way, naturally, because you wonder what you did to prompt such a big reaction. But for a long time we didn't talk about it, just went on making music. We could afford to because *Phaedra* sold a million copies and we could live off the money very well. Later on, after me and Franke had left, money did become an issue for Edgar. I earned almost a million marks at the age of 20. I bought new instruments with the money. Everything was great and I never thought about saving it for my old age.

Steve Schroyder: Tangerine Dream was never into following existing models, only into seeing what didn't yet exist: what are notes? What are frequencies? What is silence? Those were the things we thought about. It was an attempt to get different sounds out of the usual instruments. Later, they switched entirely to synthesizers, unlike the many other bands where synthesizers only played a supporting role. When I was in the band with my organ, I said to myself: standard harmonies don't exist any more, I have to find my way around this system of keys differently.

Simon Draper: It's surprising, all the places where people are into Tangerine Dream. I once went to New Orleans to make an album with the reggae band The Mighty Diamonds. What I wanted most though was to work with Allen Toussaint. I asked him what he thought of our band, and he said: "Well, it's reggae, isn't it?" He didn't have any more to say about them. Then I wanted to chat with one of Toussaint's technicians, but all she wanted to talk to me about was Tangerine Dream. It was really bizarre. We were in the deep South, black musicians playing the blackest music, but somehow everyone only wanted to talk about Tangerine Dream. **Ⓜ**

Extracted from Neu Klang: The Definitive History Of Krautrock by Christoph Dallach, translated by Katy Derbyshire, and published by Faber & Faber on May 2, price £25.

Something inside:
Labi Siffre in
Germany, 1979.

ONE FROM THE HEART

Killer grooves and stark, emotional songs have turned
LABI SIFFRE's '70s albums into cratedigger gold-dust.
Failure to fit a mould clapped a ceiling on his success. And yet,
as he concedes, stardom would have stirred unwelcome
scrutiny in unenlightened times. "I'm gay, black, an atheist,
and an artist," he tells TOM DOYLE. "So, I became wary."

United Archives/Getty Images

J UNE 6, 1973, AND THREE British pop stars find themselves staying in the same hotel, the Hallam Tower in Sheffield, on the same day. David Bowie is in town to play two shows with the Spiders From Mars at the City Hall on the Ziggy Stardust tour. Lulu, at the time a prime time TV star and household name, encounters the cocaine-withered Bowie in the lobby and is shocked by how "emaciated" he looks. Still, before the night is out, they'll have begun a brief affair and hatched a plan to record together.

Earlier that afternoon, the phone had rung in the room at the Hallam Tower occupied by Labi Siffre, a 27-year-old west London singer-songwriter with a handful of hits.

"I got the cold call from David," he recalls today. "He said, 'Oh, I've heard you're in town. Come on up.'" Bowie at this point was very much in thrall to the random creativity of William Burroughs' cut-up technique to help him create new lyrics. "We spent the afternoon doing cut-ups, sitting on the floor with cups of tea, and sandwiches with the crusts cut off," Siffre laughs. "It was totally un-rock'n'roll."

David Bowie and Labi Siffre, on the face of it, couldn't have seemed more different: the drugged-out, glammed-up weirdo and the slightly cosy acoustic balladeer regularly seen, by something in the region of 15 million viewers, guesting on Cliff Richard's BBC1 television show.

But Siffre was far from the MOR light entertainer of popular perception, being a black, gay, forward-thinking individual who as a teenager had set out to become an "artist philosopher" before veering into music.

"I don't really like describing myself as shy," he offers. "But at a very early age, I became wary of people. I'm gay, black, an atheist, and an artist. So, I became wary."

Unsurprisingly, then, mainstream fame as a singer-songwriter perched with a guitar on a stool on Saturday evening telly made Labi Siffre uneasy.

"At that time, if you were black, you had to be ➤

The singer and the song: Siffre during his hit-making '70s; (below) portrait of the young Labi – "Yes, I was adorable," says Siffre.

≺ ethnic," he points out. "If you were gay, you had to be camp. And I was neither ethnic nor camp. I knew I was totally out of place. Although, of course, it ended up being, no, I wasn't *totally* out of place."

TODAY, THE 78-YEAR-OLD LABI Siffre sits in the Champagne Bar in the atrium of London's Landmark Hotel, sipping a double espresso. Dapper in dark blue suit, white open-necked shirt and oval glasses, he's in town to promote reissues of his '70s recordings, one of which – his exquisite 1972 single, Crying, Laughing, Loving, Lying – beguiled cinemagoers last year as the keynote song in the Paul Giamatti-starring movie The Holdovers. It's prompted a wider appreciation of his catalogue, yet not so much by Siffre himself, who claims he almost never plays his old records.

"No, I don't listen to my stuff," he says, in a polished accent that is close to Received Pronunciation. "On my last trip here, I had lunch with a couple of good friends, and they put one of my albums on. I thought, Yeah, I suppose it's all right (*laughs*)." Home for him now is "halfway up a mountain in the middle of nowhere" in Catalonia. "It's really good for me," he stresses. "I do need the calm that comes from living like that."

Born "the penultimate one of five brothers" in Hammersmith in 1945 and brought up in Notting Hill and Cricklewood by his Nigerian property developer father and English/ Afro-Barbadian mother, Claudius Afolabi Siffre's first musical epiphany arrived at 11 when he heard his dad playing Frank Sinatra's 1947 recording of One For My Baby (And One More For The Road). Instantly, he was drawn to the melancholy within the song.

"It really was *bang*," he says. "I was totally floored by it. Although the song itself was amazing to me, I understood that here was somebody who had found love and thrown it all away through his own stupidity. I played it for the next three weeks almost continuously."

Siffre was a serious, deep-thinking youth, whose experiences at the Catholic monastery school of St Benedict's in Ealing turned him against religion. His second epiphany came at the age of 13 when his jazz-loving elder brother, Kole, took him to see British vibes player Bill Le Sage at the 100 Club.

"He was on-stage and he had a girl singer," remembers Siffre. "And you're going to have to excuse the arrogance here… because I'm looking up at her singing and I thought, I can do that. And almost immediately after, I thought, I can do that *better*. And I decided I was going to be a jazz singer. And then, of course, everything went horribly wrong, and I ended up doing what I do (*laughs*)."

Inspired by Jimmy Reed and Wes Montgomery, he picked up a guitar, then made a pilgrimage to Ronnie Scott's jazz club in Soho to study the latter's percussive technique in close-up. But he was so overcome with excitement that he passed out before

Guitar boss: Wes Montgomery, who caused Siffre to faint; (inset) Sinatra's One For My Baby epiphany.

Montgomery took the stage.

"I got there really early so I could be the first into the club," he smiles, "and I positioned myself in the seat where his thumb would be just *there*. And whilst waiting I had a bowl of tomato soup. They announced, 'Ladies and gentlemen, Wes Montgomery…' I felt heat coming up from my feet, and I woke up in the taxi."

From 1963 and the age of 18, Siffre was himself a professional musician, taking over from Ray Davies as guitarist in Hamilton King's Blues Messengers, finding a position in jazz singer Annie Ross's group, then forming his own band, Safari, playing loose interpretations of Beatles and Bacharach songs. In 1964, he met Peter Lloyd, 19 years his senior and set to be his partner for close to 50 years.

Siffre, who says he knew he was gay "from four", insists he wasn't overly troubled by the fact that homosexuality was still considered a criminal offence in Britain. "We were always together," he says of himself and Lloyd. "Only an idiot would have not known that we were a gay couple."

A trip to the far more liberal Amsterdam in the late '60s was an eye-opener. "They had come to the conclusion that love is love," he states. "And we in the UK were still drinking bigotry every morning with our tea."

It was while in the Dutch capital that Siffre experienced his third revelatory moment. Plucking up the courage to step on-stage at a folk club, solo with an acoustic guitar, he performed his hushed

© Labi Siffre, Alamy, Getty (4)

Take the blues away: (clockwise) peak BBC light entertainment gold as Siffre joins Olivia Newton-John, 1971; Siffre rocks on, 1972; Siffre (back row, second right) among the stars including George Harrison, Ringo Starr, Jeff Lynne, Eric Clapton, Spandau Ballet, Level 42 et al at the Prince's Trust Rock Gala, Wembley, 1986.

ballad Make My Day, in which the narrator's low spirits are lifted by the sight of a "pretty little girl in a blue dress playing in the sand".

"It's a song about depression," he admits, "which I've lived with since I was 11 years of age."

On that Amsterdam club stage, Siffre found his future musical direction. "I'm sitting up there and I'm thinking, This is what I should have been doing all the time. It was the first time I really felt that I was doing the *me* thing. It just all seemed to fit."

"Me and Bowie spent the afternoon doing cut-ups, eating sandwiches with the crusts cut off. It was totally un-rock'n'roll." LABI SIFFRE

BACK IN LONDON, Siffre gained a manager, Peter Gormley (whose other charges included Cliff Richard and Olivia Newton-John) and a record deal with Pye International, who in 1970 released his self-titled debut album: a mixture of funky folk, flutey jazz and baroque ballads that failed to chart.

Siffre took some comfort from the fact that his favourite artists at the time – Laura Nyro, Randy Newman and Harry Nilsson – were similarly commercially-challenged outsiders. *Labi Siffre*

featured a cover of Nilsson's Maybe, which the singer believed deserved to be a huge hit. In the end, it wasn't even issued as a single. "So what do I know about what's commercial?" he laughs.

For his second long-player, 1971's *The Singer And The Song*, he surprised himself by wresting control from his producer, Ian Green, resulting in a co-production credit. Siffre vividly recalls the moment when, listening back to the unsatisfactory mixes, he bashfully suggested to Gormley that he could oversee the completion of the album himself.

"I can still remember hearing my little voice at that time saying, 'Can I have a go?' And I went in with the engineer and we kind of rescued that album. I ended up producing the next lot of albums."

Under Siffre's sole direction in the studio, 1972's *Crying, Laughing, Loving, Lying* produced two UK hits: the strummy, joyful It Must Be Love (Number 14) and the dreamy country title track (Number 11). In Hotel Room Song, however, he expressed the frustration of trying to write new material while out on the road as an overworked celebrity: "Got to do a TV show in Manchester/Oh no." ➤

SOMETHING ON MY MIND

LABI SIFFRE: putting it out there, on five key albums. By TOM DOYLE

The Singer And The Song

★★★★

(Pye International, 1971)

Expanding on Siffre's eponymous 1970 debut, *The Singer And The Song* showcased his broad stylistic range. The slow-building, orchestrated Nothing In The World Like Love was a clear nod to Bacharach & David, Summer Is Coming found a midpoint between R&B and flamenco, and Rocking Chair took blues riffing to a decidedly funky place. You're Lovely, with its intricate folk finger-picking, got its simple message of romantic devotion across in a mere 31 seconds.

Crying, Laughing, Loving, Lying

★★★★

(Pye International, 1972)

Siffre's first entirely self-produced record focused his vision, opening with the one-two punch of the a cappella Slave ("I have been broken but my children will be saved") and the lovely, tumbling Cannock Chase, built from the same stuff as Nilsson's Everybody's Talkin'. On the cover, the singer ditched his previously "safe", besuited image, appearing as a furry-collared, guitar-slinging hipster. Featured his two biggest hits up to this point: It Must Be Love and the title track, subsequently covered by Olivia Newton-John in 1975 and American indie-poppers Whitney in 2020.

For The Children

★★★★

(Pye International, 1973)

Social commentary inspired by *What's Going On* was the central plank of an album that was sonically more often in tune with Cat Stevens' (far more commercially successful) acoustic balladry of the period. If it snuffed Siffre's hit-making potential, then it freed him up creatively. Standout Children Of Children lamented that socio-political idealists, including the hippies, changed little. Siffre listened to the song recently and says, "It did bring a tear to my eye… it kind of upset me that I had been so accurate."

Remember My Song

★★★★

(EMI, 1975)

Posing on the cover in tuxedo, cigarette in hand, red wine poured from a crystal decanter, Siffre's fifth visibly and audibly offered a new sophistication, and fuller band arrangements. The Meters-ish I Got The… provided the New Orleans-funky opener, while The Vulture sounded like Bill Withers produced by David Axelrod. Wistful ballads remained (Dreamer; the Randy Newman-esque title track), but it was for its groovier moments that it became much-valued by crate-diggers. One original vinyl copy on Discogs sold for £775.

So Strong

★★★

(China, 1988)

Even the big, gated drums and smooth digital synths couldn't smother the songs that Siffre felt inspired to write around his return '80s hit, (Something Inside) So Strong. Listen To The Voices tackled inequality, Nothin's Gonna Change found him dabbling in rap (sounding curiously like Malcolm McLaren on Buffalo Gals), while And The Wind Blows echoed Peter Gabriel. Weird, then, that even off the back of a big song, it didn't chart, and the subsequent singles pulled from it produced diminishing returns.

"I wasn't comfortable with being recognised or whatever, with the fame part," he says. "I'd never thought about fame and fortune. It was never in my plan. It just never occurred to me, the business of, Oh, I want to be famous, and I want to have a Rolls-Royce. And when I found myself in that situation, I just found it very uncomfortable."

His touring budgets didn't stretch to a band, and so he was left alone in the spotlight. "I learned how to go out on-stage at the Olympia in Paris, and open for Chicago, as one guy with one acoustic guitar," he says. "And be able to do it and make them be quiet. And then it was having to do that with The Supremes and the Carpenters.

"I realised fairly early on," he adds, "that I couldn't do what David [Bowie] did. I couldn't do the changing of my character. And I came to the conclusion that my act would have to be me being *more* me."

His fourth album, the *What's Going On*-inspired, socio-political *For The Children* followed in 1973, and didn't make the charts. Siffre remembers looking out of the window of Peter Gormley's office one day soon after its release, as his manager told him, "'We actually let you do that album. Because we were afraid that if we didn't, you wouldn't write any more songs.' It's quite likely that I wasn't able to tell people exactly what I was about."

The funkier side of Siffre's sound was brought to the fore on 1975's *Remember My Song*, with its distinct Bill Withers vibe, co-production and lead guitar by Big Jim Sullivan, surprisingly groovesome drumming by The Shadows' Brian Bennett, and guitar and bass contributions from Chas & Dave. Yet again, chart success proved elusive.

In the late '70s, Siffre relocated for a time to Los Angeles. "I went over there in the hope that I would meet black musicians. But in fact, I'm not very gregarious. I'm certainly not a networker."

Californian life however introduced him to weed and loosened him up. "Grass was very good for me," he grins.

But on his return to the UK in the early '80s, he was faced with two choices: tour the cabaret clubs playing his old hits or concentrate on being a songwriter. He chose the latter.

"It was, Why do I have to go into the studio and record these? Why do I have to go on the road and play these?" he says. "I want to write another song. I really got into songwriting at that time. And so the business of not being a commercial success didn't really matter to me."

THEN, IN 1981, IN A SURPRISE TWIST, MADNESS turned around Labi Siffre's fortunes by covering It Must Be Love and taking it to Number 4 in the UK, bettering by 10 places the original's chart position. While the Nutty Boys' version gave the song a roots reggae slant, the video – in which Siffre himself appeared as a white tuxedo-wearing violin-player – found a hint of bereavement in the lyric, with Suggs singing the opening line, "I never thought I'd miss you half as much as I do," into an open grave.

"It was a different viewpoint on the song," Siffre says. "The reason I liked the Madness cover is because they took the song apart. You can still hear that angular thing about it, but they used the song creatively."

At this point, Siffre was living with Peter Lloyd in the Buckinghamshire village of Cuddington, his creative energies still focused on songwriting. Appalled by a television documentary he'd seen in 1984, in which white policemen shot at black civilians in a South African township from a flatbed truck, he returned home from the pub one evening and quickly wrote what was to be one of his best-known songs, the empowering anthem (Something Inside) So Strong.

Siffre during his bid to represent the UK at 1978's Eurovision Song Contest.

Rise above: (clockwise) Siffre on-stage, 1970; Labi with Peter and Ruud – "A family of three husbands"; Siffre at the South Africa Freedom Day concert, London, April 29, 2001; (insets, from top) the Siffre and Madness It Must Be Love singles; Siffre's 1987 anti-apartheid hit So Strong; Eminem's Siffre-sampling My Name Is.

"I sat down at the keyboard, I played an ordinary C chord," he says. "I put my head back and I sang the first two lines straight out and cried. I realised I was writing about me as a gay man. And as the song progressed, I realised I was also writing about apartheid. I was also writing about being disabled and writing about being a woman in most places in the world. I was writing about a myriad of things. This was all in seconds (*laughs*)."

Siffre was initially reluctant to release the song himself, until Derek Green of China Records coaxed him out of retirement. (Something Inside) So Strong became his biggest hit, in 1987, reaching Number 4 in the UK. The singer was asked to perform the song at the South Africa Freedom Day concert in 2001 in Trafalgar Square (attended by Nelson Mandela), while its universal, rallying appeal has since seen it being sung by the crowd at the Grenfell memorial concert in 2017 and at subsequent Black Lives Matter protests. Siffre welcomes the continuing life of the song, but how his creations are shared isn't his greatest concern. "I get most job satisfaction," he says, "out of seemingly making something out of the shadow of nothing."

Down the years, his records have been re-evaluated and sampled by the likes of Kanye West, Jay-Z and, most notably, Eminem, who lifted the staccato funk middle eight of I Got The… from *Remember My Song* and used it as the base of his international 1999 megahit, My Name Is. Siffre cleared the usage on the strict condition that all sexist and homophobic lines were excised from the lyric, without

"I wasn't comfortable with being recognised. I'd never thought about fame and fortune." LABI SIFFRE

LABI SIFFRE
The Last Songs

realising that the rapper could then release both "clean" and "uncut" versions. "Had I known something more about rap, I would have said on *any* of the versions," he laments, gently.

After a live acoustic album, 1998's *The Last Songs*, Siffre fell silent again. Unconventionally, he was now living in Wales in a *ménage à trois* or "family of three husbands" comprising himself, Peter Lloyd and Ruud van Baardwijk. Lloyd died in 2013, van Baardwijk three years later. Twice derailed by bereavement, Siffre is only now seriously considering a return to the studio. "Recovering from both of their deaths was, and is, constantly with me," he says.

In a 2022 episode of the BBC's Imagine arts series, Siffre was filmed, visibly emotional, as he performed a new song, about loss, titled Far Away. Although he declines to say whether or not he will ever perform live again ("It's a difficult question to answer"), even with interest piqued since The Holdovers, he does now seem quietly determined to make another album.

"I didn't realise it could take quite as long as it has done to get functional again," he concludes. "But I always knew that my work would be my lifeboat." ⓜ

Labi Siffre's albums are reissued on Demon. For The Children is out on April 26.

© Labi Siffre, Alamy, Getty (2)

MINUTEMEN LAY DOWN DOUBLE NICKELS ON THE DIME

This band could be your life: Minutemen (from left) D Boon, Mike Watt, George Hurley, at Irving Plaza, New York, October 26, 1985.

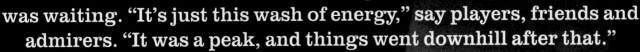

Formed in 1980, they toured endlessly and jammed econo. but in 1984, autodidact, self-sufficient San Pedro punks D Boon, Mike Watt and George Hurley were about to make hardcore's answer to Ulysses and *Ummagumma*. Their triumphant and urgent 45-track double LP blended social comment with a blistering sonic variety, though tragedy was waiting. "It's just this wash of energy," say players, friends and admirers. "It was a peak, and things went downhill after that."

Interviews by STEVIE CHICK • Portrait by RICK McGINNIS

Mike Watt: I got into music to hang with D Boon. We met when we were 12, when my family moved to San Pedro. We were both outsiders. D's neighbour Roy Mendez Lopez lived in his car and taught D guitar. I got a bass, and we made a bunch of noise. D's ma was fine with that. She preferred us staying indoors and not getting into trouble.

Joe Carducci: San Pedro was a very working-class port town, full of sailors who looked like Popeye going from bar to bar starting fights. But Mike and D were readers; Mike's brain just won't stop, he's always absorbing knowledge from books and people.

MW: First gig we saw was T. Rex in 1973. They looked so little from so far away – arena rock was like the Nurem-

burg rallies. Then we heard about punk. To us, 'Punk' meant a guy in prison who gets fucked for cigarettes. But we went to Hollywood and saw [early LA punk group] Bags up close. I felt empowered – I told D, "We can do this!" We knew Georgie [Hurley] from high school, and he wanted to play drums with us. We formed The Reactionaries in 1978, and then Minutemen in 1980. We wrote a bunch of songs, opened for Black Flag a couple times and then went on tour on our own. We had no manager, just the three of us, making it work.

Joe Baiza: The first Minutemen show I saw, they didn't leave any gaps between the songs. I figured it was all one long 20-minute song with all these stops and starts and different patterns, because otherwise their songs ➤

Rick McGinnis

Rhythm kings: (below) Watt and Hurley limber up for their gig at the Grandia Room, Hollywood, June 10, 1982; (below right) Minutemen light the way for their SST press photo shoot, 1984.

"WE WERE GONNA DRIVE SAFE AND MAKE CRAZY MUSIC."
Mike Watt

◄ would have to be 45 seconds long each or something. But that's exactly what they were.

Ray Farrell: The first time I saw Minutemen, the DJ played Pusherman before they came on, and they started playing along to it, then segued into a cover of Prelude, an incredibly obscure Tyrannosaurus Rex song. They never felt they had to follow the 'punk-rock rules' of only liking certain kinds of music.

MW: We knew genres were gulags, fuckin' 'Berlin Wall' shit. We'd play what we wanted, we didn't pay attention to any constraints. Punk taught us music was about expression. D was picking ideas up from R&B, making room for the drums and bass by playing trebly, staccato, clipped guitar, like Curtis Mayfield, like John Fogerty, like Scotty Moore. Our lyrics were us thinking out loud.

RF: Watt and D argued all the time, non-stop – it wasn't even really arguing, just two personalities that became a volcano, and were loving it. They didn't go to college, they were self-taught. Sometimes they mispronounced words, because they'd learned everything they knew from books, but they were so astute about politics, and very connected with the world around them. They were self-sufficient: they'd sleep in the van and play every night on a tour, because, as Watt said, "If you ain't playin' you're payin'". But they'd come off tour with money in their pockets; most other bands didn't.

JC: By 1983, the music was evolving. The SST bands had been through the hardcore punk vortex and were out the other side, tapping into primal influences, trying new things.

JB: 'Hardcore' suggested one-dimensional punk music, but everyone had their own ideas, and there was this environment of camaraderie that was real supportive.

Bob Mould: Hüsker Dü were on tour, driving down Interstate 5 to California. Bored, we came up with this concept LP about a kid from a broken home who escapes to Silicon Valley, and his girlfriend ODs – this narrative about abuse and wanderlust – to keep ourselves sane.

MW: The Hüskers were friends of ours – we put their debut album, *Land Speed Record*, out on our New Alliance label in 1981. When they came to California to record in 1983, we barbecued for them on Cabrillo Beach and they told us about their new double concept album, *Zen Arcade*. We thought: "We could do that too!" It was a dare, right? We'd just cut an album of songs with Ethan James at his studio, Radio Tokyo, but hadn't released them yet. So we decided to write a bunch more songs, record them in March 1984 and put out a double record of our own.

JC: SST had already put out a double album [1982 Black Flag anthology *Everything Went Black*]. Each extra disc you pressed only cost a further 50c, but

you could charge $12.98 for them, instead of $6.98 for a single. That helped dig us out of the financial hole left by the Unicorn disaster [the label had been involved in a debilitating lawsuit with MCA subsidiary Unicorn, which had agreed to co-release Black Flag's 1981 debut *Damaged* but then shelved the album for 'anti-parent' content].

MW: One thing about writing short songs is you need a lot of 'em to fill up a double album. We had to reach out to outside writers for some words – Henry Rollins, Joe Carducci, Jack Brewer. But I liked that – it pushed us to write in different kinds of ways. Georgie worked at a factory that made jet engine parts; he'd be precision-grinding steel at a horizontal mill early in the morning and having all these abstract thoughts, which he'd write down and pass to me for lyrics. D's songs were often political; Viet Nam was his version of Jimi's Machine Gun.

Ulysses was a big influence on me; James Joyce writing about everything that happened in this one day made me think what a springboard it was, to be in a band and rap about stuff with your buddy and go and explore the world. I wrote June 16th, because Ulysses was set on June 16, but also because that was D's birthday, while One Reporter's Opinion was my attempt at a song like

David Markey (2), Gail Butensky, Naomi Petersen

Paranoid chant: (from left) Watt, Boon and Hurley on-stage at The Starwood, West Hollywood, opening for Black Flag, November 18, 1980.

Gary Leonard/Corbis via Getty, Getty (6)

the section of Ulysses, with all the scientific writing. I re-read Ulysses in my forties, and it seemed much sadder than I remembered; the words hadn't changed, but I had.

George Hurley (speaking in 1985): We write all the time, experimenting and practising. If you don't keep writing new songs, you get stuck like a tyre in the sand.

MW: Hüskers had a concept for their double, but we didn't. So we made like Pink Floyd on *Ummagumma* and each took a side to curate. We drew straws and started choosing from the songs we'd recorded, and the fourth side, the 'chaff side', was leftovers. The first song D chose was Anxious Mo-Fo, which I'd wanted for my side, because his guitar solo blows me away.

RF: Their songs were like diary entries. They didn't belabour anything – they wanted to get their message out there quickly, and move on.

MW: We recorded *Double Nickels* over two three-day sessions, months apart, on an 8-track Otari machine for $1,100, and Ethan James mixed the whole thing in one night. The album title meant driving exactly at the speed limit, 55mph. D didn't like that guy Sammy Hagar, who sang I Can't Drive 55. We were gonna drive safe and make crazy music, while that clown was gonna drive crazy and make safe music. We went in the studio and played like it was a gig, but with the tapes rolling. And we let it all out, this weird, weird collection of things – everything we were about.

RF: *Double Nickels* is non-stop. It's not about hooks or pop songs. If you're not paying attention, it's just this wash of

energy. If you are paying attention, it has this dynamic that is very invigorating. Rolling Stone reviewed *Double Nickels* and *Zen Arcade* together [written by David Fricke], and that was really helpful, because it meant other magazines and radio stations would become curious about the hubbub.

David Fricke: *Double Nickels* really showed how punk rock was more than just taking things down to the fundamentals – it was about everything you could do with those fundamentals. And double albums typically had filler, but these albums were full of experiments instead, and incredible passion. And because these bands were working to SST budgets, everything had to be done fast and tight, so you had this energy on top of this incredible scope and ambition. I told my editor we had to review them, and we had to review them together. And in the same issue, we ran a four-star review of The Replacements' *Let It Be*, which just shows you what a rich era it was.

MW: Gigs were so powerful to us, everything else – interviews, photographs, even records – was just flyers to get people to the gig. But *Double Nickels* was something else. It was a peak, and things went downhill after that.

JC: Their next records, the Project: Mersh EP and [1985 LP] *3-Way Tie For Last*, were explicitly 'commercial', experimenting with verses, choruses and fade-outs – stuff they'd previously avoided.

MW: There's things on those records that make me wanna puke – too many cover versions, lots of reverb, my bass

DRAMATIS PERSONAE

● **Mike Watt** (bassist, vocalist)

● **George Hurley** (drummer)

● **Joe Baiza** (Saccharine Trust guitarist/vocalist)

● **Ray Farrell** (SST Records promotions manager)

● **Joe Carducci** (SST Records A&R/ co-owner)

● **Bob Mould** (Hüsker Dü guitarist/vocalist)

● **David Fricke** (journalist)

● **Kira Roessler** (Black Flag bassist, Watt's former wife and bandmate in Dos)

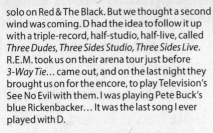

solo on Red & The Black. But we thought a second wind was coming. D had the idea to follow it up with a triple-record, half-studio, half-live, called *Three Dudes, Three Sides Studio, Three Sides Live*. R.E.M. took us on their arena tour just before *3-Way Tie*… came out, and on the last night they brought us on for the encore, to play Television's See No Evil with them. I was playing Pete Buck's blue Rickenbacker… It was the last song I ever played with D.

JC: Mike was determined to do a 'real' Minutemen record after that. But then D was killed. [On December 22, 1985, the van in which Boon and his girlfriend, Linda Kite, were travelling in ran off the highway after its rear axle broke.]

Kira Roessler: When D Boon died, Mike didn't want to play any more. He didn't want to leave his room. I was the one distraction in his life from all that, and we started jamming with our basses, making music again. I wept when I saw [2005 documentary We Jam Econo], to see that footage of Mike before D died. He'd been this giggly, gangly boy. And I hadn't seen Mike giggle since then. A hard life will change you from the eyeballs out.

JB: Later, Mike and George met Ed Crawford and started Firehose. They'd never be the Minutemen, but they had to continue, and there was good stuff there. Mike's a great guy, so supportive and inspiring.

MW: I couldn't listen to Minutemen records for years after. It was too sad. When I listen to *Double Nickels* now, I can push the personal part aside, so D's not jumping out of the speakers at me and I don't wanna cry. There's a part of you that wants to wallow, and that might steer you away from challenges you still gotta face. *Double Nickels* is proof to me that you can make a dream work. You gotta work at it, you gotta be lucky. But it can happen. *Double Nickels* is where everything Minutemen were all about added up; it's everything it was meant to be. And really, that momentum is still with me today. Ⓜ

George Hurley quote from the We Jam Econo DVD.

Such a Bright Light

Prolific, precocious, KATE BUSH's journey from girl genius to multi-faceted art-pop phenomenon involved unlikely stops on the shelf at a sceptical label and the outer reaches of London's pub rock circuit. Meanwhile, between her early demos and *Never For Ever*, childhood enthusiasms morphed into adult insights over music bold and bewitching. Still, for Bush, turning her visions into records would never be straightforward: "It's frustrating to see something that you have been keeping transient for years suddenly become solid."

Words: TOM DOYLE   Portrait: BRIAN ARIS.

T HE YOUNG CATHY BUSH PRESSED THE 'PLAY' AND 'RECORD' BUTTONS ON THE Akai reel-to-reel tape machine and her songs began to flow. Sat at the grand piano in her family home, East Wickham Farm in the suburb of Welling, south-east London, she began to capture the many, many compositions that she'd accumulated by the age of 14.

"I was writing a song, maybe two songs a day," the grown-up Kate Bush later told MOJO. "I must have had a couple of hundred. I would put stuff onto tape, but I *was* the tape machine. I used to practise, practise, practise in order to remember the stuff."

Having first begun songwriting at the age of nine, she'd developed fast. One of her earliest lyrics was themed around a typically childlike fascination with colours, but it went on and on for far too long. When she played it to her family, she noticed them growing bored.

"They could only take so much before they had to leave the room," she noted in the foreword to the 2023 paperback of her How To Be Invisible lyric anthology. "An honest response can be a very useful thing, so I worked on trying to make the next songs a little shorter."

From here, Bush's early compositions were more carefully edited, while at the same time increasingly involving an entire universe of her own creation, filled with elaborate world building and vivid character creation. When these home-recorded tapes – much to her annoyance – were inevitably bootlegged in the '80s and then leaked online in the '90s, they offered a fascinating glimpse into the early flights of imagination of a unique talent. ➤

Passing through air: Kate Bush, Old Street Studios, London, 1979.

Brian Aris

Some of these works-in-progress, later abandoned, deserved to have been completed. Something Like A Song, demoed in 1973, matched a wordless "ooo-ooo-ooo, aaa-aaa-ooo" chorus to descending piano chords, punctuating verses in which it seemed a vision of the god Pan appeared to the young singer in her garden, piping a haunting melody that she attempted to voice. In another song, Atlantis, Bush imagined a drowned world (an early draft of the one that later appeared in A Coral Room on 2005's *Aerial*) replete with shoals of herring swimming through the sails of sunken ships, to the accompaniment of her ornate arpeggios.

Other pieces were sketchier. Cussi Cussi spoke of some secret knowledge shared with the titular individual. The vaguely religious Sunsi found her drawn to the pursuit of spiritual enlightenment. You Were The Star was a pretty paean to a fallen idol, with hints of Joni Mitchell's Woodstock. Queen Eddie detailed the emotional turbulence surrounding the breakup of a gay couple.

Having access to a reel-to-reel also allowed Bush to conduct her first playful experiments in sound: recording a vocal melody, then reversing the tape, phonetically learning it backwards before recording it again so that when played forwards it took on an eerie quality.

Cathy Bush was clearly a startling, precocious talent. But capturing her complex song worlds on record would prove an endless challenge, and it was years before she'd be remotely satisfied with the results.

ON MAY 26, 1972, BRIAN BATH, A 19-year-old guitarist friend of Bush's elder, folk fan brother Paddy, drove to East Wickham Farm for the first time to have a jam with him. Surprising Bath on more than one level, Paddy's 13-year-old sibling joined in.

"I went to Paddy's, and he had his mandolin and my amp," Bath recorded in his diary. "His little sister sang through a mike and amp and sounded really incredible." Two weeks later, he was invited back. "Fit some guitar on Paddy's sister's song," he wrote. "Really feel honoured to do it."

"She had loads of songs," Bath said in 2018. "I remember a few of her family were in the room and she was on a grand piano. She was really sweet and pleasant. She had this great voice, and her songs were really kind of interesting and beautiful. They were a bit special."

Kate's eldest brother, John, brought her homemade tapes to the attention of his friend, Ricky Hopper, a record plugger. Hopper was to become the singer's earliest champion, touting these lo-fi recordings around labels and publishers, though to no avail. Then, Hopper played a cassette to his old friend from Cambridge, David Gilmour.

"I listened to it with him," Gilmour remembered, "and he said she was brilliant, and I said I agreed. I thought a bit more was needed to be brought out of it. She was

Koh Hasebe/Shinko Music/Getty Images; Gered Mankowitz/Iconicimages

Doing it for the kicks: Bush at the Zōjō-ji Temple, Tokyo, June 1978.

THE EARLY ALBUMS #1

The Kick Inside

(EMI, 1978)
SAMPLED FROM Dr Roger Payne's 1970 New Age touchstone *Songs Of The Humpback Whale*, the cetacean lowing that opens Kate Bush's debut album initially seems part of the hippy esoterica scattered across these songs – a Sanskrit mantra here, a reference to "Gurdjieff and Jesu" there. Of its time, and yet, in 2024, an announcement that a far-reaching transmission is about to begin. The thrillingly novel Wuthering Heights might have positioned Bush as a one-hit exotic, but *The Kick Inside* resonates beyond its febrile fanfiction, merging innocence with experience, sexual frankness with rich lyricism, her bold femaleness working against the music's old-world ornament.

Feel It, Oh To Be In Love and L'Amour Looks Something Like You have a lust for lust that's wonderfully shame-free ("it will be fun"); there's nothing naïve about the disconcerting bloom and fade of The Man With The Child In His Eyes or the title track's incest-and-folk-tragedy rapture. Moving, the liquid tribute to her dance mentor Lindsay Kemp, exhibits a kinetic drive towards self-realisation. "You crush the lily in my soul" does not describe a violent act, but welcome liberation from piety and cowardice. Having pondered supernatural forces in Strange Phenomena – a touch of The Exorcist in its tubular pull – Bush offers a more Blakean assessment of humanity on Them Heavy People: "Every one of us has a heaven inside." *The Kick Inside* embodies that messy bliss, Bush – not for the last time – stepping into the sensual world. *VS*

a girl plonking away on a piano with a rather squeaky voice and I didn't trust most of the A&R men that I'd come across to be able to spot what was in it."

In 1973, the Pink Floyd guitarist travelled to the farm with his own recording equipment and taped upwards of 50 of Bush's songs. Selecting a handful, in August, he organised a session at his home 8-track studio involving drummer Pete Perrier and bassist Pat Martin of Surrey country rock band Unicorn, with himself on guitar and Bush moving between acoustic and electric pianos. One track, Maybe, had been originally titled Davy and appeared to have been born of the now-15-year-old's love of David Bowie. Another, Passing Through Air, bore the stylistic imprint of her other hero, Elton John (and was the only officially released cut from the session, later appearing on the B-side of the Army Dreamers single in 1980).

"They didn't really achieve what was required," Gilmour reckoned of the demos. Two years on, in the summer of 1975, massively upping the ante, he offered to fund a full-scale master session at George Martin's AIR Studios, situated four storeys above Oxford Circus in central London.

Gilmour enlisted Andrew Powell, a producer and arranger whose recent credits included Leo Sayer and Steve Harley & Cockney Rebel, to oversee the recording. Three tracks were laid down: The Saxophone Song, Maybe and, astonishingly, what would prove to be the master version of The Man With The Child In His Eyes, recorded live by the 16-year-old Kate with the accompaniment of a 30-piece orchestra.

When EMI's Bob Mercer popped into Abbey Road the following month to visit Pink Floyd during the mixing of *Wish You Were Here*, Gilmour pulled him into another room to play him the AIR recordings. Mercer immediately expressed interest in signing Bush and at this point Gilmour effectively stepped away, and was later reimbursed for his initial investment.

"Then it sort of sat for two years," the guitarist noted. "This has generally come out as looking like they were nurturing her. There seems to be an element of revisionist thinking in the things I've read about it, because it seems to me that [EMI] then [considered] nearly every record producer who produced girls. Because for some reason they didn't want to use Andrew Powell."

Gilmour bumped into Mercer at a party and remembered the latter telling him, "'C'mon, this one just isn't working. You found the only good songs.' Or words to that effect. I said, 'Well, why don't you go back to Andrew Powell?' and he sort of ummed and ahhed. Eventually, they did go back to Andrew Powell and that's when it all started rolling."

Chris Moorhouse/Evening Standard/Hulton Archive/Getty Images; Barry Plummer

Something like a song: Bush in London, 1978; (below, left) outside her parents' home, East Wickham Farm, south-east London, and (right) at the family piano, 1978.

"I went to Paddy's, and he had his mandolin and my amp. His little sister sang and sounded really incredible." BRIAN BATH'S DIARY

≺ In the February 1977 issue of EMI's in-house magazine Music Talk, A&R man Nick Mobbs was interviewed, revealing the company's plan for their new artist — the eventual release of her debut single still nearly a year away. "Kate was signed in the knowledge that releases may not be immediate," he said. "But we have a belief in her long-term potential and are anxious to give her a chance to blossom even more."

It was a challenge for Kate Bush to blossom in the side room of a south London pub, but that became the next part of the plan. In urgent need of some live experience, on March 17, 1977, the 18-year-old first stepped on-stage at the Rose Of Lee pub in Lewisham, fronting the KT Bush Band, comprising Brian Bath on guitar, Del Palmer on bass and drummer Vic King.

For the most part, their set consisted of the era's standard covers band fare: Honky Tonk Women, Come Together, Free's The Stealer, along with Robert Palmer's funky slant on Little Feat's Sailin' Shoes and Shirley & Company's disco smash Shame, Shame, Shame. A recording, made in a Catford studio, later surfaced of the singer's take on the *Abbey Road* opener, sounding unmistakably Kate Bush and with not a trace of Lennon in her delivery.

At the same time, some of her own songs crept into the set, with the rocking James And The Cold Gun designated as the set's climax. Here Bush developed the stage routine she would later use in her 1979 Tour Of Life, involving her mock-shooting the rest of the band and even audience members with a fake rifle.

"She was just brilliant," Del Palmer recalled to Kate Bush

"We all looked at each other, like, What the hell is all this? No one had ever seen anything like it before."
GRAHAM HEWISON ON THE KT BUSH BAND

fan magazine HomeGround. "She used to wear this big, long white robe with coloured ribbons on, or a long black dress with big flowers in her hair. She did the whole thing with the gun, and they just loved it."

Bob Mercer caught the show one night at the Rose Of Lee and, impressed by the dynamic James And The Cold Gun, put Bush and the band in De Wolfe Studio in Soho in April '77. None of the tracks were ever to be released from what was essentially a test recording, including a lost song titled Dear Dead Days concerning the notion of trying to slow the passage of time. Similarly, none of the musicians were destined to be involved in the sessions for *The Kick Inside*, commencing in July.

In the meantime, alongside their residency at the Rose Of Lee, the KT Bush Band played other pub and club shows in King's Cross, Tottenham, Putney and Chelsea, before venturing further afield for one-nighters in Essex and Sussex. Graham Hewison was a bassist for a rival south London pub rock band, Stage Fright, who caught the KT Bush Band at the Lewisham pub.

"We were doing the same circuit and we were just checking out other bands," he remembers. "One of our band said, 'Well, there's the KT Bush Band.' We thought, Never heard of them, but we'll go and have a look.

"It wasn't a rock band… it was obviously way more theatrical. I guess there were probably 150 people there. She had this kind of chiffon-y dress on, and she was floating around and through the audience.

"We all looked at each other, like, What the hell is all this? No one had ever seen anything like it before." ➤

Gered Mankowitz/Iconicimages (3), Barry Plummer, Brian Aris, Andrew Phillips

Symphony in blue: Kate Bush, breaking the mould, 1978.

Out of her tree: Kate poses for Record Mirror's Andy Phillips in Manchester Square, London, 1980; (left) the Gered Mankowitz leotard shoot, 1978.

Don't box me in: Bush in a frame from the cover-shoot for *The Kick Inside*'s US sleeve; (below, left) Kate tools up for Melody Maker's Barry Plummer, 1978; (right) a 1979 Brian Aris portrait.

"There was no hair, no make-up, no stylist, just the two of us. That would never happen with artists now."
ANDY PHILLIPS

FLASH BACK

Kate Bush's early portraits, by the snappers who took them. "Give her a space and she'd burn it up," they tell LUCY O'BRIEN.

IN 1978 Gered Mankowitz went to a meeting at EMI and they played him a song by a new young female artist. "That was Wuthering Heights," he remembers. "I was knocked sideways by the sound of it." EMI wanted a publicity portrait, so Mankowitz, whose vibrant use of colour and composition spawned iconic '60s shots of the Stones and Jimi Hendrix, advised: "We need to make a picture that people will want to see again, the same way you want to hear the music again and again."

The 19-year-old Bush was energetic and enthusiastic, photographed in his studio wearing a pink leotard that "reflected the dance and movement so important to her expression" – an image EMI had plastered on buses and billboards.

"Kate had strong, collaborative ideas and presented a sensual image," says Mankowitz, who went on to shoot definitive photographs of the singer – folded in a box for the US edition of *A Kick Inside*; dressed in theatrical animal costume for *Lionheart*, haloed in red on the single sleeve for Hammer Horror. "The photo sessions were always exciting and energetic. Give her a space and she'd burn it up, make it her own."

Bush was happy to do informal pictures as well. In May 1978, Barry Plummer went to East Wickham to take snaps for Melody Maker. "The brief was, 'Just go and get some pics,'" he recalls. There were soft, ethereal shots of her sitting on a doorstep and at the grand piano, but most bizarre was a shot of the singer posing with a rifle on a bearskin rug. "For some reason she picked that up from the mantelpiece," says Plummer. "I learned later that she's against guns, but she used it spontaneously like a prop."

As a young Record Mirror photographer, Andy Phillips remembers going to the EMI office in 1980 and Bush's PR giving him the keys to a garden in Manchester Square. "I went with Kate; no hair, no make-up, no stylist, just the two of us. That would never happen with artists now – you'd have six lawyer meetings and an approval form."

Wearing a zippered Vivienne Westwood top and leather boots, Bush propped herself against a tree and said with a grin, "They expect me to be wacky Kate."

As the '80s progressed Bush demanded more control over her image and made herself much less available. "I felt very flattered that people should think of me [as a] sex symbol," she told Melody Maker. "But what I really want to come across as is as a musician, and I think that sort of thing can distract."

Those early snappers realise now how lucky they were. Brian Aris, for instance, whose striking 1978 image graces MOJO's cover this month. "I got her to pose as a dancer," he says, "with that combination of boldness and power. She was very experimental."

For Gered Mankowitz, Bush's emergence coincided with a peak time for pop visuals. "It was fantastic, a new avenue for expression," he says. "And Kate was at the centre of that."

"By the end of the second record, I was thinking, I don't want to be produced by somebody who sees it differently from me."
KATE BUSH

Roar power: Kate shows a feline friend who the real lionheart is, at the Bush family's home, East Wickham, London, September 26, 1978.

I N THE SUMMER OF 1977, KEYBOARD player Duncan Mackay was sitting in the control room at AIR London alongside his Cockney Rebel drummer bandmate Stuart Elliott, plus bassist/guitarist David Paton and guitarist Ian Bairnson of the Scottish pop-rock band Pilot. Moonlighting from their regular groups, the four were booked as a session team to play on the debut album by an unknown singer named Kate Bush.

"Andrew Powell hadn't turned up yet, so we were just having a chinwag," Mackay remembers today. "This little girl comes into the studio and says, 'Hello, would anybody like a cup of tea?' And we went, 'Yes, please,' and carried on chatting away to each other. We thought she was the studio tea girl.

"Three or four minutes later, Andrew Powell turned up and led her in and said, 'So, hi guys, have you met Kate?' (*laughs*)

"She was a most delightfully down-to-earth, ordinary person, no airs and graces. Then she sat down at the piano and opened her mouth, and you went, Holy shit…"

"She was 19, I was only 24," Stuart Elliott recalled to MOJO in 2018. "She was this little hippy chick. We thought nothing of it, y'know, another session. Then as soon as she sat at the piano and started playing songs like Wuthering Heights, our jaws dropped. We just thought, Flipping hell, this is unbelievable."

The team quickly developed a modus operandi: they'd listen closely to Bush play through a composition, working out the chords and absorbing the lyrics, and then immediately try to evoke the song's atmosphere in their parts. From the off, they were cutting three tracks a day.

"It was really led by Kate because it was a complete picture," Elliott said.

THE EARLY ALBUMS #2

Lionheart

(EMI, 1978)

BY ACKNOWLEDGING she dislikes *Lionheart* – "I'm not really happy with it," she said in 1989 – Kate Bush has not aided her second album's reputation. Yet it is much more than *The Kick Inside*'s disappointing sequel. Gered Mankowitz's cover shot – turning The Wizard Of Oz's Cowardly Lion into a generation's psychosexual nightmare – underlines the album's even more extreme theatricality. Coffee Homeground's two-bob take on the Threepenny Opera stars a Mitteleuropean poisoner; the rock-operatic Don't Push Your Foot On The Heartbrake is an interpretation of a Patti Smith song like *The Kick Inside*'s Kite was an interpretation of a Bob Marley song. Hammer Horror hits the eldritch switch.

Yet it is the failing actor of Wow who is the album's emotional core: "We're all alone on the stage tonight". It's a loneliness that seeps through Kashka From Baghdad's compassionate voyeurism. If *The Kick Inside* sought new sensation, *Lionheart* can't help looking back. Psychedelia's nursery nostalgia is given a modern therapeutic twist with In Search Of Peter Pan; JM Barrie's child-kidnapper turns up again in Oh England My Lionheart, an elegy for the previous generation's deathly past: "dropped from my black Spitfire to my funeral barge."

It's an album that knows there's something dark out there: poisoners, ghosts, malign lost boys. On Fullhouse, it's even closer: "I am my enemy." The ominous gong that closes Hammer Horror is the reverse of *The Kick Inside*'s opening whale song: a fade out, uncertainty. The soundstage goes black. What happens next is uncertain, but she needs to be brave. *VS*

Kate Bush
Lionheart

"I just sat down at the drums, and I largely played to her vocal." In particular, the drummer imaginatively accompanied Bush as she slipped through the changing time signatures in the chorus of Wuthering Heights that lent the song its entrancing effect, like mist on the West Yorkshire moors. "Everything I did was in response to her top line melody," he stressed, "and in the gaps she would leave, I'd jump in with a little fill."

Mackay was for the most part employed to play supportive electric piano and Hammond organ, while on Strange Phenomena he added fast-moving synth sequences to enhance Bush's twinkling piano and narrative involving curious coincidences and moon-phased menstruation. As one piano player viewing the skills of another, Mackay was wholly impressed.

"Kate just played 100 per cent the correct stuff for what she was singing," he says. "I probably would have played something slightly different, and it wouldn't have been as good."

Meanwhile, Bush was soaking up every last detail of the recording process. "You couldn't keep Kate away from the sessions even if you had wild dogs and bazookas," engineer Jon Kelly later recalled to Sound On Sound writer Richard Buskin. "She was just drinking it all up, learning everything that went on. The first moment she walked into the control room, I could tell that's where she wanted to be, in control of her own records. She was so astute and intelligent."

Stylistically, it was clear that Kate Bush was not to be easily poured into the piano-based, female singer-songwriter mould of a Carole King or Lynsey de Paul. In an interview with Melody Maker's Harry Doherty shortly after the release of *The Kick Inside*, she stressed that "all the songwriters I admire and listen to are male. I feel closer to male writers."

At the same time she expressed a certain amount of creative frustration when it came to

Chris Moorhouse/Evening Standard/Hulton Archive/Getty Images, Mondadori Portfolio/Angelo Deligio/Camera Press

In the fast lane: (left) Bush keeps her feet off the heart-brake, 1978; (right) with fellow Melody Maker award-winner Bob Geldof, November 1979; (below) Billy Cobham "wasn't doing it right," Kate said.

the indelible aspect of the record-making process.

"There's your expression going down there, and there's no way you can change it," she gently fretted. "It's there forever. It's very frustrating to see something that you have been keeping transient for years just suddenly become solid. It's a little disconcerting… but exciting."

QUIETLY DETERMINED TO EXERT MORE INFLUENCE over the recording of what would become her second album released in 1978, *Lionheart*, Kate Bush invited Brian Bath over to the flat where she was now living in Brockley, to work together on arrangements and guitar parts.

"I'd sit with her at the piano, and we'd go through songs. I'd write up some rough kind of bar charts and we'd try to knock them into order. Like, 'Where's the intro, Kate? Are you really going to use that chord?' And we'd suss out what the chords were and just work out where we were with the guitar."

One of Bush's newest creations, Coffee Homeground, rendered in a Brecht-Weill style, centred on a character visiting someone they are convinced is secretly trying to poison them by slipping arsenic or belladonna into their drinks.

"It had really heavy guitars on it, and that idea wasn't used in the end," Bath recalled. "The lyric was so interesting: 'Where are the plumbers/Who went missing here on Monday?' Her subject matter was just outrageous." The singer herself described the song as being about the "humorous aspect of paranoia".

Bush convinced EMI and Andrew Powell to use the latest line-up of the KT Bush Band – Brian Bath and Del Palmer, along with new drummer Charlie Morgan – for the *Lionheart* album sessions at Super Bear Studios, tucked away in the mountains north-east of Nice. But only two satisfactory backing tracks, for Wow and Kashka From Baghdad, were cut before the label and the producer forced a rethink.

"We started doing our versions of the songs and they gave us a good go for a couple of days," Bath said. "It was really hot outside but freezing in the studio. You'd open the door up, the hot air would come in, and all the instruments kept going out of tune. Things started not working out and there were a few meetings about what was going to happen and what was not going to happen."

The *Kick Inside* team of Elliott, Paton, Bairnson and Mackay were quickly sent to France to complete the *Lionheart* sessions. "She went out with her band," says Mackay, "and probably Andrew said, 'I want my chaps because I know how to talk to them to get them to play better.' I'm not saying [the others] played rubbish, but obviously that plan didn't work. And then we flew out and entered the album."

Mackay instantly proved his value by adding spooky synth arpeggios to Wow. In the overdubbing process, he felt Powell was relaying Bush's ideas. "I'd be speaking more with Andrew and assume, rightly or wrongly, that he was coming across with instructions from Kate. Everybody was in the room to make the best piece of music."

Thematically, the songs on *Lionheart* moved from Wow's study of the artifice and loneliness of performance to the adult corruption of childhood wonder of In Search Of Peter Pan. The quasi-title track Oh England My Lionheart, meanwhile, took a rose-tinted look at the nation and its past and, as Bush put it, "how beautiful it is amongst all the rubbish."

Elsewhere, in Symphony In Blue ("The colour of my room and my mood") and the self-admittedly "probably quite autobiographical" Fullhouse there were glimpses of the mental pressures Bush was suffering: "paranoia, anger, that sort of thing," she confessed to writer Colin Irwin. As much as she hid it at the time, the making of *Lionheart* was a frustrating one for the singer.

In a recorded interview for EMI, issued on cassette as a promo for the album, she admitted it had presented for her a "difficult situation… I felt very squashed in by the lack of time. That's what I don't like, especially if it's concerning something as important for me as my songs are."

"By the end of the second record," Bush later told MOJO, "I was thinking, I don't want to be produced by somebody who sees it differently from me. So I thought, if I could, I would try and take over."

Del Palmer witnessed Bush's creative determination break dramatically to the surface. Invited to New York to appear on Saturday Night Live in December 1978, she was rehearsing a performance of Them Heavy People with the show's house band when she suddenly stopped to tell the drummer he was playing his part wrong, before proceeding to demonstrate the correct beat. She didn't know, or care, that the drummer was Billy Cobham.

"When she found out she just said, 'Well, he wasn't doing it right,'" Palmer told HomeGround magazine. "An awe-in- ➤

Jim Bamber / The Sun / News Syndication, Michael Putland/Getty Images

"She Created This Whole Massive World"

Illusionist **SIMON DRAKE** was Kate Bush's co-conspirator on the ground-breaking, never-to-be-repeated Tour Of Life. "She was a pioneer," he tells **DANNY ECCLESTON**.

REHEARSING KATE BUSH'S Tour Of Life was nearly the end of then-budding illusionist Simon Drake. He was emerging from under a walkway at the back of the stage, when a section of plywood slid loose and cracked him on the head.

"I was knocked right out," he recalls today. "And I came to with Kate sort of holding me in her lap. I was sick for a couple of days."

Drake was lucky. If one of the section's metal braces had hit him he might not have lived to tell the tale. It was, sadly, one of several instances where the ambition of Bush's staging for her single tour as a star outstripped the experience of the team lashing it together, a situation that ended in tragedy after the warm-up show at Poole Arts Centre, with the fatal fall of young lighting engineer Bill Duffield.

It was an outcome unthinkable in the innocent pre-dawn of Drake's involvement with the tour, which had begun the moment he first heard Wuthering Heights on the radio in January '78. Bowled over, Drake – a former plugger at Decca and EMI – sent a note to Bush through Capital Radio producer Eddie Puma.

"I knew Eddie was seeing her that night. I just wrote that the record was amazing and if she ever toured, I wanted to be a part of it."

Later, Drake invited Bush to a magic show he was performing at J Arthur's, a club run by Krays associate Freddie Foreman at the "wrong end" of the King's Road, Chelsea, a party for Roxy Music. "I was on a little half-circle stage. And I distinctly remember her sitting there watching me, sat on her own."

Subsequently, Drake was invited to tea-fuelled meetings at Bush's flat in Lewisham. He watched the singer scribbling designs for the ankh-shaped set that later clobbered him ("she's very aware of esoteric matters") as the pair swapped ideas for bringing Bush's already-theatrical songs to the stage.

"She was a pioneer," says Drake. "There wasn't anyone doing anything quite that ambitious then. Maybe Peter Gabriel with Genesis. Certainly not with that amount of dance. Now it's normal."

Drake's key scenes with Bush included two 'dancing cane' demonstrations on L'Amour Looks Something Like You and Strange Phenomena, and a spidery turn as a crazed fiddler during Violin.

"The violin was Kate's own from when she was a kid. I cut out a bit of the back and put homemade pyro in it. The idea being I'd play the violin so fast, it would start smoking."

For the paranoid murder fantasies of Coffee Homeground, Drake had two liquids – one pink, another yellow – that turned black when mixed: "You know, like a poison. Then I'd come up behind her and try to strangle her. They were all these rather 'panto' attempts at assassination."

Drake and Bush dubbed the assassin 'Hugo'. The vibe was Berlin '30s cabaret, Paris Moulin Rouge. "He's partly based on 'Valentin The Boneless One' who you see in a couple of paintings by Toulouse-Lautrec with this very big, pointy chin, pointy nose and cheekbones."

The tour itself – 24 shows between April 2 and May 14, 1979 – was a roller coaster: traumatic for Bush on account of Duffield's death and the exposure to her own mounting fame. "I mean, fans would almost throw themselves in front of the coach," says Drake. "I mean, it was scary."

Factor in the demands of the show – its athletic challenges, the costume changes – and it's miraculous that only one health scare (Bush lost her voice temporarily in Sweden) threatened to end the tour prematurely. "She was amazing every night for two and a half hours," says Drake. "I mean, extraordinary. She created this whole massive world."

Drake's work on the Tour Of Life proved the beginning of a rise through the showbiz ranks, and a relationship with Bush that continued, providing magic at several of her son Bertie's birthday parties. In 1990 and 1991 he acquired another level of fame fronting Channel 4 TV show Secret Cabaret, and at 67 continues to make a career from magic at the heart of Simon Drake's House Of Magic. In 2014 he was pleased to receive an invite to Bush's Before The Dawn residency at the Hammersmith Apollo. Why does he think it took her so long – over 37 years – to get back on the stage for a comparable run of shows?

"I don't know. I can only guess," says Drake. "Basically, a production like the Tour Of Life is hard to control. The fact that when she did do anything again, it was all in one place, with a stage crew from more of a theatre background, something extremely controlled, I think that's probably a clue. For someone like Kate, who's that good, it's hard for anything to be good enough. It's just got to be better."

What did he make of the show?

"I was so pleased and proud to see her do this incredibly grown-up version of what she'd done all those years before. It was really like walking into a dream, wasn't it?"

After the gig, Drake was ushered into VIP drinks, then the super-VIP drinks, "which was weird – only six people in there." When Bush entered with Bertie, they hugged and she asked what he thought, whereupon Drake endeavoured to reassemble his blown mind.

"I just said, Fuuuuuuck! And she said, 'Is that all you're gonna say? Fuuuuuck?'"

Simon hosts private and occasionally public shows at his own London theatre, where Tour Of Life memorabilia can be found. See houseofmagic.co.uk

Sticking to her guns: Bush the Cowgirl is locked and loaded for Tour Of Life, 1979.

> "I was knocked right out. And I came to with Kate sort of holding me in her lap."
> **SIMON DRAKE**

◄ spiring musician and she says, 'No, that's not how I want it. I want it like this.' Says a lot about her."

ALTHOUGH EXHAUSTED BY THE MAKING OF two albums and the 24-date Tour Of Life, which ended at London's Hammersmith Odeon in May 1979, Kate Bush was back in the studio by September of that year, notably co-producing her third record with Jon Kelly. As a result, *Never For Ever* was arguably the first of her albums that sounded like *her*.

"Yeah, I think so," she said in 2005. "I discovered things like the Fairlight, and I was using the musicians that I wanted to use. No offence to the musicians on the second record.

"I mean there were obviously restrictions because we were paying a studio. It took six months to make that record, which is actually very quick for me. But at the time it was a very long time to spend making a record. It was really fun working with the musicians that we had on that album as well. It was a laugh again, I suppose."

The core players Bush used for the initial tracks recorded for *Never For Ever* – The Wedding List, Blow Away (For Bill), Egypt and the stomping, Roxy Music-ish Violin – were those who'd appeared on Tour Of Life: Brian Bath, Del Palmer, guitarist Alan Murphy and drummer Preston Heyman.

"The band was a real good working unit," said Bath, "and a couple of the songs we'd actually performed live already, although the arrangements were changed for the album. You could see it was taking a new direction. There was the influence from the Steely Dan type of thing. It had a different kind of spark to it."

When the sessions moved from AIR to Abbey Road in January 1980, Steely Dan-like standards of precision were much in

(top) in Amsterdam, April 29, and (below) Copenhagen, April 26, 1979, with Simon Drake (left and below right).

"I think music is very visual. On *Never For Ever* there was quite a bit of that, trying to imagine being there."
KATE BUSH

evidence, along with a similar revolving door policy when it came to sourcing exactly the right musicians for specific parts.

"It was always a problem with the bass or the drums," Bath said. "We'd all be sitting around waiting for the next player to turn up. There'd be logs of names of people turning up at the studio and we'd run the song and if it didn't work… they'd get another one.

"But finally Stuart Elliott came in, and he's very orchestrated. Fabulous drummer. He's so inventive and he gives you hints of where you could put things afterwards."

"I came in halfway through," Elliott remembered. "That's when we recorded Breathing and Babooshka. It was not a case of, y'know, the hits have all been recorded, we'll just do a few album tracks. That was one of the most fruitful sessions."

When it came to learning further nuances of the recording process, Bush had also gained outside experience with a key mentor. Ahead of the Abbey Road leg of the record, Bush had become a friend and collaborator of Peter Gabriel, contributing spectral backing vocals and counterpoint melody to No Self Control and the "jeux sans frontières" hookline to the UK Number 4 hit Games Without Frontiers, both from his third self-titled album.

But while Gabriel was thanked by Bush in the credits of *Never For Ever* "for opening the windows", she claimed to Melody Maker he had been less a direct musical influence and more someone who had "let some light in for me", particularly in the sense of being able to maintain a public face and yet also a regular personal life. "Offstage he's very normal," she told Record Mirror, "and that's the kind of thing I believe in."

Gabriel was a central figure in her 44-minute-long BBC2 TV special, simply titled Kate, which aired on December 28, 1979, and featured songs from her first two albums and three already recorded for the work-in-progress *Never For Ever*. If its shot-on-video, lit-for-TV production values lent it an am-dram quality at certain points, it was both an addendum to Tour Of Life and a signifier of where Bush's next live production might have been heading.

It opened with full band performances of Violin, Symphony In Blue and Them Heavy People, before Gabriel first appeared as special guest for a powerfully stark, voice-and-electric-piano reading of Here Comes The Flood from his first, 1977 solo album. Kate, wearing a weirdy beard, then debuted Ran Tan Waltz (set to be the B-side of Babooshka), a comedic folk tune in which the hapless narrator is a lad left holding the baby as his wife goes out gallivanting. Next, at the piano, she sang her festive piano ballad December Will Be Magic Again (released as a single the following year).

Aside from a Play For Today rendering of The Wedding List, in which the singer cast herself as a new bride moved to murderous revenge when her husband is shot, the standout moment came with the return of Peter Gabriel for a duet cover version of Another Day from Roy Harper's 1970 album, *Flat Baroque And Berserk*.

The TV performance of this song of regret for a fading love affair depicted them as a worn out couple sitting at either end of a fold-down table, as an alternative scenario blue-screened into a picture frame on the wall revealed the former to be a desperate and violently angry man (and likely the source of their troubles). An important staging-post in Bush's quest to give pictorial life to the dramas of her songs.

"I think music is very visual," said Bush in 2005. "On *Never For Ever* there was quite a bit of that, trying to imagine being there. It's that thing of being in this place, isn't it? That you're talking ➤

Rob Verhorst/Getty Images (2), Jorgen Angel/Getty Images (2), Gai Terrell/Getty Images

> ## "When I heard *The Wall*, I thought, There's no point in writing songs any more. Because they'd said it all." KATE BUSH

"I'm still just me": the public face of Kate Bush, 1981; (left) coffee hotel-ground, London, 1978.

< about or singing about, so you're trying to create what it looks like and who's there."

WITH *NEVER FOR EVER*, KATE BUSH seemed poised to fully realise the kinds of characters and scenarios she'd been reaching for since her childhood songwriting. But she was both inspired and disheartened midway through its recording by the release of Pink Floyd's double album opus, *The Wall*, in November 1979 – particularly side three, from Hey You to Comfortably Numb.

"When I heard it, I thought, There's no point in writing songs any more," she admitted. "Because they'd said it all. When something really gets you, it hits your creative centre and stops you creating."

After two weeks in which her sense of purpose was temporarily lost, Bush set her bar higher. The ominous, apocalyptic Breathing benefited from stately Floyd-like pacing. Elsewhere, the sampling marvel that was the Fairlight was put to good use, rendering rifle cocks as a rhythmic component of Army Dreamers.

"What an extraordinary machine at the time," Duncan Mackay says of the Fairlight, which he played – at Bush's prompting – on Army Dreamers and All We Ever Look For. "There was a viola sound that obviously would have been sampled within the range of what that instru-

THE EARLY ALBUMS #3

Never For Ever
(EMI, 1980)

MAKING THE video for Breathing, the apocalyptic horror that closes *Never For Ever*, Kate Bush was zipped tightly into three womb-like inflatables, the crew pumping oxygen to the singer through the plastic. "Then it would steam up and they had to open it out so the air blasted into me," Bush explained in 1980. "It felt so good."

There's a similar release around Bush's third album, a sense of windows thrown open, of exciting new technology cracking the glass dome around her songwriting. The perfect synthesis comes with the sampled loading of a gun on Army Dreamers, turning a delicate waltz of grief into a relentless death march, but there's a similar blast on the footsteps and chants of skittish madrigal All We Ever Look For, or the elliptical drum-machine blips of Delius (Song Of Summer). Breathing's narrative of an unborn baby sensing the poisonous post-nuclear world around it, meanwhile, is raw speculation, imagination tempered by political reality.

This time, the greasepaint remains on the dressing table, and aside from Babooshka's plate-smashing hell-hath-no-fury folk-tale or its vengeful-bride counterpart The Wedding List, there's a subtlety to Bush's role-playing here. Turn Of The Screw reinvention The Infant Kiss, for example, is all the more disturbing for its calm clarity. Like the seekers on All We Ever Look For, Bush knows what it means to be on a quest – looking for space, looking for truth. With *Never For Ever*, though, it seems all the doors are opening. VS

ment plays. But then I started messing around with it. And I played some part that was much, much, much higher than the instrument and this strange and completely unique sound appeared. And people said, 'What the bloody hell's that?' I said, It's meant to be a viola. But it sure ain't (*laughs*)."

A similarly exotic soundscape was created over the analogue beatbox pulse and piano base of Delius, with Paddy Bush adding sitar strums and the imagined bassy voice of the titular composer. The song's lyric was inspired by Bush's TV viewing of Ken Russell's 1968 film Song Of Summer, detailing how Frederick Delius, with tertiary syphilis, had spent his final years croaking his last compositions to an amanuensis, Eric Fenby. The tale of creative frustration and resolve stuck in her mind. Remarkably, she was only 10 when it first aired.

Now, incredibly, upon the release of her third album on September 8, 1980, she was still only 22. Soon *Never For Ever* would be her first UK Number 1; also the first chart-topping album by any British female solo artist. But it caught her at a critical point, where she was finally on the right path creatively, but still unsure as to what to make of her own celebrity.

"I'm not a star," she insisted, although the lengthy queue of fans down Oxford Street waiting to have copies of *Never For Ever* signed by her at a Virgin Megastore appearance on September 12 told a different story. "My name is, but not me," she added. "I'm still just me."

It appeared to be true. To those around her, Kate Bush hadn't changed at all.

"That was the delightful thing," Duncan Mackay attests. "Kate would still say, 'Would you like a cup of tea?'" Ⓜ

Thanks to Seán Twomey of Kate Bush News www.katebushnews.com for additional research.

Camera Press/Steve Emberton, Camera Press/Clive Arrowsmith

MOJO FILTER

YOUR GUIDE TO THE MONTH'S BEST MUSIC

EDITED BY **JENNY BULLEY** jenny.bulley@bauermedia.co.uk

"The Youngs'
iron certainty
that there is
nothing a great
riff won't cure
or conquer."

**THE GENIUS OF
AC/DC, BY DAVID
FRICKE. REISSUES P94.**

CONTENTS

INDEX

Alone again, naturally

Thirty years after Portishead's debut, their singer makes her first solo album.
By **Victoria Segal**. Illustration by **Ben Giles**.

Beth Gibbons

★★★★

Lives Outgrown

DOMINO. CD/DL/LP

"**GOD KNOWS** how I adore life," sang Beth Gibbons on Mysteries, the opening track on *Out Of Season*, her 2002 collaboration with Talk Talk bassist Paul 'Rustin Man' Webb. Such hello-birds-hello-sky sentiment isn't generally associated with Portishead's singer – not unless the birds are the kind that circle hungrily overhead and the sky is falling down.

Her sparse output since *Out Of Season* underlines how her voice has become a prized totem of misery, a gift for those wishing to convey despair, desolation – or just sometimes – fragile hope. Inevitably, she was the presiding dark spirit of Portishead's starkly contorted 2008 comeback *Third*, but neither genre nor language obstructed Gibbons' ability to communicate. When, in 2014, she courageously performed Górecki's Symphony No. 3 with the Polish National Radio Symphony Orchestra, conducted by Krzysztof Penderecki, it was announced she was learning the piece without speaking "the mother tongue", finding emotional depth beyond grammar.

That same year, she guested with Bristol metal band Gonga on their version of Black Sabbath (or, as they rightly preferred, "Black Sabbeth"). In 2022, she sang on Mother I Sober, the raw dissection of intergenerational trauma on Kendrick Lamar's album *Mr. Morale And The Big Steppers*, while last year she covered Joy Division and David Bowie with Afghan girl group Miraculous Love Kids.

With *Lives Outgrown*, though, she is officially (if not literally) alone, her first solo album carving a path through its own Lonesome Valley. Recorded with Talk Talk drummer Lee Harris and producer James Ford (on an incongruous hot streak after working with Arctic Monkeys, Blur, Depeche Mode and Pet Shop Boys on their latest records), it has taken 10 years to emerge, a fitting span of time for an album so profoundly concerned with its passing. Despite her habitual elusiveness, Gibbons has stepped out to explain that these are songs shadowed by death, songs that deal with loss, grief and the menopause – a life-phase she describes as a "massive audit" that "cuts you at the knees". In other words, *Lives Outgrown* asks – back to Black Sabbath – "what is this that stands before me?"

On Floating On A Moment, the answer is largely "nothing good" – or maybe, just nothing at all. "Without control/I'm heading for the boundary that divides us," she sings over the track's stately Plain Gold Ring rhythm, "travelling on a voyage where the living/They have never been." The backing vocals are divided between cowled, monkish chanting and Gibbons' own kids sweetly singing "all going to nowhere". It's a more medieval take on The Flaming

> "*Lives Outgrown* is a record alert to shed skins, sensitive to the inexorable damage caused by the years."

**BACK STORY:
AHEAD OF
THE HERD**

● "Anywhere she wanted to go, I went," drummer Lee Harris has said about his work with Beth Gibbons on *Lives Outgrown*. The singer's association with Harris and his former Talk Talk bandmate Paul Webb goes back to pre-Portishead days, when Gibbons applied to be the singer in their band 'O'Rang. With Portishead's trip-hop star suddenly rising, however, she only ended up as a guest vocalist on their 1994 debut LP *Herd Of Instinct* (above).

Lips' cosmic-uncle hit Do You Realize?? ("…that everyone you know someday will die"), an acutely painful and lovely rendering of the old "life's a killer" line.

From the stormy opening swell of Tell Me Who You Are Today, Linda Perhacs if she'd been raised in a Somerset barn, *Lives Outgrown* is a record alert to shed skins, sensitive to the inexorable damage caused by the years. On Lost Changes, Gibbons is in full Cassandra mode, calling out the oblivious – "hey you, over there" – before declaring "forever ends/ You will grow old." On its swinging pendulum of a chorus, as across the whole album, the instrumentation is richly varied: hammered dulcimer, vibraphone, flute, Raven Bush's violin and viola and Harris's inventive percussion (a box of curtains, a paella dish). The record might have taken years to create, but it still feels intimate, natural, sometimes threateningly unpredictable, sounds rising and falling against Gibbons' vocals like a tide.

There are moments of high drama: the car-chase brass on Reaching Out echoes Portishead's early cinematic stylings; Rewind, an environmental lament flooded by strings and percussion, insists "we all know what's coming" before ominous audio of children playing in water. Beyond The Sun, meanwhile, thunders onto the record like it's crashing through undergrowth, bass clarinet and bowed saw increasing the sense of hectic ritual, feverish, *Hounds Of Love* pursuit. Yet *Lives Outgrown* more often feels dense rather than lush, a subtle, sepia-and-grey shading reminiscent of Warren Ellis-era Bad Seeds, or P.J. Harvey's *I Inside The Old Year Dying*.

As Bill Callahan might say, this is her apocalypse, in all its forms – the death of a relationship (Reaching Out), the extinguishing of dreams (For Sale), the loss of a beloved "soul" (Burden Of Life). It's impossible, though, to escape the ultimate existential dread that suffuses *Lives Outgrown*. Over time, the music industry has realised that not everyone hopes they die before they get old and has come to accept the Not Dark Yet school of songwriting, happy to frame Johnny Cash or Leonard Cohen as biblical prophets facing down their doom. An artist addressing the specific challenges of female midlife is still rare, however – a few comic songs about hot flushes, Tori Amos's 2014 LP *Unrepentant Geraldines*, or Tracey Thorn's witty yet poignant Hormones (from 2010's *Love And Its Opposite*) come to mind. *Lives Outgrown* is hardly a Davina McCall wellness DVD, but there's a real sense of being repeatedly slammed up against mortality by biology, especially on the salt-scoured Oceans. Gibbons sings of ovulation and exhaustion in an unusually porous, chalky register, the song ending with her sinking to the (rock) bottom of the sea, "not afraid any more".

If that all sounds bleak, it is. Yet *Lives Outgrown* is also very beautiful, not least when Gibbons quietly sings "it's not that I don't want to return" during Floating On A Moment's contemplation of death. It's an echo of Mysteries, a reminder that you can only be this sorrowful about losing something when you love it so much. It would be too easy to say it ends on a note of redemption or hope – after what's gone before, it's clear there are no last-minute reprieves – but the closing Whispering Love does feel like quiet acceptance, a patch of sun after all the cold truths, the odd little chirrup that punctuates the song suggesting a small blip of happiness. As she sings on Floating On A Moment, "all we have is here and now." Keep in the company of *Lives Outgrown*, and that's no sad thing.

Branching out: The Lemon Twigs dream on.

Stephanie Pia

The Lemon Twigs

★★★★

A Dream Is All We Know

CAPTURED TRACKS. CD/DL/LP

Brand new, you're retro: Long Island brothers make swift return with fifth album.

"EVERY DAY IS like a memory/Of someone I knew a thousand years ago/I've never heard or seen." As suggested on insomniac's lament They Don't Know How To Fall In Place, there's an unnerving glitch in Michael and Brian D'Addario's musical matrix, their newest record again suggesting that two skinny New York musicians became jammed in a pop wormhole sometime between 1968 and 1974 and still haven't wriggled free. As with 2023's downbeat *Everything Harmony*, what might just be a Beatles-Beach-Boys-Big-Star data-scrape is elevated through high-calibre songwriting, My Golden Years soaked in insta-nostalgia, the Sean Ono Lennon-produced In The Eyes Of The Girl sinking into the psychedelic surf. It's impossible to shake the uncanny-valley unease, though, especially during Peppermint Roses, a nervous breakdown in ruffles and lace. A dream, maybe, but there's something of the nightmare about them.

Victoria Segal

A DREAM IS ALL WE KNOW   THE LEMON TWIGS

Various

★★★

The Power Of The Heart: A Tribute To Lou Reed

LIGHT IN THE ATTIC. CD/DL/LP

Velvet understatement: respectful homage to the ex-titan of sleaze.

Curated by long-term ally Bill Bentley, this set of newly-commissioned covers takes in some of Lou Reed's career highlights as well as detours into his curly-mullet era. Keith Richards does a pleasingly fey job on The Velvet Underground's I'm Waiting For The Man, while Joan Jett And The Blackhearts (I'm So Free), Rufus Wainwright (Perfect Day) and Rickie Lee Jones (Walk On The Wild Side) spray their various scents over selections from 1972's career-defining *Transformer*. Elsewhere, The Afghan Whigs warp 1984's I Love You, Suzanne into a Kings Of Leon-style stadium belter, Lucinda Williams drawls stylishly through Legendary Hearts and fellow Americana titan Rosanne Cash finds the darkest of twinkles in Magician. No ding-dong sucking and not many dirty needles, but with its hushed, reverential tone, *The Power Of The Heart* is the kind of tribute the professorial Reed of his tai chi years would have appreciated.

Jim Wirth

Michael Head & The Red Elastic Band

★★★★

Loophole

MODERN SKY. CD/DL/LP

Strong sequel to MOJO's Best Album Of 2022.

"I'm just loving the future," Mick Head announced in MOJO 365, a singer-songwriter finally parlaying 40 years of cultish and critical acclaim into something akin to success. Nevertheless, this fairly swift follow-up to 2022's *Dear Scott* more often negotiates with the past, as Head memorialises formative Liverpool events and Shack-era road tales, revisiting old musical touchstones as he goes. Love, of course, remain sine qua non (Ciao Ciao Bambino, the especially superb Ricochet), but there's a bossa-adjacent throwback to his '80s band The Pale Fountains too (You Smiled At Me), and a new curio in You're A Long Time Dead that's roughly Rhapsody In Blue, Dixieland-style. It all makes for a scrappier and less cohesive set than *Dear Scott*, but possibly a more characterful one, with even better songs. Start with Merry Go Round, elegiac psych-baroque co-written by Shack alumnus Pete Wilkinson that impressionistically mentions Mussolini, Thatcher and, perhaps more positively, the Bunnymen's Will Sergeant.

John Mulvey

Neil Young With Crazy Horse

★★★★

Fu##in' Up

REPRISE. LP

'Neil & The Horse' revisit (and rechristen) most of *Ragged Glory*.

Those overwhelmed by Young's *Archives* onslaught lately may be considering sitting this one out: *Fu##in' Up* presents latterday Crazy Horse, with guitar foil Nils Lofgren, plus Promise Of The Real's Micah Nelson (piano/guitar), performing 1990's beloved *Ragged Glory* in sequence, bar closer Mother Earth (Natural Anthem), last November at Toronto's 200-capacity Rivoli club. In a move that some may deem wilfully misleading, the songs have been retitled using relevant lyric fragments, "allowing them to be here now", and Young's refusing to calling it a live album. Though 1991's *Weld* definitively documents *Ragged Glory*-concurrent performances, there's an undeniable zip to these ones. In January, Young revealed he'd been fighting arthritis in his hand, but that at Rivoli he'd

"finally discovered a way around the pain". Certainly, he bashes his strings with renewed vigour, if not always fluidly, and on 15-minute A Chance On Love (AKA Love And Only Love) summons a feedback tsunami worthy of 1991's noise-only *Arc*.

Andrew Perry

Blue Öyster Cult

★★★★

Ghost Stories

FRONTIERS MUSIC. CD/DL/LP

Is this goodbye from the Long Island pioneers of heavy rock?

Still touring, 50th anniversary been and gone, BÖC bring familiar playfulness and unbridled melodicism to *Ghost Stories*. Billed as their final studio LP, it uses Peter Jackson-adjacent AI technology to de-mix and help refurbish unreleased vault material largely recorded between 1978-83, enabling a posthumous appearance by co-founding keyboardist Allen Lanier and inspiring new input from the classic line-up's brothers Albert and Joe Bouchard, alongside shepherding co-frontmen Eric Bloom and Donald 'Buck Dharma' Roeser. We get unheard studio versions of the MC5's Kick Out The Jams and The Animals' We Gotta Get Out Of This Place (both were covered by BÖC on 1978 live outing *Some Enchanted Evening*), plus such

fine, previously fabled originals as Gun and The Only Thing. Palette cleanser? A mellifluous acoustic take on The Beatles' If I Fell. Manna for Cult devotees.

James McNair

Isobel Campbell

★★★

Bow To Love

COOKING VINYL. CD/DL/LP

Belle of Belle & Sebastian fame get back on track.

"I'm the tortoise/You're the hare," sings Isobel Campbell on Dopamine. Hamstrung for a decade by record biz red-tape post 2010's *Hawk*, her third, by then not so unlikely LP with Mark Lanegan, she's back in the race with this successor to 2020's *There Is No Other*. With its intimate and enveloping production, there's much to applaud about *Bow To Love* as Campbell targets toxic masculinity (Everything Falls Apart) and the distancing, dehumanising aspects of social media (4316), but you sometimes feel only the shallows of her rhyming dictionary are being plumbed. Props, all the same, for the way Do Or Die's arrangement suddenly opens onto a *Bryter Layter* vista with strings and piano, for Take This Poison's drone-based haunting and Matmos-like electronica, and for the album's hipster-baiting cover of Dire Straits' Why Worry.

James McNair

Bleachers

★★★★

Bleachers

DIRTY HIT. CD/DL/LP

Fourth album from whizz producer's group offers nocturnal atmospheres.

In parallel to his work as a songwriter, musician and studio bod for St. Vincent, Lana Del Rey and Taylor Swift, New Jersey's Jack Antonoff has pursued a hit-and-miss career as the frontman of indie poppers Bleachers. 2021's *Take The Sadness Out Of Saturday Night* featured a vocal cameo from Bruce Springsteen on Chinatown, apparently further inspiring Antonoff on this self-titled LP. The try-too-hard Modern Girl shoots for The Boss doing Subterranean Homesick Blues but lands closer to Billy Joel's We Didn't Start The Fire, though it's thankfully not representative of the record as a whole. Instead, there's taut New Wave (Tiny Moves; Jesus Is Dead), but mainly moody electronic balladry (think Streets Of Philadelphia), with Del Rey turning up to fulfil the intent of her one repeated line ("I'll make it darker") on Alma Mater.

Tom Doyle

Primal *Screaming*:
St. Vincent's, AKA Annie
Clark, latest is a thrilling,
unpredictable listen.

Hear my cry

Seventh album from Annie Clark
brings darkness, then light.
By Tom Doyle.

St. Vincent

★★★★

All Born Screaming

VIRGIN/FICTION. CD/DL/LP

AFTER THE out-of-time 1970s masterpiece
that was 2021's *Daddy's Home*, it was perhaps
inevitable that Annie Clark would feel the pull
of bubbling synths, dirty guitars and conspicu-
ous modernity once again. Entirely self-pro-
ducing for the first time, here Clark has made a
more difficult record than its predecessor – at
least in its first half – and one created in the
wake of unspecified loss.

The spiralling English folk rock of Hell
Is Near, in which Clark assumes vocal tones
clearly indebted to Beth Gibbons, is a misdi-
recting opener. Second cut, Reckless, is where
the darkness begins to close in, in an impressionistic depiction of bereavement, watching
someone fade away in the "London sun" as the

narrator begins "cracking
up". It's one of two con-
secutive songs to feature the
latter phrase. Broken Man,
with its '83 Eurythmics
synth pulses and a guesting
Dave Grohl's artfully syncopated drum fills,
sees her assume the role of a peacocking, macho
character who, as the title makes explicit, isn't
all he seems.

Stylistically, *All Born Screaming* pinballs
madly between dream pop, prog, grunge,
electronica and industrial, making for thrilling,
unpredictable listening, with Clark's voice the
cohesive glue. The moment when the heaviness appears to lift is meanwhile deceptive: the
parasitic relationship of Flea (in which Grohl
revives his shuffling In Bloom beat) gives way to
the Grace Jones (think Pull Up To The Bumper)
groove of Big Time Nothing, the sashaying
moves of which belie the fact that it's essentially a self-empowering mantra attempting to
destroy negative thinking.

Part two attempts to search for the beauty
in chaos and tragedy. Sweetest Fruit, with its
Hounds Of Love-era Kate Bush synth quirks and

tom-tom beat, is a tribute to
Scottish electro-pop artist
Sophie, who fell to her death
from a rooftop in Athens in
2021 while trying to photo-
graph the full moon ("But
for a minute, what a view,"
Clark imagines). Meanwhile,
The Power's Out transcribes
the skipping rhythm of Bow-
ie's Five Years to an '80s beatbox, as a national
outage (as opposed to looming doomsday) leads
to episodes of murder and suicide amongst a
city filled with desperate characters.

While Clark has confessed that *All Born
Screaming* was her toughest LP to make so
far, both due to personal trauma and her sole
overseeing of the recording process, support
comes from bassist/programmer Justin Meldal-
Johnsen (Beck, Nine Inch Nails) and the
increasingly omnipresent Cate Le Bon, fresh
from producing Wilco and Devendra Banhart.
The latter lends additional production to a
handful of tracks but earns a feature vocal credit
on the near-seven-minute title track, wherein
she and Clark layer up an operatic coda over an
insistent, ravey beat. It's a celebratory ending
to a clearly cathartic album that further proves
Annie Clark to be a brilliant and multifaceted
musical force.

Kind of blue: Iron & Wine, AKA Sam Beam, conjures a beautiful lushness on his new LP.

Kim Black

Iron & Wine
★★★★
Light Verse
SUB POP. CD/DL/LP

Sam Beam's first full-length I&W album in seven years.

AFTER HIS LAST album, a second collaboration with Calexico (*Years To Burn*, 2019), the world shut down and Beam did too. It took several years and a tour with Andrew Bird for his songwriting mojo to come back. You might assume, given the title, that Beam's seventh full-length album as Iron & Wine is lightweight and whimsical. Actually it's pretty magnificent. He wrote it, he says, as an "album" album, to listen to from beginning to end. It starts hushed and intimate (You Never Know), then as the band gradually comes in, it takes on a beautiful lushness throughout. There's drums, keyboards, bass, mandolin, slide guitar and, with a 24-piece orchestra, a whole lot of strings.

Highlights include the lovely one-man harmonies on Tears That Don't Matter; the rhythmic, percussive Anyone's Game, and All In Good Time, a soulful, churchy duet with Fiona Apple.

Sylvie Simmons

different life, Same Water might be a huge rock ballad. These songs may sound simple, but they have heart-bursting depth.

Andy Fyfe

Various
★★★★
Under The Bridge 2
SKEP WAX. CD/LP/DL

More maverick pop from former Sarah Records' stable.

It's hard to pick out songs on this sequel to the 2022 compilation of groups who recorded for '90s Brighton label Sarah Records. Mainly because each act on its 20 tracks is still questing, still pushing to create fresh new material. Amelia Fletcher and Rob Pursey's The Catenary Wires, for instance, have made eerie, eviscerating dream pop with Alone Tonight, while Jetstream Pony provide contrast in the swoonsome shoegaze of Look Alive. The Orchids are there, with the short but sharp A Final Love Song, alongside the audacious punk pop of Boyracer's Unknown Frequencies, and the soaring choruses of Robert Sekula (14 Iced Bears). Unlike the innocence of their '90s output, these bands sing indie pop with a twist – songs about burn-out, regret and long lost flings, but there's also room for quiet joy and hope.

Lucy O'Brien

Tidiane Thiam
★★★★
Africa Yontii
SAHEL SOUNDS. DL/LP

Guitarist from Senegal's northern border insists Africa's time has come.

Hailing from Podor, home to Baaba Maal on the Senegal/Mauritania border, Thiam grew up listening to Manding music on distant Malian radio stations, which perhaps explains stylistic similarities with the great Boubacar Traoré's more reflective pieces. That, and the fact the two men grew up beside water – you can definitely imagine whiling away a day listening to *Africa Yontii* on a riverbank, before wondering where the time went. There's a message, too, about opportunity, development and destiny, but as the album is fully instrumental, you may have to dig deep to find it. Instead, just lie back and allow the field recording Yewende transport you to Senegal after dark, and let the twin guitars of Yangue lift your spirits. Simple music,

perhaps, but one of those records you'll find yourself returning to again and again when the sun comes out.

David Hutcheon

Keeley Forsyth
★★★★
The Hollow
FAT CAT. CD/DL/LP

Yorkshire singer's third LP doubles down on her elemental voice and performative skills.

It's fitting that Keeley Forsyth's last screen appearance was in Poor Things. Like Yorgos Lanthimos's eccentric blockbuster, the TV actor turned singer's latest shows little regard for convention. Whether paying tribute to grandmother Mary (Eve) or re-imagining Mihály Víg's The Turin Horse score (Horse) over circling synths, these non-linear creations are vehicles for an incredible contralto that echoes Anohni, Diamanda Galás, Jarboe, even late-era Scott Walker. The latter comparison holds for Turning, given a noirish ambience by Colin Stetson, and A Shift, which repurposes Mal Finch's protest song We Are Women, We Are Strong into a vortex of sax, strings and baleful bass synth. Intimate and intense, operatic and

guttural, Forsyth paints her world's rugged beauty in tones that could stop listeners dead.

Andy Cowan

Larry Campbell & Teresa Williams
★★★★
All This Time
ROYAL POTATO FAMILY. CD/DL/LP

Americana power couple deliver a fourth winner.

The duo's fourth album is a song cycle about living and working as a wedded team, barrelling out of the chute with Desert Island Dreams, a statement of marital bliss featuring Campbell's virtuosic country-rocked guitar and Williams' wailing vocals. All This Time and Ride With Me are more Campbell originals that examine a shared life, emphasised by the couple's pitch-perfect harmonies. The George Jones/Gene Pitney classic That's All It Took (also covered by Gram Parsons and Emmylou Harris) shows off their deep country roots, particularly Williams' Tennessee heritage. Campbell's ode to comedy giants Laurel and Hardy is a poignant look through a child's eyes, while his guitar, mandolin and pedal steel are proof that the Dylan/Levon

Helm vet remains one of the finest contemporary instrumentalists. Little Feat's Bill Payne guests throughout on keyboards.

Michael Simmons

The Secret Sisters
★★★★
Mind, Man, Medicine
NEW WEST. CD/DL/LP

Actual sisters make canyon-deep soul country on fifth album.

Muscle Shoals natives Laura and Lydia Rogers long ago moved beyond their early 1940s/'50s revivalist sibling country act, but *Mind, Man, Medicine* takes them into new territory entirely. The country pop of Bear With Me and Paperweight are the duo's bread and butter, but the Sisters have also landed on that deep-soul sweet spot of James Carr, where love and passion writhe on a hook, exciting, inescapable and likely damaging. Take the hushed, creeping If The World Was A House: "If the world was a house and it was on fire/Would we just put it out or let it burn higher... I'd save you, you'd save me." But you know they won't. Elsewhere, Anna Calvi would be jealous of Never Walk Away's Orbison-esque crescendo, and in a very

Chris Smither
★★★★
All About The Bones
SIGNATURE SOUNDS. CD/DL/LP

Venerable folk-bluesman's 20th album.

Eighty this year with five-and-a-half decades of LPs behind him, Smither sounds as good, maybe better than ever. The deft guitar-picking and floorboard-stomping are still there. So are his fine songs with their wry, wise, trenchant words, timeless melodies and languid ash-and-gravel voice. It opens with the title track, featuring a visit from the Grim Reaper – sparse folk-blues with an aptly skeletal arrangement from a small but perfect ensemble of electric guitar, drum, harmony singer and moody lone saxophone. There's a great feel to the LP, like it was recorded in the dead of night in an old jazz bar beside a graveyard in New Orleans. There are two covers – Eliza Gilkyson's lovely Calm Before The Storm; Tom Petty's Time To Move On, the album closer – and eight originals, whose highlights include Completion, Down In Thibodaux, and beautiful ballad Still Believe In You.

Sylvie Simmons

Collective conscience: the sense of togetherness is "electrifying and urgent" on Kamasi Washington's latest.

Be not afraid

Reared on hip-hop, the saxophonist invites lyrical friends into his open world. By Grayson Haver Currin.

Kamasi Washington
★★★★

Fearless Movement
YOUNG. CD/DL/LP

KAMASI WASHINGTON's album covers feel like feints, singular portraits of his imposing figure that give the onlooker the sense that his music is egocentric and self-interested. But since his toddling days in a casual family band that featured Ronald and Stephen 'Thundercat' Bruner, the second-generation Los Angeles saxophonist has depended upon the collaboration of community, of musicians chasing strains of transcendence together in a room. From his days as a "Young Jazz Giant" and his inaugural tour with Snoop Dogg to his sprawling two prior albums, each rendered by a cast of dozens, Washington has indeed functioned as a very

bright star in his artistic constellation but never the one around which everyone else revolves. "Each of the musicians I have with me I respect as being a genius," he told The Fader website in advance of 2018's *Heaven And Earth*. "I would never try to block that."

This idea has never been more clear or powerful on Washington's records than on *Fearless Movement*, his first album in six years and, even at 86 minutes, his most concise statement by half since the breakthrough run that began with 2015's *The Epic*. On these dozen tracks, Washington creates a playground and invites friends in to be themselves, shaping a dizzying crosshatch of ideas where George Clinton's lounge croon sets up a trumpet-chased pep talk from rapper D Smoke, or André 3000 slips – with flutes in hand – into a nocturnal haze that feels like some futuristic Debussy state of bliss.

Perhaps most telling is Asha The First, framed by a loping melody his pandemic-born daughter penned on piano before she was two. The song crashes in with a Doug Carn-like

spiritual jazz proclamation before cousin Thundercat steps in for a whirlwind bass solo. Washington then rips through the lead, all passion. When rappers Taj and Ras Austin slide into the track's back half for a tangle of rapid-fire verses as the drums and keys surge forward as if carried by a riptide, the sense of togetherness is electrifying and urgent, as if Washington had a message he needed help delivering right now.

It is easy to imagine Washington disappearing here, his restless tone shrouded beneath the features and tizzy of ideas. And, sure, this is not a saxophone record, not something that will convince you he is a titan of the instrument itself. (There are, however, many moments where he cooks, like his steady climb toward a bellow during Prologue and his ever-winding lines during The Garden Path.) That hardly seems like the point, anyway: *Fearless Movement* is an unabashed, cross-country, transgenerational manifestation and celebration of Black American music, pushing it forward from a deep love of its past not just in the spirit of community but in its actual presence.

Organ grinders: Arab Strap's Aidan Moffat (left) and Malcolm Middleton at their most streamlined, visceral and direct.

Arab Strap
★★★★

I'm Totally Fine With It; Don't Give A Fuck Anymore

ROCK ACTION. CD/DL/LP

Falkirk duo fuse modern disconnection with dramatic pop on their second LP since re-forming.

THE GLOVES are off on Arab Strap's eighth album. While Aidan Moffat skilfully dissects social media addiction (Allatonceness) and post-lockdown social anxiety (Summer Season), his unflinching depictions and grizzled meditations are backed by some of Malcolm Middleton's most out-there scores, with fuzzed-up bass and thrash metal chords to the fore. Whether intoning over analogue techno (Bliss), fingerpicked melancholy (Molehills) or ornate Scottish gothic (Dreg Queen), Moffat poetically eschews the obvious as he essays the horror of ageing alone (Safe & Well) and discovers "the truth isn't out here" after all (Turn Off The Light). Thrillingly raw, it captures the pair at their most streamlined, visceral and direct, disproving F Scott Fitzgerald's theory about second acts.

Andy Cowan

Amaro Freitas
★★★★

Y'Y

PSYCHIC HOTLINE. CD/DL/LP

Brazilian pianist's fourth LP – an electric homage to the Amazon rainforest.

As on its forerunners, Amaro Freitas's latest is flush with future-facing jazz heavily inspired by his ancestry. A verdant homage to Manaus, deep in the Amazon basin, Y'Y shows his fluid piano technique – a hard to quantify mix of Monk, Ibrahim, Corea and Shipp – let loose on looping patterns that trace ever more surprising arcs and mood variations. It weaves from ominous to euphoric amid the thunder drums of Uiara, Freitas using his piano as part of his percussive armoury, while two collaborations with a flute-wielding Shabaka Hutchings (Y'Y, Encantados) are blessed with light but lyrical solos that quiver with emotional resonance. Freitas's pearling tone and fluid technique peaks on Dança Dos Martelos, as he summons moments of intense drama and supreme gentleness within the same song.

Andy Cowan

Kat Gollock

Fat White Family
★★★

Forgiveness Is Yours

DOMINO. CD/DL/LP

Depraved South Londoners' fourth act of degeneracy.

In a blog post last September, Fat White Family leader Lias Saoudi argued that "punk's spirit is broken", that today's artists are too mindful of pleasing everybody to challenge taboos. Certainly, nobody can level that accusation at FWF, who've transgressed with manful abandon these past 13 years. After peaking on 2019's Serfs Up!, the brothers Saoudi struggled to get this fourth album made amid ructions with guitarist Saul Adamczewski, who, for the umpteenth but apparently final time, departed acrimoniously mid-sessions. Consequently, Forgiveness Is Yours feels inconsistent, patched together. At best, John Lennon simmers with keys, strings and flute, while Lias imagines encountering Yoko Ono and becoming possessed by her late husband. Without Adamczewski, however, a certain rock'n'roll energy is lacking: Work and Bullet Of Dignity veer towards the hi-NRG disco of Lias's Decius project; others are little more than vaudeville pastiche, or oppressively grim spoken-word with background rustling. Think: transitional.

Andrew Perry

Rafael Toral
★★★★

Spectral Evolution

DRAG CITY. DL/LP

Experimental Portuguese composer abandons oscillators and returns to his first love.

Between 2004 and 2017, Rafael Toral embarked upon a sonic investigation. Forgoing the guitar with which he'd created such minimalist works of tone-field ambience as 2001's Violence Of Discovery And Calm Of Acceptance, he began a 13-year 'Space Program'. Utilising oscillators and sine wave generators, Toral created a kind of spontaneous bleep-and-bloop hard bop futurism that he dubbed "post-free jazz electronic music". Now, with those years of accrued sonic knowledge behind him he's returned to the guitar to create Spectral Evolution. Beginning in a deceptively simple fashion with the hum and pluck of an over-amped electric guitar, these 12 seamless tracks evolve and expand, finding in feedback, distortion and drone sounds that emulate jungle birdsong, trumpets, flutes, choirs and grand church organs. The Space Program instruments have been retained, adding passages of big-band jazz chaos to proceedings, but ultimately this is a work of lush, immersive harmonic beauty and escape.

Andrew Male

Mick Harvey
★★★

Five Ways To Say Goodbye

MUTE. CD/DL/LP

Ex-Bad Seed's collection of melancholy farewells.

Since leaving his three-decade role as Nick Cave's musical director, Harvey's been busy: working with P.J. Harvey until 2017, extending his Serge Gainsbourg series, soundtracking movies, duetting with Mexico's Amanda Acevedo, and here serving up a solo mix of self-compositions and covers. As on 2013's Four (Acts Of Love), the songwriterly ratio favours other artists, majoring in deep cuts from fellow Aussies like The Triffids' David McComb (a torrid Setting You Free) and The Saints (both Ed Kuepper's Demolition, and Chris Bailey's Ghost Ships). While dignified sideman Harvey may seem a reluctant songsmith, he does personalise Marlene Dietrich's A Suitcase In Berlin with hazy memories of that city's mid-'80s all-night hostelries Ex'n'Pop and Risiko, and on When We Were Beautiful & Young offers a sombre post-punker's take on George Harrison's When We Was Fab. While his voicing is low key, the real treat is the string-arranging, which dramatises the melancholy with world-class opulence.

Andrew Perry

The Flowers Of Indulgence
★★★

Dylan's Lost Songs Vol 1.

TBS. CD/DL

Dylan covers album recorded in Scotland by a band of UK Bob devotees.

In recent years we've had a female singer cover a Dylan album (Mary Lee's Corvette's fine Blood On The Tracks) and another cover a Dylan concert (Cat Power's brilliant …Sings Dylan: The 1966 Royal Albert Hall Concert). Here we have an unknown band covering 12 of Dylan's most obscure songs. All the tracks are from Dylan's 1967 Basement Tapes with The Band – the 138-song complete sessions that were finally released as Vol. 11 of Dylan's Bootleg Series 10 years back, to the delight of ardent fans. Judging by their name (from Every Grain Of Sand), the six-piece The Flowers of Indulgence are ardent fans. More we can't say since they go by amusing pseudonyms, but they sound more like enthusiasts or semi-pros than a Traveling Wilburys. Still, it's good to hear some of these little-known songs. Best: She's On My Mind Again, A Rainy Afternoon and Wild Wolf.

Sylvie Simmons

|||||||||||||||||||||||||||||||||

Roots Architects
★★★★

From Then 'Til Now

FRUITS. CD/DL/LP

Adventurous instrumental album cut by Jamaican heavyweights.

In 2017, Swiss keyboardist Mathias Liengme conceived the Roots Architects project, gathering 50 of Jamaica's greatest living musicians under the direction of revered session keyboardist Robbie Lyn. Wisely letting Lyn take charge, the assembled cast became a who's who of legendary players, the Black Ark rhythm section of Boris Gardiner and Mikey Boo gracing Whitewater, and Sly Dunbar, Lloyd Parks, Bo Pee Bowen and Bubbler Waul recreating the core of Joe Gibb's Professionals on Rose Hall's Birds. Lyn and Ernest Ranglin pull us into Studio One territory on Squirrel Inna Barrel, and on 45 Charles Street Flabba Holt and Dwight Pinkney reach for a Roots Radics vibe. The players keep the action on-point throughout, and the unhurried nature of the sessions has yielded something inspired and organic, rather than a staid mishmash. An excellent result that sounds better with every listen.

David Katz

Follow the light

His first 'proper' solo LP in years. Rosanne Cash, Weyes Blood, and Jess Wolfe and Holly Laessig from Lucius guest. By James McNair.

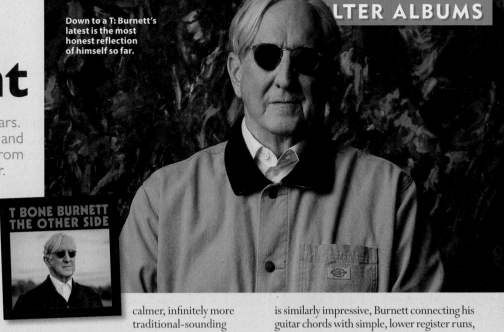

Down to a T: Burnett's latest is the most honest reflection of himself so far.

T Bone Burnett

★★★★

The Other Side

VERVE FORECAST. CD/DL/LP

PLAYING GUITAR on Dylan's Rolling Thunder Revue; bringing the O Brother, Where Art Thou soundtrack to life; producing everyone from Roy Orbison to B.B. King to Brandi Carlile: however high the stakes, T Bone Burnett has always delivered. Indeed, the diversity of this 76-year-old son of St Louis, Missouri's canonical output boggles the mind, and sparks a thought: how do you tread pastures new when you've already been pretty much everywhere?

Burnett did so, though, on 2019's *The Invisible Light: Acoustic Space*, and on 2022's *The Invisible Light: Spells*. Made with drummer Jay Bellerose and film composer Keefus Ciancia, these unnerving, sci-fi-oriented LPs tapped electronic and spoken-word elements, and were part influenced by a dystopian dream about tech-ruined humanity Burnett had as a kid. For a man synonymous with roots music, it was quite the odyssey.

Having journeyed to The Twilight Zone, Burnett now presents *The Other Side*. It's a calmer, infinitely more traditional-sounding record, but some of these spare country-blues songs are not for the faint-hearted either. With Burnett's co-producer Colin Linden on dobro and Kalamazoo guitar, and Dennis Crouch on string bass, Waiting for You seems conceptually straightforward until you learn it portrays a love affair between ghosts, while the graveyard-set Sometimes I Wonder, with Natalie Mering, AKA Weyes Blood, on bv's, ponders transition to the sweet, or perhaps not so sweet hereafter.

Happily, there are also mood lighteners. All horses'-hooves percussion and Everly Brothers harmonies, (I'm Gonna Get Over This) Someday is a charming Burnett/Rosanne Cash duet; the kind of song that would have bedded-down nicely on either of the LPs T Bone produced for Robert Plant and Alison Krauss. The structural integrity of Come Back (When You Go Away) is similarly impressive, Burnett connecting his guitar chords with simple, lower register runs, and making a little orchestra out of nothing. Yes, there is cuatro, clarinet and violin on *The Other Side*, but it's mostly just Burnett and an acoustic guitar. Songs this good need little ornamentation.

There is fine, often textural use of the Lucius singers' spectral harmonies, but Burnett's beautifully abraded voice stars, calm and quietly authoritative on The First Light Of Day. He attributes the new tone he has found at 76 to singing from his chest, rather than his head, and we benefit from his onward journey.

A record producer's role often involves great tact and a nurturing largesse, but it's taken him until now, Burnett has said, to treat himself with the kindness he'd automatically afford other artists. He's an old dog with new tricks then, *The Other Side* probably the most honest reflection of himself he's ever made.

Pet Shop Boys

★★★★

Nonetheless

PARLOPHONE. CD/DL/LP

Arch-archbishops carry on regardless with fifteenth album.

In 2020, Pet Shop Boys concluded their own Berlin trilogy with the downbeat *Hotspot*, companion to 2013's *Electric* and 2016's *Super*. While it's improbable Neil Tennant and Chris Lowe will ever disown the club (proof: the submerged throb of Loneliness), the duo have stretched out with *Nonetheless*, luxuriating in imported storytelling (Dancing Star; Bullet For Narcissus) and high-thread-count drama (The Secret Of Happiness; Love Is The Law). While the disco end of their spectrum is lavishly furnished – "sexy sexy sexy," sings Tennant alarmingly on The Schlager Hit Parade – their melancholic strain is most potent here. New London Boy's trembling scene memories hit the sweetest spot between West End Girls and Being Boring ("plastic and showy" rhymed with "Roxy and Bowie"), while the heartbreaking A New Bohemia upgrades Piano Man to the First Class lounge. As that peppery title suggests, *Nonetheless* shows the duo pulling themselves up to full songwriting height, not just forging on, but flourishing.
Victoria Segal

Pokey LaFarge

★★★

Rhumba Country

NEW WEST. CD/DL

Retro country stylist gets a makeover on tenth studio album.

Indiana-born busker turned songwriter and occasional actor, Pokey LaFarge (Andrew Heissler, on his birth certificate) has been making records since 2008, including a stint on Jack White's Third Man label. *Rhumba Country* is his first since 2021's *In The Blossom Of Their Shade*, after which LaFarge went off-grid to work on a farm in Maine. Time spent ploughing fields revived his creativity and gave him a sunnier perspective. *Rhumba Country* is brighter than his last album and seasons its country songs with gospel, mambo and Tropicália. There's a cheeriness to For A Night, Run Run Run and Sister André (the last about a centenarian French nun), and a filmic quality to the character with "a farmer's tan, hotel slippers and a Margherita in his hand" in So Long Chicago. Occasionally slight and throwaway, everything here is nevertheless fun.
Mark Blake

Tom Rush

★★★★

Gardens Old, Flowers New

APPLESEED RECORDINGS. CD/DL/LP

The folk veteran's first album in five years.

The baritone folk rocker has been delivering dependably quality albums since his 1962 debut. His latest is his first release in five years and while he's known for his covers (he introduced songwriters like James Taylor and Joni Mitchell) this one consists primarily of originals. (He wrote folk classic No Regrets in 1968, so his track record is short but impressive.) His percussive acoustic rhythm guitar creates a bed on which lies dobro, mouth harp and other instruments that accentuate the blues central to Rush's sound. He excels at the folk tradition of bawdy songs, like his own Gimme Some Of It and Nothin' But A Man. And while he also delves into more romantic approaches to relationships in To See My Baby Smile, album closer I Quit is a quintessentially witty break-up ditty.
Michael Simmons

Kid Congo & The Pink Monkey Birds

★★★★

That Delicious Vice

IN THE RED. CD/DL/LP

Sinister, noir-ish thrills from garage rock bastion.

Charter member of The Gun Club, one-time Cramp and occasional Bad Seed, Kid Congo Powers' punk cred is unquestionable. However, his Pink Monkey Birds have evolved past the primal thrills of punk rock, coining instead a suspenseful storytelling rich in mood and playfulness. Their seventh full-length goes heavy on the noir ambience, established by the twang and sigh of Powers' guitar and his unsavoury tales. The macabre Wicked World channels the inner monologue of a serial killer with the lurid vibe of a Roger Corman exploitation movie, while the brilliant closing Murder Of Sunrise delivers a suspenseful 18 minutes of menace via shimmering cymbals, speaker hum and fathoms-deep bass lines. There's beauty here too, in Ese Vicio Delicioso's giddy, skronky calypso and the swooning Hawaiian guitar of The Smoke Is The Ghost, but it's only ever a brief respite from the impressively all-pervading creepiness.
Stevie Chick

Dan Winters

Raymond Richards
★★★★

Sand Paintings
ESP INSTITUTE. DL/LP

These expansive pedal steel pieces radiate from the shadow of Death Valley.

With deserts as sprawling as seas, mountains as gnarled as roots, and colours as intricate as kaleidoscopes, the American Southwest is a familiar muse for contemplative instrumental music, its features like prompts for wanderlust. But on his second LP of gilded pieces for the pedal steel, longtime Portland producer, studio owner, and session ace Raymond Richards augments expected motifs and textures with a rarer emotional openness and compositional imagination. As dream-drunk synths circle beneath sighing steel and forlorn Dobro lines, Rattlesnake Pass suggests abiding apprehension, a worry for the future that seems insurmountable. Saguaro, meanwhile, is warm and wistful, conjuring one of Bill Frisell's rootsy units lit by campfire glow and cold whiskey. With help from

Calexico's John Convertino, 2 Cent Mambo scorches funk in the sun, while the stuttering horns and hazy delays of Deer On Hwy 80 frame untold troubles on unseen horizons.
Grayson Haver Currin

Khruangbin
★★★

A La Sala
DEAD OCEANS. CD/DL/LP

Texas trio's first in four years tweaks their signature mix of dub, blues and global grooves.

A decade in, Khruangbin remain as elusive as ever. Cinematic sounding instrumentals such as A Love International and Ada Jean cleave to the Houston band's core strengths, Laura Lee's pulsing dubby bass and DJ Johnson's understated percussion (all handclaps, timbales, cowbells) underpinning guitarist Mark Speer's cascading melodies and lightly wrought arpeggios. As with predecessor *Mordechai*, vocals are more to the fore – albeit low in the mix and reverb drenched – on Todavía Viva and Hold Me Up (Thank You), efforts that capture Khruangbin at their most simple and infectious, whispered motifs floating on a breeze of instinctual-sounding moody exotica. Never overwrought, *A La Sala* is a cool exercise in the beauty of restraint and understated groove mastery, exploring

new vistas without subverting Khruangbin's blueprint.
Andy Cowan

Bibi Club
★★★★

Feu De Garde
SECRET CITY. CD/DL/LP

Second LP of hazy avant-pop from Québécois duo.

The lovely *Feu De Garde* is the second LP by the French-Canadian duo Adèle Trottier-Rivard and Nicolas Basque, who operate as Bibi Club. Initially – as the bulk of the songs are sung by Trottier-Rivard in French and due to a bossa nova-via-motorik sensibility – it seems Stereolab is the touchstone, but as second track Parc De Beauvoir hits its groove it becomes clear a yen for the directly poppy wins out over any indie tendencies. Take the misty, reflective You Can Wear A Jacket Or A Shirt: it could be a Lana Del Rey ballad with a slightly different arrangement. Le Feu's ascending chorus is ready for a mass sing-along. It's subtle, but Bibi Club are aiming high. Ultimately, the only benchmark springing to mind

is the similarly-styled early-'80s Franco-Belgians Antena. *Feu De Garde* is that good.
Kieron Tyler

Charles Moothart
★★★

Black Holes Don't Choke
IN THE RED. CD/DL/LP

Ty Segall sideman's powerpop bonanza of "love songs for the apocalypse".

As supporting guitarist in Segall's Freedom Band, and lead guitarist in Fuzz (where Segall drums), Moothart clearly shares his bandmate's hyper-productivity, having somehow found time for three late-2010s outings with his CFM quartet. For this full-name debut, he recorded alone in LA, yet *Black Holes Don't Choke* has a feel of 'Ionerism' *à la* Tame Impala's Kevin Parker, as if its ideas, musical and thematic, were unloaded into Pro Tools in frenzied wee-hours sessions on a tour bus, then later organised. As such, it's anything but live-in-the-room, with opener Roll, Little Egg and Clock Rats each taking dramatic left-turns mid-song, from acoustic to electric or vice versa, like entirely separate tracks have simply been spliced together digitally. Out of all that chaos, however, some memorable tunes emerge: One Wish recalls

Matthew Sweet's honey-harmonised hyper-pop, while Anchored And Empty echoes Fuzz's doom metal, amid prevailing themes of alienation in these precarious times.
Andrew Perry

Elizabeth King
★★★★

Soul Provider
BIBLE & TIRE RECORDING CO. DL/LP

Gospel star's follow-up to 2022's *I Got A Love*.

Her third album in four years, Elizabeth King's *Soul Provider* is full of energetic exclamations over thrust-and-parry R&B, the octogenarian, who first sang gospel in the early '70s for Juan D Shipp's D-Vine Spirituals label, chasing ever higher connection with and surrender to the Lord while hymning peace and unity. King's voice takes centre-stage throughout; deep and rich and a lot like her peer Mavis Staples'. With her daughters providing sweet backing vocals on the uproarious Tables In The Temple, she mines the same gospel funk territory that the Staple Singers did. On Stretch Out, a song dating back to her early days, distorted whooshes of fuzz and wah wah summon a more apocalyptic feel as she screams, "His eyes are like balls of fire." Indeed.
Lois Wilson

Emily Barker
★★★★

Fragile As Humans
EVERYONE SANG. CD/DL/LP

Aussie songwriter's excellent fifth solo LP.

It's an irony that two of Western Australia's greatest musical talents – Emily Barker and the late David McComb – write songs filled with a deep noir ennui, the exact opposite of their native climate. Barker's career has been a mazy one over 13 albums, including collaborations with Marry Waterson, as Applewood Road with Amber Rubarth and Amy Speace, and also her previous band The Red Clay Halo. *Fragile As Humans* revisits the territory of 2008 track Nostalgia, used as the theme song for Kenneth Branagh's Wallander series, where the gloom of heartache and self-doubt is gently illuminated by the hope of fulfilling new dreams. Whether it's the melancholy drift of The Quiet Ways, the Joni Mitchell-like Call It A Day or finding contentment in life's small things on the beautiful With Small We Start – a Wallander reboot theme in waiting – Barker's writing has never been so pin sharp.
Andy Fyfe

Kelley Stoltz
★★★★

La Fleur
AGITATED. CD/DL/LP

San Fran's psych-pop wizard continues to cast his spell.

LATELY BUSIED producing an LP for former Osees keyboardist Brigid Dawson and by session-sitar stints for Robyn Hitchcock, Kelley Stoltz also became a first-time dad recently. The latter fact is pertinent since *La Fleur*'s itchy psych-pop evokes the sleep-deprived world of new parenthood, the mind racing, but fatigued. If Reni's Car, a two-minute jangler about borrowing a BMW owned by The Stone Roses' drummer, is pure escapism, Losing My Wild's brilliantly sliced and diced guitars seem to propel a tale of wings newly clipped, but our new dad dotes and philosophies on About Time, pondering his baby daughter's future. Jason Falkner (Jellyfish; Beck) helps out on two songs, but *La Fleur* is your typical Stoltz as multi-instrumentalist splurge, paint hitting canvas with gusto as '60s US psych and '80s UK psych fraternise.
James McNair

Top trumps: Kelley Stoltz paints a psych-pop splurge.

Tar quality

Californian enigma back in black on slow-cooked fourth LP. By Jim Wirth.

Pitch perfect: Jessica Pratt charts diffuse interior states.

Jessica Pratt
★★★★
Here In The Pitch
CITY SLANG. CD/DL/LP

BACK IN 2012, when her self-titled debut became something of a word-of-mouth sensation, Jessica Pratt explained that her yen for a slightly distant sound was down to growing up listening to music on cassette. "That real dreamy, cloudy sound," she said. "That's kind of always what I wanted to go for."

One way and another, Pratt has stayed true to that vision. *Here In The Pitch* is only the fourth LP the perfectionist songwriter has managed to let go of, but on the belated follow-up to 2019's much-feted *Quiet Signs*, her ethereal songwriting, uncannily pitched vocals and penchant for Shangri-Las séance music continue to mark her out as an eerie one-off: Laura Nyro as painted by Joan Miró.

Pratt calls lead track Life Is a "false flag" in terms of the rest of *Here In The Pitch*, its kitchen-sink drama production and carpe diem spirit somewhat at odds with the record's murky MO. "Life is/It's never what you think it's for," she announces over stabbing Street Hassle strings. Ryley Walker is on guitar somewhere in the mix, but Pratt is the frosty Shirley Bassey centre-stage, a splendid ambling melody leading her to her fridge magnet-worthy pay-off line: "It's the age of what's to come/And baby you're on."

However, if Pratt has the chutzpah to deliver a killer affirmation, it is not something she makes a habit of. While on World On A String she sings, "I want to be the sunshine of the century", her natural place remains the shadowy corners, with *Here In The Pitch* imagining Scott Walker's moody *Scott 3* on starvation rations: grand metaphysical drama, but with the gigantic orchestrations boiled down to acoustic guitar, ghostly keyboards and echoey wood-block percussion.

There are fragments of a tale of woe scattered across its *Desertshore*-style run time. All chewed fingernails, Pratt yearns for cosmic vengeance on Better Hate, and for lost things on her beached samba Get Your Head Out ("I keep comin' back to what I left behind"). However, as with Aldous Harding, Jana Horn or Aoife Nessa Frances, her words tend to sidestep the confessional to chart more diffuse interior states, By Hook Or By Crook, Empires Never Know and Nowhere It Was all venturing far into automatic-writing dreamland.

It ends somewhere a little more lucid. The Last Year offers something like a resolution. "You'd wonder if ever there's been hope for me," Pratt sings as she picks out another redemptive, Dusty Springfield-at-35rpm melody. Times have been hard, but the future suddenly looks bright: "I think it's gunna be fine, I think we're gunna be together, and the storyline goes forever." The finer details of that plot are a little hazy, but *Here In The Pitch* prefers to keep it that way. It's cloudy, dreamy. Don't worry so much about what it all means, lie back and let the tape hiss.

Dog Unit
★★★★
At Home
BRACE YOURSELF. CD/DL/LP

East London post-rock reactivators' unguessable debut.

One of Dog Unit's two interweaving guitarists, Sam Walton, has talked of how the instrumentals-only four-piece meticulously sculpted this first album as an unfolding plotline. Initially, they created some "tent-pole tracks", then constructed around them, writing to order "a midway breather, a climactic moment that led from civility to menace, a 'closing credits' song…" The listener soon twigs onto *At Home*'s linear narrative, as metronomic Kraut-y rhythms, and Walton and Henry Scowcroft's skilfully enmeshed six-string picking, variously recalling first-wave post-rockers Ui and even an upward-elevating Television, culminate in second track Lab Coats' measured blasts of Dinosaur Jr-style feedback. With that fiercer propensity noted, In A Magic World, Then Yes feels a doubly lovely "breather", before John X

Kennedy's "menace" meltdown sets the pulse racing. By the time The Dogs Are Barking Again's clarinet-tinged "closing credits" roll, you've heard one hell of a movie, directed with all the mastery of a Hitchcock or a Truffaut. Sequel, please!
Andrew Perry

III
E
★★★
Living Waters
SILVER ROCKET. DL/LP

Thalia Zedek and friends sculpt No Wave din into a mature noise of their own.

When not fronting her eponymous band, former Come singer/guitarist Thalia Zedek is one-third of E. Their fifth album is firmly rooted in the No Wave sound she helped coin with mid-'80s post-punks Live Skull, but also develops a more mature, eloquent dialect of noise all their own. A democratic outfit, vocals are split between the trio, with the moody title track foregrounding Jason Sanford's guitar (which he welded from steel wire) in terse conversation with drummer Ernie Kim's brooding saxophone. Kim's melodic burr, meanwhile, guides Jumprope's melancholic investigation of loss into a fruitfully vulnerable place, while Zedek's own Null is a primal maelstrom that uses No Wave as a thrilling vehicle for tension and release. It's bracingly cacophonic stuff, but balanced by a confident feel for songwriting that ensures *Living Waters* holds its own against the later work of Sonic Youth.
Stevie Chick

IIIIIIIIIIIIIIIIIIIIII
The Zutons
★★★★
The Big Decider
ICEPOP. CD/DL/LP/MC

They're back and they're produced by Ian Broudie and Nile Rodgers.

It's been a torrid time for The Zutons since 2008's blues-tinged *You Can Do Anything*. Following their 2009 split, singer Dave McCabe was convicted of assault and spent time in rehab. A couple of subsequent reunions never quite took flight until the remaining members – McCabe, drummer Sean Payne and saxophonist Abi Harding – started living together at their studio. Hence, the uplifting, rueful and expertly crafted *The Big Decider*. A first producer, Nile Rodgers, drawls a bonkers spoken coda to Disappear, which swings without turning into a Chic knock-off. A second producer, Lightning Seed Ian Broudie (who helmed the 2004 debut *Who Killed… The Zutons?*), brings taut urgency to the surging title track. Elsewhere, Harding curls some gorgeous saxophone over Company, opener Creeping On The Dancefloor is a call-and-response stomper loosely related to Valerie, and the life-affirming closer Best Of Me suggests a band finally at ease with themselves.
John Aizlewood

IIIIIIIIIIIIIIIII
Villagers
★★★★
That Golden Time
DOMINO. CD/DL/LP

Irishman's sixth studio album: mellow melody meets hard truths.

As Conor O'Brien retreats from band mode – 2021's *Fever Dreams* was his most maximal yet – to bare-boned ballads here, the intensity never wavers. Lockdown evidently suited him. With the world in meltdown, O'Brien seems to have embraced it all – omnipresent mobile screens, the invasiveness of ideologies, political corruption – but this is his finest collection of melodies yet, reflecting candour, tenderness and pathos with no bare polemic to disrupt the intimate tone, with judiciously deployed guests including Planxty's Dónal Lunny (bouzouki) and Katy Kelly (soprano). A sudden gust of strings elevates No Drama, while the Acker Bilk clarinet folded into woozy electronica shifts Behind That Curtain from serene piano bar to drunken cabaret entertainer, as O'Brien laments, "the air of confusion that doesn't sit right… I just don't know who we are any more."
Martin Aston

Samuel Hess

Mdou Moctar (far right) and band spirit up an amps-on-11 polemical masterpiece.

Mdou Moctar
★★★★
Funeral For Justice
MATADOR. CD/DL/LP

Tuareg shredder and band's sixth official long-player, in all senses their heaviest.

WHEN NIGER'S democracy was overturned in a military coup last July, the country's foremost Afro-blues ambassadors were stranded in the US, and required a GoFundMe campaign to remain Stateside amid the chaos. Fury at that situation palpably fuels *Funeral For Justice*: where even 2021's international breakthrough *Afrique Victime* found time for songs of seduction and unrequited love, here the much-travelled band – named after singer/guitar-mangler Mahamadou Souleymane, and propelled by another fearsome instrumentalist in drummer Souleymane Ibrahim – channel all their collective power at political targets. The explosive title track urges Niger's democratic leaders to rise up and serve their people, while the swingeing Oh France castigates imperialist exploitation. Underscoring such urgent messaging, the MM quartet spirit up a uniquely hard-driving and frenziedly danceable Afro-rock, with Moctar's warp-speed picking quite electrifying to behold. Only relenting for the odd Tinariwen-esque chill moment (Takoba; Imajighen), this one's an amps-on-11 polemical masterpiece that warrants worldwide respect.

Andrew Perry

corporate, more like their original idiosyncratic selves.
James McNair

IIIIIIIIIIIIIIIIII
Bab L' Bluz
★★★★
Swaken
REAL WORLD. CD/DL/LP

Franco-Moroccan quartet rocking harder than ever.

Bab L' Bluz's debut, *Nayda!*, arrived without fanfare in 2020 and was a proper eye-opener: a bovver-booted North African psychedelic blues album that gave Yousra Mansour and her crew a crowd-pleasing set wherever they played. "We adapted our sound for festival crowds, made it heavier, rockier," she says. "More courage. More fire." Their second LP, then, arrives with greater expectations, but a gig-tested muscularity to blow the cobwebs off that four-year gap, with the rock of Led Zeppelin rather than the roll of more familiar Saharan bands. Crucially, though, the band use traditional lutes, flutes and percussion – awisha, ribab, guembri, qraqeb, ney – giving their music a different texture to groups with similar dynamics. There's a trance-like swing to AmmA, no-nonsense boogie on Zaino, and if apocalyptic freak-outs (*à la* I Am The Resurrection) are your thing, Mouja will definitely not disappoint.

David Hutcheon

Les Savy Fav
★★★★
Oui, LSF
FRENCHKISS. CD/DL/LP

New York art-punks return from 14 years in the wilderness, revivified.

Even amid a mid-'90s post-hardcore scene pushing post-punk energy in radical new directions, the way Les Savy Fav studded their pugilistic riffage with wry perversity and unexpected hooks set them apart from the pack. More focused than their previous work, *Oui, LSF* remains firmly in the group's idiosyncratic wheelhouse, equally foregrounding their bristling dissonance and acerbic pop flourishes. Guitarist Andrew Reuland embraces this duality, swinging between Keith Levene-esque shrapnel (on the sardonic character study Legendary Tippers) and blue, longing lines like The Edge (Somebody Needs A Hug). As ever, though, vocalist Tim Harrington is the true focus, leading the rowdy gang choruses of Void Moon, revelling in the gnomic riddles of What We Don't Want, and firing off the occasional unforgettable couplet: "This thing we call love/Feels more

like Afghanistan", off Barbs, is one of his best.
Stevie Chick

IIIIIIIIIIIIIIIIII
Arild Andersen, Daniel Sommer, Rob Luft
★★★★
As Time Passes
APRIL. CD/DL/LP

Folk undertones peek through the first instalment of jazz drummer Sommer's Nordic trilogy.

2017's *Duets* album showed Daniel Sommer was an empathic drummer with an acute ear. A similar improvisational approach is at the heart of *As Time Passes* as Sommer softly punctuates the rhythm of Fifth Winter and the minimal title track with his sticks. While his controlled brushwork and atypical rhythmic impetus fits easily with Arild Andersen's spacious and serene pizzicato bass lines, Luft's intricate reverbs and fluid phrasing supply textural depth. A lyrical guitarist whose warm wafts of sound contain echoes of Metheny, Frisell and Abercrombie, Luft peaks on Evening Song, snatching a melody from the ether that's

Satie-like in its simplicity. Continually unfolding, motifs rising and falling with distinct ECM vibes, it's mellow testament to their ability to shape forms in the moment.
Andy Cowan

IIIIIIIIIIIIIIIIII
James Elkington & Nathan Salsburg
★★★
All Gist
PARADISE OF BACHELORS. CD/DL/LP

Two busy pals convened for two winter writing sessions.

Since James Elkington and Nathan Salsburg released their last album of guitar duets, 2015's *Ambsace*, they have each issued the most distinctive works of their respective careers. Elkington's library music compendium, *Me Neither*, was a late-2023 highlight, while Salsburg's ongoing *Landwerk* series is a hauntological hymnal. Their third set together radiates the esprit of friends enjoying a staycation, two incisive guitarists writing, laughing, and imbibing together at a common kitchen table. They are peppy and impeccable during the Breton medley Rule Bretagne, pensive then powerful during their expansive suite within a song, Nicest Distinction. There are occasional flourishes, like Wanees Zarour's winding fiddle solo during Death Wishes To Kill or a buzzing well of upright bass and splashes of pedal steel during

closer Buffalo Stance – yes, a contemplative five-minute interpretation of the Neneh Cherry classic. But mostly, here are two ace and erudite guitarists, deep in the delight of friendship.
Grayson Haver Currin

IIIIIIIIIIIIIIIIII
Kings Of Leon
★★★
Can We Please Have Fun
POLYDOR. CD/DL/LP

The Followill family attempts to lighten-up.

When they arrived, unintelligible lyrics and all, with 2003's *Youth & Young Manhood*, Kings Of Leon's gnarled garage-country and irresistible Southern Gothic backstory fired many a column-inch. Now nine albums into the major leagues and mindful of possible relegation, *Can We Please Have Fun* sees them re-boot, the enlistment of producer Kid Harpoon (Harry Styles, Miley Cyrus) signalling necessary change after 2021's somewhat fatigued-sounding *When You See Yourself*. Though fun, per se, isn't overtly audible and Caleb Followill's brow is still furrowed, his strong millennial-generation-Bono energy taps fine melodies on Ballerina Radio and Mustang, while ingredients such as heavily-modulated guitars and treated wind-chime loops evidence a new sonic daring. KOL say making this record between albums deals was liberating. They do sound less

IIIIIIIIIIIIIIIIII
Angus & Julia Stone
★★★
Cape Forestier
PIAS. CD/DL/LP

Australian siblings' sixth album heads back to their roots.

It's sometimes hard to keep up with releases from the Stone siblings, whether it's their albums as a duo, solo releases or Angus's jam band Dope Lemon. As much as their separate muses may lie elsewhere, it's the duo's work together that really butters their bread, even if last album *Life Is Strange*, the 2021 soundtrack to the video game, was over-contrived and underwhelming. *Cape Forestier* harks back to the more carefree sound of earlier albums, its strength lying in doing the familiar that much better. Key track, The Wedding Song, an old live favourite written for a friend's celebration, finally gets a studio version, and they even inject a rare touch of menace and mystery into the Fleetwood Mac-inspired Down To The Sea. Looser and less polished than ever, *Cape Forestier* is all the better for it.
Andy Fyfe

Ebru Yildiz

Moris Tepper
★★★★
Building A Nest
CANDLEBONE. CD/DL

Long-awaited return of the Captain Beefheart guitarist.

On Secret Life here, Moris Tepper sings "I abide by my secret rules", and while pretty much out of the loop since 2010's *A Singer Named Shotgun Throat*, he's been busy painting and now he delivers a generously filled seventh solo album high on invention and songwriting chops. These 21 songs are a mix of personal reflection and observational vignettes. His CV includes playing with Frank Black and Tom Waits, and Broken Cups carries a Waits-ian poignancy. Musically his remit encompasses the gnarly acoustic blues of Blackbone Chicken; tough, wiry rock songs; and slices of Americana like Between Us, which nods back to The Band. It's all subtly coloured with mellotron, organ and synthetic brass, but what really sets Tepper apart is his animated guitar playing, which is allied to his melodies and song structure in a way that's sometimes elliptical but always individual.

Mike Barnes

|||||||||||||||||||||
Bill Frisell
★★★★
Orchestras
BLUE NOTE. CD/DL/LP

The master guitarist comes with strings attached.

If you were to pick an electric guitar player likely to team up with symphonic forces then the self-effacing Bill Frisell might not seem your man. The blend of Americana and jazz he has explored over a pioneering 50-year career has always seemed intimate, personal, self-contained – no need for battalions of fiddles and French horns. So this hook-up with the near 60-strong Brussels Philharmonic on one disc,

and the smaller Umbria Jazz Orchestra on another, takes some getting used to. But persist: arrangements by Michael Gibbs are sympathetic and subtle, sustaining a mood that is recognisably Frisell-ian. Among tunes from across his career, a few sag under the weight of brooding brass and strings – Lookout For Hope, Doom – but others soar – Beautiful Dreamer, Electricity, We Shall Overcome. Ultimately it's a winner.

John Bungey

Alan Braufman
★★★★
Infinite Love Infinite Tears
VALLEY OF SEARCH. CD/DL/LP

Fire burns brightly on second comeback LP from '70s NY loft-jazz pioneer.

Since his 'lost' debut *Valley Of Search* was reissued in 2018, saxophonist/flautist Alan Braufman has established an enviable live rapport with drummer Chad Taylor, bassist Ken Filiano and tenor saxophonist James Brandon Lewis. *Infinite Love…* brings Veracruz vibraphonist Patricia Brennan into the mix, supplying a trippy textual dimension to the swinging Chasing A Melody and sprightly Spirits, each instrumentalist veering off on impulsive sprints of solo abandon. Yet it's the highly flammable chemistry between Braufman and Brandon Lewis that cuts deepest, their hard-blown saxes playing teetering call-and-response around Edge Of Time's nervy groove and Liberation's jagged melody. With subtle nods to John Coltrane and Don Cherry, Braufman's spiralling, uplifting compositions occupy an evolving space where jazz's past and future collide.

Andy Cowan

Ambarchi/ Berthling/Werliin
★★★★
Ghosted II
DRAG CITY. CD/DL/LP

Australian composer/ guitarist and the Fire! rhythm section create further harmonic possibilities for guitar/bass/drums.

The team-up between this trio was one of MOJO's albums of 2022, a gorgeous, transportive record that perfectly showcased the telepathic connection between guitarist Oren Ambarchi, bassist Johan Berthling and drummer Andreas Werliin. "Just one problem," we said at the time, "at 38 minutes it's all over far too soon." Well, maybe they were listening. Returning to Daniel Bengtsson's Studio Rymden in Stockholm, this is defiantly a sequel record, but is it Gremlins II or Basic Instinct II? All improvised, each of the four discursive tracks here possess the same serotonin-suffused warmth as *Ghosted* but divested of the former's motorik drive. That's not a criticism, just a qualification. This is to *Ghosted* what Layla Part 2 is to Layla, the transcendent, ambient coda to the hit record and, to those in the know, the place where you go for calm, peace and release.

Andrew Male

|||||||||||||||||||||
Adam Wiltzie
★★★★
Eleven Fugues For Sodium Pentothal
KRANKY. CD/DL/LP

First self-named LP in nine years from erstwhile Stars Of The Lid soundscaper.

Apparently inspired by a recurring dream wherein "if someone listened to the music I created, then they would die", Adam Wiltzie's second solo LP doesn't immediately augur the listener's imminent demise, its wordless essays fitting squarely into the chamber-ambient terrain of a Winged Victory For The Sullen, his collaboration with Dustin O'Halloran. Typically, the granular keyboard textures and swirling strings of Pelagic Swell sound like Henryk Górecki reimagined by *On Land*-era Eno, while Tissue Of Lies' droning synths are etched with quivering electric guitar. Elsewhere, the saturnine waves of As Above Perhaps So Below suggest the torpor induced by the titular barbiturate, while We Were Vaporised proffers further subterranean tectonics offset by cosmic keyboard drifts that might have been plucked, like much here, from an art-house sci-fi movie score.

David Sheppard

Thobias Faldt

Spirited away: more ghostly transcendence from Ambarchi/ Berthling/Werliin.

EXPERIMENTAL
BY JOHN MULVEY

Shane Parish
★★★★
Repertoire
PALILALIA. DL/LP

Journey In Satchidananda and Europe Endless, John Fahey-style? Yes please!

In his notes to this album of solo performances, Shane Parish refers to an Andrés Segovia quote about the guitar being "an orchestra in miniature". Parish has lately been on manoeuvres in an actual guitar orchestra of sorts, as part of the heavy-duty, electrified Bill Orcutt Guitar Quartet. Here, though, he uses exceptional fingerpicking technique on acoustic to tackle a canon of mostly non-guitar tunes: jazz by Mingus, Dolphy, Ornette, Alice Coltrane and Sun Ra; electronica by Aphex Twin and Kraftwerk; prepared piano by John Cage. Parish's label boss Orcutt made experimental capital out of the Great American Songbook on 2013's *A History Of Every One*, but on *Repertoire* Parish is almost flipping those polarities, taking some pretty outré music and exposing the accessible melodies at their core. And while Parish is candid about his process, discussing how his take on Roland Kirk's Serenade To A Cuckoo is informed by Davy Graham's Angi, the album plays less like a scholarly treatise, more a love letter to great music – and to its enduring flexibility.

ALSO RELEASED

Horse Lords
★★★★
As It Happened
RVNG INTL. DL/LP

The Baltimore-formed quartet's rigorous and vigorous attack on musical norms continues apace with this rethink of the live album: a radically-edited collage of 2022 and 2023 European shows. As with 2022's ace *Comradely Objects*, though, the theorising is comprehensively overwhelmed by the ecstatic vibes of the music, as math-rock, avant-jazz, minimalist composition and much more are reconstituted into party jams.

Phill Niblock/ Anna Clementi/ Thomas Stern
★★★
Zound Delta 2
KARL. CD/DL/LP

When the minimalist composer Phill Niblock died in January, obits tended to focus on his imposing monolithic drones. This first posthumous release, though – performed by Italian-Swedish singer Clementi and ex-Crime And The City Solution bassist Stern – works on a microbial scale, as multiple agonised vocals, tiny sonic adjustments and various unidentifiable squelches accrue into a mass

hum with the eerie potency of ancient Tibetan ritual.

Mind Over Mirrors
★★★★
Particles, Peds & Pores
BANDCAMP. DL

Jaime Fennelly has been busy recently as one-third of Appalachian kosmische champs Setting, but here he's back in solo synth-jockey mode with the first Mind Over Mirrors album in six years. It's a good one, too, packed with vibrational lunar ragas in the zone between Tangerine Dream and Bitchin Bajas. Serene drones in excelsis, then, but try Suprachiasmatic for an accelerated route to transcendence.

Magic Tuber Stringband
★★★★
Needlefall
THRILL JOCKEY. DL/LP

The North Carolinan duo of Courtney Werner and Evan Morgan, meanwhile, fit into a more orthodox Appalachian tradition of guitar, banjo and fiddle-driven folk music. But as on 2023's great *Tarantism*, they stray easily towards wilder realms, into improvised music that evokes the landscape as well as the culture of their region and which sounds, occasionally (cf The Hermit's Passage), like a deep backwoods AMM. *JM*

Baby Seals
★★★
Chaos

TRAPPED ANIMAL. CD/DL/LP
Cambridge punk trio's snarling debut is packed with spiky tracks like Yawn Porn and Mild Misogynist satirising gender stereotypes and amplifying absurdity. The sludgy title track's barbed reflection on sexual assault subverts their 'empower pop' template for something more darkly resonant. *AC*

The Blow Monkeys
★★★
Together/Alone

LAST NIGHT FROM GLASGOW. CD/DL/LP
Dr Robert continues his purple patch with this rewarding follow-up to 2021's *Journey To You*: his songs about love, loss, history and legacy delivered in his soulful croon, and set to horn and string arrangements that reference The Beatles and Bacharach. *LW*

Céu
★★★★
Novela

URBAN JUNGLE/ONE RPM. CD/DL/LP
After 2019's *Apká!* took Brazilian chanteuse Céu deep into digital pop, she and drummer/producer Pupillo team with Adrian Younge (Kendrick Lamar/Wu-Tang) in LA for a live-in-the-room affair, with crisp beats, ornate strings, retro-spangly guitar and sublime singing. Think Black Pumas go Tropicália, and groove! *AP*

Fireball Flingaz
★★★★
Giants Of Defiance

INFLAMER. CD/DL
Edgy breakbeats drive Exile and Remark's tag-team rhymes, pumped-up ageing B-boys exorcising demons over strings, pianos and frantic scratches. While tapping into the urgency of Britcore acts like Hijack and Gunshot, the album's political pulse is focused squarely on current events. *AC*

Oliver Hohlbrugger
★★★★
Nothing's Changed, Everything Is New

REVIR/MOONFLOWER. DL/LP
Norwegian art rocker's second LP seeks truth in louche poetry and fourth world ambience. Be it pulsing Bright Lights, VU-rocker Velveteen or the dramatic title track, it's a mash-up of Coltrane, Brel, Floyd and Tindersti cks. *AC*

Cassie Kinoshi's Seed
★★★★
Gratitude

INTERNATIONAL ANTHEM. CD/DL/LP
A saxophonist/composer/arranger with symphonic heft, Kinoshi's follow-up to 2019's *Driftglass* channels the energy of British jazz's brave young things into a widescreen suite. With an MVP performance by Shirley Tetteh on guitar. *JM*

Scott Lavene
★★★
Disneyland In Dagenham

NOTHING FANCY. CD/DL/LP
Craig Finn and Golden Dregs help out on eccentric Essex songwriter's third LP. Tragi-comic Custard and Debbie are Lavene's stock-in-trade, mixing Baxter Dury-like roughshod poetry with Robyn Hitchcock's surrealist flair. Flute-looped Little Bird reveals a more delicate balladeer. *AC*

Sunburned Hand Of The Man
★★★★
Nimbus

THREE LOBED. CD/DL/LP
The first family of New Weird America at their most amiable here on (roughly) Album Number 762. Freeform mulch is mostly sidelined for more streamlined psych and communal campfire singalongs. Plenty of beat poetry for the true heads, mind. *JM*

Transmission Towers
★★★★
Transmission One

É SOUL CULTURA. CD/DL/LP
Liverpool machine soul duo Mark Kyriacou and Eleanor Mante's debut spans jazzy exotica (One), sonic whirlpools (Everything) and lunar escapades (Cosmic Trigger). A fusion of Shabazz Palaces, Sun Ra and wonky space funk, the results are addictive. *AC*

Vanderwolf
★★★
The Great Bewilderment

ANOTHER RECORD LABEL. CD/DL/LP
Max Vanderwolf's second set of soulful glam-pop features a rumination on political failure entitled Gaza (written in 2016, despite its ominous currency). With reverberant, Floydian guitar by Adrian Utley, it's a highlight of this eclectic blue oddity. *JB*

EXTENDED PLAY

Nina Simone
Nina's Back!

Making its digital debut with new artwork, this forgotten curio from Simone's storied back pages shocked her fanbase on its release in 1985 by the Santa Monica-based VPI label. It found Simone, then 52, allowing producer Eddie Singleton to update her style with a smooth soul makeover defined by prominent slapped bass, twinkling synths, and cooing female background vocals. Simone sounds uncomfortable with her slick backing tracks but can still summon righteous fire, as the solidly grooving message song It's Cold Out Here shows. Another highlight, the tightly funky dance cut You Must Have Another Lover, channels the groove of The Valentine Brothers' Money's Too Tight (To Mention). Overall, though, *Nina's Back!* is an uneven affair where '80s production values often diminish her power.
Charles Waring

Relight the fire: Nina Simone, still righteous in 1985.

Simon Wells
★★★★
Blankets

CRIME PAYS. CD/DL/LP
Former Snuff guitarist's lilting cut of The Specials' Do Nothing conceptually bookends Snuff's warp speed '90s version. The rest is mostly folk covers, simply arranged, warm and true. One knotty original (Should've Done) stands its ground between such as RT's precious Beeswing and two by Ted Hawkins. *JB*

Jim White
★★★
All Hits: Memories

DRAG CITY. CD/DL/LP
The tirelessly inventive drummer – Dirty Three, Xylouris White, most everyone else – goes it alone for a set of fervidly improvised stickswork against subdued keyboard tones. Octopoidal, Milford Graves-style free jazz, miraculously achieving a sort of zen clarity. *JM*

Ferrandis/Dalle/Cache Agency

MARCUS KING

Mood SWINGS
THE WORLD TOUR

TUE 5 NOV / LONDON EVENTIM APOLLO
WED 6 NOV / MANCHESTER ALBERT HALL
THU 7 NOV / GLASGOW BARROWLAND BALLROOM
SAT 9 NOV / BIRMINGHAM O$_2$ INSTITUTE
SUN 10 NOV / CARDIFF THE GREAT HALL

METROPOLISMUSIC.COM   GIGSINSCOTLAND.COM

A METROPOLIS MUSIC + DF CONCERTS PRESENTATION BY ARRANGEMENT WITH X-RAY

PAPER LOVES TREES

European forests, which provide wood for making paper,
paper packaging and many other products, have been
growing by 1,500 football pitches every day!

Discover the story of paper
www.lovepaper.org

LOVE PAPER

Source: Forest and Agricultural Organisation of the United Nations (FAO), 2005 - 2020
European Forests: EU27 + Norway, Switzerland and the UK

Love Paper is a registered trademark for Two Sides Ltd. Registered in the UK, U.S. and other countries and used with permission.

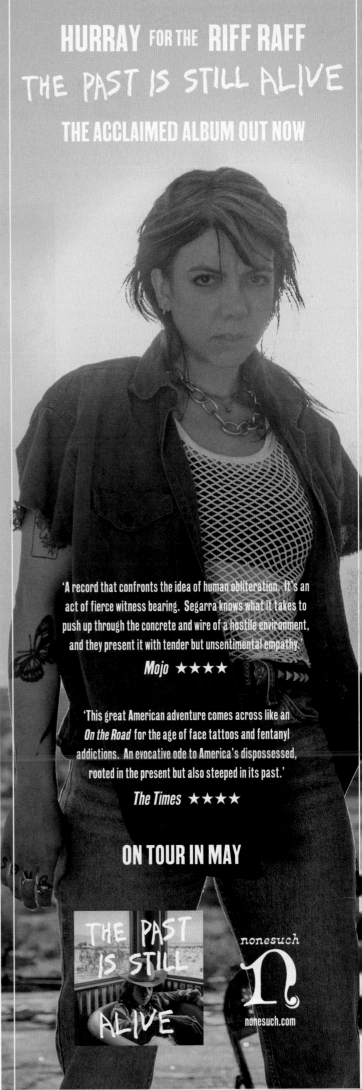

HURRAY FOR THE RIFF RAFF
THE PAST IS STILL ALIVE
THE ACCLAIMED ALBUM OUT NOW

'A record that confronts the idea of human obliteration. It's an
act of fierce witness bearing. Segarra knows what it takes to
push up through the concrete and wire of a hostile environment,
and they present it with tender but unsentimental empathy.'

Mojo ★★★★

'This great American adventure comes across like an
On the Road for the age of face tattoos and fentanyl
addictions. An evocative ode to America's dispossessed,
rooted in the present but also steeped in its past.'

The Times ★★★★

ON TOUR IN MAY

THE PAST IS STILL ALIVE

nonesuch
nonesuch.com

Black gold

The first wave of 16 studio and live LPs getting remastered on gold vinyl to celebrate the group's 50th anniversary. **By David Fricke.**

AC/DC

★★★★

AC/DC 50 Reissues

COLUMBIA/SONY LEGACY. LP

THINK OF EVERYTHING you expect from an AC/DC album – and get each time, with varying degrees of headbanging transcendence, because there is no deviation in formula and execution: the chugging power-chord assault and flying-gravel tone of the rhythm guitar; the train-kept-a-rollin' beat; howlin'-wolf singing and macho-lyric lust. Then think of what lead guitarist and duck-walking stage imp Angus Young brings to that controlled mayhem – the curt razor-wire fills and frantic, crabwalk solos – and imagine this: he does it all, in rehearsals and in the studio, sitting down, head bent in concentration as he plays. Honest – I've seen it.

"I have to have substance first, to feel it in me, before I can do the show," he told me in 2008 referring to his psycho-schoolboy act, a signature of AC/DC shows since he and his late, older brother, riffmaster Malcolm, founded the band in Sydney, Australia in 1974. Angus recalled an exchange with producer Rick Rubin during the sessions for 1995's *Ballbreaker*, one of 16 studio and live LPs getting the remastered, coloured-vinyl treatment across 2024 for the group's 50th anniversary. "He asked me, 'Don't you ever get off that stool and move around?' No," Angus replied. "I'm not going to put on a show for myself. I want the music to be right first."

The first instalment of these reissues is strict business (original US/UK track listings) from all over the first third of AC/DC's half century, starting with 1976's *High Voltage* ★★★★, their international debut with feral, vocal powerhouse Bon Scott. A mix of two '75 Australian LPs, it was fair warning of the band's mission – It's A Long Way To The Top (If You Wanna Rock'N'Roll), sealed with Scott's parade-ground lark on bagpipes – and ruthless method, meaning no ballads (The Jack was slow but hardly tender) or harmonies. As Angus put it, "The Beach Boys always reminded me of the nice kids in school." This was hard rock, not heavy metal, produced by ex-Easybeats Harry Vanda and George Young (the brothers' elder sibling) with severe attention to the Chuck Berry and '65 Rolling Stones in AC/DC's blues-gene pool. The title track and Scott's hard-partying promise in T.N.T. ("Watch me explode!") have never left the setlist.

At the other end, with Brian Johnson's sandpaper larynx, are 1990's *The Razor's Edge* ★★★★ – a return to form after a dry-spell '80s, starring the fret-tapping hail storm Thunderstruck – and 1992's *AC/DC Live* ★★★, basically a double-LP best-of with stadium ambience. (The superior '78

"This was hard rock, not heavy metal, with severe attention to Chuck Berry and the '65 Rolling Stones."

**BACK STORY:
GOODS TO
DECLARE**

● In April 1980, AC/DC flew to the Bahamas to record *Back In Black* at Compass Point Studios. They got into trouble as soon as they landed. As the band were clearing immigration at the airport, a customs inspector grabbed a guitar case containing Malcolm Young's (above) trademark Gretsch White Falcon. As Brian Johnson recalled, "Malcolm pulled it off him and went, 'You fuckin'…' Fortunately someone held him back. We'd just come down to do the album, and he would've ended up in prison."

Getty, Fin Costello/Getty

havoc, *If You Want Blood You've Got It*, is in the next batch of gold wax.) Malcolm's contention that AC/DC was always his and Angus's enterprise ("We've lived it from the beginning") is clear in the personnel merry-go-round, especially in the engine room with the prime-time rhythm section, bassist Cliff Williams and drummer Phil Rudd, on only four of these reissues.

But that's a mighty run, including AC/DC's twin peaks with producer Mutt Lange: 1979's *Highway To Hell* ★★★★★, Scott's last album before his death in February 1980; and the rapid multi-platinum rebirth with Johnson on *Back In Black* ★★★★★, released that July. (Disclosure: my essay for a 2003 CD reissue of *Back In Black* is reprinted in this vinyl edition.) Then there are the records before and after that Waterloo, 1978's *Powerage* ★★★★ and 1981's *For Those About To Rock (We Salute You)* ★★★. Together, they are a stampeding testimony to the Youngs' rough-hewn genius and their iron certainty that there is nothing a great riff won't cure or conquer.

Powerage is the almost-*Highway*, produced by Vanda and Young but with Williams's melodic grip on bass and in the street-gang chorale of Rock And Roll Damnation hinting at Lange's FM-radio savvy in the wings. There is buried treasure too, eclipsed by the hits to come, in the Creedence-SWAT-team crunch of Down Payment Blues and Riff Raff's straight-line frenzy. But *Highway To Hell* was nearly a dead end. AC/DC spent three weeks in Miami going nowhere with producer Eddie Kramer (Hendrix, Kiss) before reaching out to Lange, then coming off a UK Number 1 with The Boomtown Rats' Rat Trap.

The best thing that came out of Miami was a Malcolm-and-Angus guitar intro that ultimately triggered Highway To Hell, a brawling jubilee ("No stop signs/Speed limits/Nobody's gonna slow me down") that only rang like a death wish after Scott's passing. Lange did not receive writing credits on *Highway* (as he later did with Def Leppard) but his focus on hooks and an enriched, studio framing of AC/DC's raw gifts are composition nonetheless. He put enough commercial spin on Girls Got Rhythm, Touch Too Much and Scott's "season ticket on a one-way ride" to get AC/DC into the Top 20 on Billboard's album chart – a first with a vengeance.

Back In Black followed like an arena-scale Irish wake, the world finally showing up for the party after Scott left early. Johnson came to the job with laddish cheer and a high-pitch sustain in his Geordie rasp, able to carry the Armageddon in Hells Bells while actually expressing something like gratitude for the bedroom marathon in You Shook Me All Night Long. Malcolm and Angus, in turn, returned to their spiritual well for Back In Black, a hymn to Scott built on a stuttering-avalanche lick inspired by Johnny Kidd & The Pirates' Shakin' All Over.

For Those About To Rock, AC/DC's first Number 1 album in America, can't help being a lesser blast in comparison. Lange brought the panoramic muscle one more time, but only the title cannon fire has endured. Notably, it was the lone song from that record in the show when AC/DC returned to live work at the Power Trip festival last year. As for *Dirty Deeds Done Dirt Cheap* ★★★, this later variation on a 1976 Aussie release has great Bon but is uneven early days. And *Who Made Who* ★★★ was a 1986 soundtrack for a Stephen King film with one new song, some catalogue tunes and a genuine surprise: a stomping napalm-guitars instrumental called Chase The Ace that is pure, primal Youngs – with Angus, no doubt, sitting down.

Ain't a bad place to be: AC/DC's Angus Young gives Bon Scott a lift to the highway, London, August 1979.

Laibach
★★★★
Opus Dei
MUTE. CD/DL/LP

Slovenian provocateurs' Freddie-powered 1987 hurrah.

LAIBACH'S AUDACIOUS first LP for Mute made an impact with a Wagnerian, German-language reinvention of Queen's One Vision. The titanic, martial posturing suggested subversion of a Leni Riefenstahl film ("Ein Fleisch, ein Blut"). Forming in Tito's Yugoslavia, between communism and capitalism, Laibach's self-proclaimed "totalitarian" rock music featured adaptations of Stalinist socialist realism and "Nazikunst", but their long game has revealed much more of Mel Brooks' Springtime For Hitler than any kind of Third Reich apologia. Meanwhile, pop music's twin infinities of awe and absurdity would be investigated across entire re-workings of The Beatles' *Let It Be* album and the Sound Of Music soundtrack. Here, the astronomic ambiguity is underscored on The Great Seal, featuring recitation of Churchill's "fight them on the beaches" speech. This reissue is impressively augmented by 16 live tracks plus new artwork and sleevenotes.

Roy Wilkinson

Industrial strength: Laibach's *Opus Dei* has an astronomic ambiguity.

feeding, and a huge influence on The Stone Roses.
Lois Wilson

||||||||||||||||||||||
Soundtracks & Head
★★★★
Daga Daga Daga
GLASS MODERN. LP

First issue for lost album by Swell Maps rhythm section.

This one's been a long time coming. Epic Soundtracks and Jowe Head first played in a duo together in 1972, making experimental home recordings, then by 1977 they were respectively the drummer and bassist in Swell Maps, in which they reworked a few of those earlier musical ideas. In 1981, a year after the Maps split, the pair cut the 10, largely improvised tracks which make up this previously-unreleased LP, only two of which saw the light before the money ran out – the haunting single Rain Rain Rain and its B-side, Ghost Train. Conventional instruments such as guitars, bass and drums are skilfully deployed alongside more left-field elements such as VW engine sounds, the overall mood subtle and elusive, with the occasional vocal. If you're an admirer of the more avant-garde side of the Swell Maps repertoire, seek this out.
Max Décharné

Brian Eno
★★★★
Eno OST
UMR. CD/DL/LP

Eclectic soundtrack to Gary Hustwit's career-spanning film portrait of the enduring ambient potentate.

Eno the movie promises to go beyond documentary stereotype, generative technologies ensuring no two screenings will be alike. The accompanying soundtrack is perhaps less ground-breaking, its 17 tracks cherry-picked from Eno's five post-Roxy Music decades, although it opens with an anomaly – the previously unreleased All I Remember finding habitually future-facing Brian looking yearningly backwards, recalling scenes from his youth ("flickers in windows and 40-watt bulbs and TVs") – and ends in a dream, a heat-hazed By This River, captured in August 2021 at a stifling Athens Acropolis. In between, airings of Eno benchmarks like Third Uncle and Sky Saw are complemented by deep cuts such as the elegantly buoyant Motion In Field, a collaboration with pianist Tom Rogerson, while the clattering Lighthouse #429, plucked from Eno's capacious Sonos Radio outtake dump, is surely the epitome of his self-styled "jazz that nobody asked for".
David Sheppard

||||||||||||||||||||||
Robin Trower
★★★★
Bridge Of Sighs
CHRYSALIS. CD+BR/LP

Trower's power trio's finest just got louder, clearer and bigger.

Robin Trower's life changed in September 1970 when Jimi Hendrix's death prompted him to make a rare foray into writing. After Song For A Dreamer appeared on Procol Harum's fifth album, the guitarist quit to form his own trio. 1974's *Bridge Of Sighs*, the second and most mellifluous of his Jimi-fired titles, is Trower's masterpiece. While awash with Uni-Vibe effects, controlled wah wah lines, even a Peter Green-like solo on About To Begin, this meticulously recorded, deeply melancholic work is distinctly Trower's. The title track, with its tolling bells, Trower's windswept, reverberating guitar lines and a throaty vocal from bassist James Dewar, is a downbeat stoner classic. Now stretched to four discs, a set taped at New York's Record Plant showcases the band in its natural habitat – in front of a crowd eager to cheer a single note of tightly-held feedback.
Mark Paytress

||||||||||||||||||||||
Labi Siffre
★★★★
For The Children
DEMON. LP

Fourth studio LP from the folk-soul British singer-songwriter, remastered from original stereo tapes.

His previous album, 1972's *Crying, Laughing, Loving, Lying* had reached Number 11 in the charts and garnered two hit singles. But when his record label, Pye, first heard For The Children they were not pleased. "My manager said: 'Every word on the album is true,'" Siffre told The Guardian in 2022, "but people don't want to hear that." Moving on from the diaristic romantic honesty of …Loving, Lying, Siffre turned his attention to humanity, religion and the environment. Produced and arranged by Siffre, For The Children might be seen as an atheistic, misanthropic *What's Going On*, with Gaye's orchestral funk-soul arrangements replaced with an acoustic folk urgency. Yet behind the bright melodies and Siffre's seductive vocals there is darkness here, a despair for the future, and a contempt for humanity that works its way into your soul. An iron fist in a velvet glove.
Andrew Male

||||||||||||||||||||||
The Rain Parade
★★★★
Emergency Third Rail Power Trip
LABEL 51 RECORDINGS. CD/DL/LP

Their neo-psych first album from 1983 plus bonuses.

Heading up the Paisley Underground, Rain Parade began as The Sidewalks, a Brit Invasion-indebted outfit, which after a year holed up in a rehearsal studio turned to recreating '60s psychedelia for a new generation. Mixing Byrdsian 12-string, waspy drone and reverb-cloaked vocals with sitar, Farfisa etc, they distinguished themselves from their forebears with contemporary lyrics. Signed to Enigma, they debuted with 1982's dreamlike What She's Done To Your Mind, one of several bonuses included here along with demos, rehearsals and an extraordinary live take on Syd Barrett's No Good Trying which replicates the Pink Floyd down-the-UFO sound. Their debut album, meanwhile, is paradigmatic Paisley Underground, a gentle, jangly soundworld both warm blanket and imagination-

||||||||||||||||||||||
Skip Mahoaney And The Casuals
★★★★
Your Funny Moods
NUMERO GROUP. DL/LP

Rare vocal harmony soul album from 1974.

From Washington DC, Skip Mahoaney started out singing on street corners before forming The Casuals with school mates in 1965. A model vocal harmony troupe built around his glistening falsetto, their 1973 debut single Your Funny Moods, penned by Mahoaney and keyboardist/drummer James Purdie, was issued on DC International Records. An earnest ballad, it taps into the emotional overload of contemporaries The Delfonics, Stylistics and Dramatics and was a minor hit. The album of the same name followed in 1974, but a dispute with the label over the artwork – a head shot of a black female with Afro with no photos of the band – led to an acrimonious group split. The album does them proud though, its seven songs elaborate, billowy mini masterpieces, with Town Called Nowhere's social protest bringing a tougher edge.
Lois Wilson

Andy Catlin

**Bound for glory:
Sister Rosetta Tharpe
turns it up.**

Photo by Tony Evans/Getty Images

Sacre bleues

Previously unreleased recording
of the mother of all rock'n'roll
guitar. By David Fricke.

Sister Rosetta Tharpe

★★★★

Live In France: The 1966
Concert In Limoges

DEEP DIGS/ELEMENTAL MUSIC. LP

IN NOVEMBER, 1966, Britain's founding
class of rock guitar gods was in high-speed
ascent. Eric Clapton and Peter Green juggled
studio dates, BBC sessions and one-nighters
with Cream and John Mayall's Bluesbreakers
respectively. Jimmy Page toured the US with
The Yardbirds while former bandmate Jeff Beck
was about to launch his own group, and the
American émigré Jimi Hendrix was blowing
minds in his first gigs with the Experience.

That same month, the mother of all
rock'n'roll guitar was working in France
without a band, like history in twilight on a

cruelly tight budget. At 51,
the gospel star Sister Rosetta
Tharpe was many hard miles
from her 1940s and '50s hit-
record prime and nearing the greater reward
promised in her songs. Four years after this
concert at the Grand Theatre in Limoges (taped
by French radio and previously unissued), Tharpe suffered a stroke on tour, then lost a leg to
diabetes; she died in 1973 after another stroke,
buried in Philadelphia in an unmarked grave.

But here is the Arkansas-born, Chicago-
raised woman who took the blues and swing
to Pentecostal worship, then turned it up so
everyone could feel the healing – still raising the
roof, all the way to heaven, armed with nothing
more than the electricity of her faith, a white
triple-pickup Gibson SG (with gold hardware)
and a voice as titanic as James Brown, Otis
Redding and Howlin' Wolf combined. Opening
with her 1939 Decca smash This Train, Tharpe
jumps out of the station like a sunnier John
Lee Hooker, thumping her foot on the floor
for a backbeat and crying "All aboard, let's go"

before a soloing jubilation of
spearing-treble jabs, land-
slide licks and ingenious,
natural wah wah in the way
Tharpe presses and pulls at
her vibrato bar. Another signature 78, Didn't It Rain (a
1947 duet with singer Marie
Knight), is here and gone like a Buzzcocks
single, Tharpe washing your blues and sin away
in under two minutes.

Unlike many black singers who first let loose
at Sunday communion then struggled with
censure and guilt as they crossed over to soul
and pop, Tharpe knew you couldn't have bap-
tism without procreation (she cut I Want A Tall
Skinny Papa with Lucky Millinder's Orchestra
in 1941). You'll have no trouble hearing where
Tina Turner and Etta James found their raw, sul-
try certainty when Tharpe holds the joy ("Fe-e-
e-l so good") in Down By The Riverside, on the
way to a guitar break of nimble, skittering chops,
lined in natural amp-stress distortion, like she's
just waiting for the call to join ZZ Top.

Tharpe was, in fact, soon to meet her Maker.
But as she sings at one point, "He give me a
guitar/Told me to play it!" In an era of gods, she
was here to serve. And salvation was assured.

The in sounds from way out: *Ghana Special 2* stars Delips Apo (left, from The Godfathers and Dadadi) and Andy Vans.

Future shock

Cultural upheaval and technological advances shake up West African emigrés. By David Hutcheon.

Various

★★★★

Ghana Special 2: Electronic Highlife & Afro Sounds In The Diaspora 1980-93

SOUNDWAY. CD/DL/LP

STRANGE THINGS happen when the compulsion to keep moving forward means artists collide with the harsh realities of economic turmoil. In the 1960s, boom-time countries across Africa promoted new forms of indigenous music, sponsoring big bands comprising the finest musicians. Shit-hot guitarists; peerless, soul-scorching singers; batteries of percussionists; nightlife that would shame Manhattan or Soho. To be young was very heaven as independence blossomed.

By the late 1970s, however, the wheels were coming off: turbulent times brought recession, authoritarian governments clamped down on joy, record sales dried up, clubs closed and the cost of keeping orchestras on the road spiralled. With many of the best musicians seeking opportunities abroad, obsolescence or innovation were the stark choices facing entrepreneurial scenesters. It was the end of a golden age of African music… and that's when things got weird.

You can imagine the furore in Congo when the great rumba ensembles came under pressure from smaller funk outfits (see *Congo Funk!* on p101); in Senegal, mambo-mimicking orchestras were elbowed aside by tyros such as Youssou N'Dour; similarly, in Ghana, the venerated highlife giants were replaced by punks who could record quickly and cheaply using synths. Many of them were based in Europe or North America, where they had access to not only state-of-the-art studios and better equipment – Ghana's rulers had imposed tariffs on such luxuries – but also a fuller spectrum of musical influences with which to feed their heads.

The new sounds of R&B and disco seeped in (M.C. Mambo by Pepper, Onion, Ginger & Salt is a riot), as did Caribbean soca and reggae, and the original, colourblind, new wave of NYC. Curiously, however, the heart of this revolution was Germany – the great vocalist Pat Thomas, for example, recorded Gaye Wani in Berlin, and worked with Marijata, whose Otanhunu also features (buy everything they ever recorded) – leading to the dismissive term "burger highlife" being coined by the old guard. For a new generation, though, these innovations and experiments came to be seen as a modern, relatable identity, significantly fresher than anything that came with a whiff of the colonial era.

While it's true you can often hear what upset the highlife connoisseurs, the bulk of this collection of outsider art holds up 30-plus years on. Just as Nigeria's William Onyeabor proved you didn't need virtuoso musicians to make tracks that resonate perfectly in a time and place he could never have predicted, so the burgermeisters land in 2024 just as there's a renewed love for 45-year-old synth-pop, for Roland 303s (see Starlite's exceptionally squelchy Anoma Koro), and for that exhilarating sense of standing on the cusp of a promise-laden, forward-looking age. Just because it never arrived doesn't mean we can't be nostalgic about it…

Air

★★★★

Moon Safari: 25th Anniversary Edition

RHINO. CD/DL/DVD

French duo's '98 landmark of chill, expanded.

Straight out of Versailles, Nicolas Godin and Jean-Benoît Dunckel's halcyon debut as Air went Top 10 in Britain and bagged three Top 30 singles, preparing the ground for downtempo successors like Zero 7 and impacting the world of advert music. Twenty-six years on, though, it's *Moon Safari* and Eurodisco/soft-rock earwormers including Sexy Boy and Kelly Watch The Stars that remain the clever, persuasive sell. As devotees of the sophisticated pop of Michel Polnareff and Gainsbourg (strange how they were lumped in with the French house scene), the duo transmit romance, melancholy and nostalgia via unsweaty grooves, Fender Rhodes piano and electro-acoustic finesse, like woodier takes on Daft Punk's cyborg reflections on lost innocence. This edition comes with the album in

Spatial Atmos audio and extras not on the 2008 reissue: Mike Mills' oddly wistful tour doc Eating, Sleeping, Waiting And Playing appears in HD.
Ian Harrison

Conrad Schnitzler

★★★

Slow Motion

BUREAU B. CD/LP

Accessible 1979 soundtrack by the oft-challenging kosmische titan.

The 14 short tracks on *Slow Motion* accompanied the 1979 film of the same name, directed by abstract painter Karl Horst Hödicke. They were first issued in 2010 as two limited-edition albums: 26- and 300-copy pressings. For watchers of German sonic individualist Conrad Schnitzler (1937-2011), this easily available release is welcome. Some of what's here are concentrated bursts of what he is known for: Slow Motion 9 condenses the oscillator-driven rumbling vortex of Kluster's 1971 album *Zwei-Osterei* into a two-and-half-minute eruption.

Contrastingly, the pulsing Slow Motion 3 is akin to the more abstract aspects of *Metamatic*-era John Foxx. Opening cut Slow Motion 1 could actually be a post-punk-era synth explorer. With his short-stay memberships of Tangerine Dream and Kluster far behind him, this found Schnitzler at his most accessible and sits well with his equally user-friendly 1978 album *Con.*
Kieron Tyler

Brian Auger's Oblivion Express

★★★★

Live Oblivion Volumes 1 & 2

SOUL BANK MUSIC. CD/DL/LP

Marking their 50th anniversary, the organ auteur's live albums get first ever vinyl reissue. Sold separately.

These live albums were recorded at LA's Whisky A Go Go over two nights in 1974 when jazz funk and fusion were at their mainstream height. Both capture Hammond organist Auger and his Oblivion Express (a fledgling Steve Ferrone on drums, Barry Dean on bass, Jack Mills on guitar, Alex Ligertwood on vocals) in simpatico improvising their greatest hits. The results are melodious, spontaneous lengthy jams that often better the studio versions. A case in point on *Vol. 1*, their 10-minute take on Bumpin' On Sunset, Auger's best ever recorded take on the Wes Montgomery number, his marauding runs and jubilant vamps leading into calm, cosmic reverberation. Even better is Freedom Jazz Dance on *Vol. 2*, where infinite possibilities are glimpsed in an ostinato frenzy.
Lois Wilson

Chet Baker & Jack Sheldon

★★★

In Perfect Harmony: The Lost Album

JAZZ DETECTIVE. CD/DL

West Coast luminaries' shelved studio project emerges from the shadows.

In 1972, Chet Baker was coaxed out of a semi-retirement induced by his heroin addiction to pick up his horn again and record in the studio with his trusted friend, fellow trumpeter, and singer, Jack Sheldon. But following producer Jack Marshall's sudden death in 1973, the album was canned and subsequently forgotten. After 50 years of gathering dust, the 11-track collaboration proves a lost gem that deserves to see the light. Baker and Sheldon couldn't be more different in terms of their vocals, with Baker's delicate boyish tone contrasting with Sheldon's grittier, more dynamic delivery. Sheldon's bebop-steeped horn, too, is livelier than Baker's, but the stylistic differences between the two create a delicious dramatic tension that is strongest on You Fascinate Me, where Sheldon's voice injects an irreverent hipster vibe. (Also available as a limited-edition RSD LP).
Charles Waring

HUGH CORNWELL
ALL THE FUN OF THE FAIR TOUR

NOVEMBER 2024

20 READING SUB 89
21 LEEDS OLD WOOLLEN
22 EDINBURGH QUEENS HALL
23 SUNDERLAND FIRE STATION

27 SOUTHAMPTON THE BROOK
28 LONDON ELECTRIC BALLROOM
29 MANCHESTER ACADEMY
30 NORTHAMPTON ROADMENDER

MOJO 4/4 STARS - "CORNWELL'S STILL DOING THINGS HIS WAY AND OFTEN WITH STRIKING RESULTS"

Very Special Guests

GIG CARTEL IN ASSOCIATION WITH FRUIT PIE MUSIC PRESENT

WITH SUPPORT FROM SEB WESSON

nik KERSHAW AND BAND

2024

28 JUN - OXFORD - O2 ACADEMY
29 JUN - NORWICH - EPIC STUDIOS
12 JUL - NORTHAMPTON - ROADMENDER

THE GIG CARTEL BY ARRANGEMENT WITH FRUIT PIE MUSIC PRESENTS

NIK KERSHAW
the 1984 tour

CELEBRATING
40 YEARS OF HUMAN RACING & THE RIDDLE

2024

03 OCT LINCOLN ENGINE SHED
04 OCT SUNDERLAND FIRE STATION
05 OCT EDINBURGH QUEENS HALL
06 OCT HOLMFIRTH PICTUREDROME
08 OCT CAMBRIDGE JUNCTION
09 OCT MANCHESTER ACADEMY 2
10 OCT NEW BRIGHTON FLORAL PAVILION
11 OCT WOLVERHAMPTON WULFRUN
12 OCT CARDIFF TRAMSHED
14 OCT BATH KOMEDIA
15 OCT PORTSMOUTH GUILDHALL
16 OCT LONDON O2 SHEPHERDS BUSH EMPIRE

THE UNDERTONES

OCTOBER 2024 and friends

Thursday 10 Liverpool Hangar 34 *
Friday 11 Sunderland Fire Station *
Saturday 12 Sheffield Leadmill *

*RUTS DC

Thursday 17 Lincoln Engine Shed +
Friday 18 Norwich Epic +
Saturday 19 Wolverhampton Kk's +

+ THE REZILLOS

Thursday 24 Frome Cheese & Grain #
Friday 25 London Camden Electric Ballroom #
Saturday 26 Southampton 1865 #

PETE WYLIE
THE MIGHTY WAH!

inspiral carpets

moo!

23:05 BURY ST EDMUNDS // THE APEX
25:05 CHESTER // THE LIVE ROOMS
19:07 HOLMFIRTH // PICTUREDROME
20:07 CASTLETON // THE DEVIL'S ARSE CAVE

Spell-bound: these Broadcast demos are a fitting memento of Trish Keenan's poetic songwriting and unimpeachable voice.

Broadcast
★★★★
Spell Blanket – Collected Demos 2006-2009
WARP. CD/DL/LP

Raw vignettes act as moving reminder of Broadcast's splendour.

THESE CAPTIVATING demos – some full songs, some mere sketches – were the source from which Broadcast were due to create their fifth studio album. Tragically, the 2011 death from pneumonia of co-founder Trish Keenan – who formed Broadcast in Birmingham with James Cargill in 1995 – means that this is how they'll remain. It lends added poignancy to the 36 songs and part-songs and a tantalising insight into what would have been. *Spell Blanket* meanders through Broadcast's singular world of psych, folk, avant pop and haunting electronica. Opener, The Song Before The Song Comes Out is 42 seconds long but intensely intimate. Singing into a portable recorder as she walks, you hear Keenan's footsteps, listen to her breathe between lines. Of the fuller songs, Tunnel View is a bewitching gothic nursery rhyme while Running Back To Me predates psych behemoths Goat by years with its droning, saturnine malevolence. So many ideas, so much beauty and a fitting memento of Trish Keenan's poetic songwriting and inimitable, unimpeachable voice.

Stephen Worthy

Brother Jack McDuff
★★★★
Ain't No Sunshine (Live In Seattle)
'REEL TO REAL. CD/DL/LP

Jazz organist's previously unheard "Emerald City" gig surfaces.

A prolific Illinois organist who rose to prominence in the early 1960s, McDuff (born Eugene McDuffy) was a leading light of the soul-jazz movement, which offered an accessible, blues-based antidote to the way-out experimentation of the avant-garde scene. Following stints at the Prestige, Atlantic and Blue Note labels, McDuff, who discovered guitarist George Benson, spent the early '70s at Chess's Cadet imprint, which was his recording home at the time of this previously unissued concert, taped in 1972. Leading a band comprising the twin saxophones of Leo Johnson and Dave Young alongside guitarist Vinnie Corrao and drummer Ron Davis, McDuff serves up a perfect storm of after-hours blues, hard-swinging jazz, and incendiary funk grooves. The 10-track set blends original numbers, like the propulsive Theme From Electric Surfboard, with jazz standards and a sublimely soulful take on Bill Withers' R&B hit Ain't No Sunshine.

Charles Waring

The Cat's Miaow
★★★★
Skipping Stones: The Cassette Years '92-93
WORLD OF ECHO. DL/LP

A compilation of tape material by Melbourne's early-'90s indie trailblazers.

The Cat's Miaow were vocalist Kerrie Bolton, bassist Andrew Withycombe, guitarist Bart Cummings and drummer Cameron Smith. *Skipping Stones* rewinds to the band's prolific two years of cassette recordings that initially came out via the Melbourne-based Toytown label. Its 35 tracks are full of wonders, from nearly fully-formed coming-of-age songs (Faded) to ruminative 30-second vignettes (Disappointed). Although The Cat's Miaow were purveyors of an indie sound radiating from distant shores, they amalgamated their influences into a unique palette, closer to NZ's Dunedin scene than the trendsetting Creation and Rough Trade bands. Hazy-sounding Autumn echoes Satin Doll by The Chills. Elsewhere, there's jangling guitars and chiming keyboards galore. Few tracks exceed the three-minute mark but even so, the variation between harder-edged and mellow is impressive. Standout I Hate Myself More Than You Do veils bittersweet melodic reminiscence with distorted JAMC-esque guitars.

Irina Shtreis

Various
★★★★
This Is Mod: 1964-1968
KENT. LP

First in Ace Record's 'This Is' series: a genre-specific comp at an affordable price.

'Mod' here refers to the rare soul, jazz and R&B sides that the original '60s stylists might have danced to in Soho basements late into the night and early morning. It's a fantasy soundtrack of course, but the music compiled by Dean Rudland is faultless: 14 tracks spanning 1960 to '68 and taken from Ace and its associated catalogues – Fame, Goldwax, Modern, Flip etc. It begins with the latest track, Clarence Carter's earthy Looking For A Fox and ends with Timmy Thomas's emotion-heightened cover of The Animals' It's My Life. The remainder are songs that are familiar but still retain their edge, such as The Ikettes' exultant Camel Walk, Hank Jacobs' hip instrumental Elijah Rockin' With Soul and Mary Love's sweet but grainy Lay This Burden Down.

Lois Wilson

Various
★★★★
Jah Fire: The Observer 7" Singles Collection 1976-1977
DR BIRD. CD

Peak roots reggae produced by Niney The Observer.

Known as Nine Finger or Niney because of a missing thumb, Winston Holness cut some vocal sides at Studio One in the late 1960s and worked as a record salesman for Clancy Eccles, Bunny Lee, Lee 'Scratch' Perry and Joe Gibbs before founding his Observer label in 1970, hitting instantly with the apocalyptic Blood And Fire. This 2-CD package gathers the seven-inch editions of some of the most loved Observer productions of the mid-1970s, including Gregory Isaacs' Slave Master, Horace Andy's Materialist, Jacob Miller's Moses, Junior Byles' Weeping and Tyrone Taylor's Sufferation; less familiar and equally compelling are Nyabinghi instrumentals such as Bobby Ellis's Doreth and the Soul Syndicate's Zimbabwe, as well as further gems from Junior Delgado, The Jewels, deejays Dillinger and I Roy, plus Niney himself.

David Katz

Various
★★★★
Eccentric Soul: Consolidated Productions Vol. 1
NUMERO GROUP. DL/LP

Obscure '60s R&B from Mel Alexander's LA operation.

Taking Motown as the blueprint, and with the slogan, 'Sounds Of Success', producer, songwriter, singer Mel Alexander founded Consolidated Productions in 1961 and for the next three decades hustled imprints such as Ajax, Angel Town, Car-A-Mel and Kris, to little commercial effect. Yet as this first volume from his extensive archive attests, the lack of sales had nothing to do with quality: the 28 tracks, spanning galloping dancers blending agony and ecstasy to proto quiet-storm ballads, are all exceptional. In the former camp, The Deb Tones & The Del-Reys' joyous girl group take on Knock On Wood, and BB Carter's Cool It Baby, a gorgeous call and response. In the latter, The Del-Reys again with Walk Proud, which channels the sweet, smooth tones of Smokey and Billy Williams' So Called Friend with its woozy, late-night feel.

Lois Wilson

Sun Ra
★★★
Inside The Light World: Sun Ra Meets The OVC
STRUT. LP

Lost 1986 Arkestra sessions capture jazz's foremost futurist at his most laid-back.

The vinyl renaissance has ensured Sun Ra releases keep landing thick and fast over 30 years since his death. This latest is a rare excursion into a 24-track studio, documenting a meeting of minds with rocket scientist Bill Sebastian's OVC, a sophisticated light projector that cast kaleidoscopic patterns on-stage. While the repertoire is established, languorous takes on Theme Of The Stargazers, Sunset On The Nile and Saturn Rings major on Sun Ra's abstracted piano vamps, off-the-wall percussion and polite call-and-response chants. It peaks with a breathless 22-minute version of Discipline 27-II, as tangles of interlocking horns meet deep space pulses, cosmic solos and clusters of dissonance. One can only imagine it blowing impressionable minds via the OVC.

Andy Cowan

Various
★★★★

Congo Funk! Sound Madness From The Shores Of The Mighty Congo River Kinshasa/Brazzaville, 1969-1982

ANALOG AFRICA. CD/DL/LP

Energetic compilation distils some of Africa's most potent '70s funkateers.

A flashback to an era where smaller independent labels filled the void in the ailing Congolese record industry, this fleet-footed collection shows how traditional rumba was elevated and extended by psychedelia and funk. One such obscure pressing was Petelo Vicka Et Son Nzazi's Sungu Lubuka, an eight-minute dance feast that married cool horn breakdowns with intricate electric guitar textures. Six-string mastery is similarly on-point amid the poppy immediacy of Kiwita Kumunani and yelping James Brown-ish fervour of Lolo Soulfire, two standouts by L'Orchestre OK Jazz (whose guitarist Franco Luambo ran a premium pressing plant), and M.B.T.'s party-in-a-glass M.B.T's Sound. Impeccably sequenced, with fulsome linernotes, global groovers will find this seamless mix of the known and obscure frequently revelatory.

Andy Cowan

Various
★★★★★

Holland-Dozier-Holland Detroit 1969-1977

DEMON. CD/DL/LP

Essential soul from HDH's Invictus, Hot Wax and Music Merchant labels.

ON LEAVING Motown in 1968, Holland, Dozier and Holland, the songwriting triumvirate behind the 'Sound Of Young America', launched their trio of labels with an unimpeachable run of 45s: Chairmen Of The Board's Give Me Just A Little More Time; Freda Payne's Band Of Gold; Honey Cone's Girls It Ain't Easy, etc; strong, soulful, naturally Motown-y songs that have since become a part of pop's fabric. This rewarding 4-LP or 3-CD cherry-pick of singles contains them and more, with later material such as New York Port Authority's I Got It Pt. 1 and the aforesaid Chairmen Of The Board's Skin I'm In expanding their aural identity: the first-named presaging gospel house with its thumping disco beat and the second, tense funk rock featuring members of Parliament-Funkadelic.

Lois Wilson

Solid gold: Freda Payne – one of many H-D-H-produced soul stars.

Cannonball Adderley
★★★★

Poppin' In Paris: Live At L'Olympia 1972

ELEMENTAL. CD/DL/LP

The jazz giant captured live three years before his death.

As this previously unissued Parisian live performance shows, although Austrian keyboardist Joe Zawinul quit Adderley's band in 1970 to form Weather Report, he left an indelible mark on the alto saxophonist's music. Four of the cuts in the band's set are Zawinul compositions, including the infectious Walk Tall and Adderley's biggest chart hit, the gospel-infused soul-jazz classic, Mercy Mercy Mercy, which he first recorded in 1966. Even so, Zawinul's replacement, rising piano star George Duke, then 28, can be heard shaping the band's sound via the explorative opener, the 20-minute Black Messiah, a progressive, cutting-edge piece that remains tethered, albeit loosely at times, to the jazz tradition. With its seamless blend of edgy avant-jazz (Directions), earthy street funk (Hummin'), and hard bop (Autumn Leaves), this stunning concert shows why Adderley's group, with its mixture of bold experimentation and toe-tapping accessibility, was such a popular live attraction.

Charles Waring

Glad
★★★★

A New Tomorrow: The Glad & New Breed Recordings

CHERRY RED. CD

What Timothy B. Schmit did before Poco and the Eagles.

Even in what passed for their heyday, they were hardly household names, but Sacramento's Glad (formerly The New Breed) are ones that got away. They featured pre-Poco Timothy B. Schmit; their sole LP, 1968's *Feelin' Glad* was produced by Eirik Wangberg (AKA Eirik The Norwegian when he engineered Paul McCartney's *Ram*) and James Burton played on their thunderous version of Mann/Weil's Shape Of Things To Come. They probably guessed it wasn't to be when promotional copies of *Feelin' Glad* featured another band's music, but on this evidence (*Feelin' Glad*, plus mono singles by both Glad and the more R&B-fuelled The New Breed), they deserve exhumation. With Hollies-level harmonies cascading over their mostly self-penned material (especially the impossibly catchy Pickin' Up The Pieces); the proto cosmic country of No Ma, It Can't Be and Tom Phillips's swirling psychedelic guitar, they had everything but an audience.

John Aizlewood

Hard Skin
★★★★

Gold

JT CLASSICS. DL/LP

Two chords, two fingers: neo-Oi! pranksters' Greatest Hits Volume 1.

"It stands with its boots on, chest out and bollocks swinging," writes Hard Skin's Fat Bob in his typically foul-mouthed introduction to this beginners' guide to the south Londoners' subversive take on the sound of the Cockney Rejects and Angelic Upstarts. Smart-alec ex-anarcho types with hip pop biz connections (Joanna Newsom was a notable incongruous guest on a previous LP), Fat Bob and Johnny Takeaway formed Hard Skin as a pastiche of ficko punk in the 1990s, but the killer tunes and sly gags have now been coming for 30 years. Back On The Bottle, Oi Not Jobs, Romford ("is full of wankers") and Down The Pub are all nod-and-a-wink takes on Oi!'s foundation ethos of "having a laugh and having a say", and if neo-Nazi boneheads and uptight skinhead purists continue to regard them with suspicion, anyone who appreciates both flares and slippers should hold Hard Skin dear.

Jim Wirth

Roy Montgomery
★★★★

Temple IV

KRANKY. CD/DL/LP

Vinyl reissue for beautiful New Zealand psych-noise-drone LP from 1996.

When New Zealand guitarist Roy Montgomery recorded *Temple IV* in 1996 he was returning to music after a long sabbatical. One half of doomy early-'80s Flying Nun janglists Pin Group, Montgomery quit music in 1985 to work in theatre. Then, when his partner Jo died in 1992 he went travelling, finally settling in a New York apartment where he recorded two LPs back-to-back, attempts, he told MOJO's Stevie Chick, "to reconnect with a person who's gone, [reinhabit] the relationship." Partly inspired by an overnight stay in ancient Mesoamerican pyramid Tikal Temple IV, *Temple IV* is a work of mesmerising, melancholy psych guitar simplicity. Working with a cheap Teisco guitar, wrestling with feedback and interference, utilising reverb, repetition, distortion and delay, Montgomery gradually ascends to a hypnotic form of hallucinatory guitar music, his mourning repurposed as a trance-inducing religious experience.

Andrew Male

The Cryin' Shames
★★★★

Please Stay

TEA CHEST TAPES/CHERRY RED. CD/LP

Joe Meek-produced Mod, Merseybeat and freakbeat. Brian Epstein was a fan.

From Liverpool, The Cryin' Shames started out as The Bumblies with a gritty undertow indebted to Them and The Rolling Stones. An audition with Joe Meek led to two singles and a third with a reconfigured line-up in seven months. The first, Please Stay, a desperate ballad with agitated vocals, gave Meek his last Top 30 hit. The third, Come On Back, is a freakbeat classic with a three-figure price tag, its uneasy mood proving Meek could move and shake with the psych times. A shelved album of covers, presented here with many other previously unheard tracks from the 'Tea Chest Tapes', peaks with their brilliant reading of Marvin Gaye's No Good Without You, which is enveloped in distorted fuzz and delivered with snotty attitude, and is a garage punk revelation.

Lois Wilson

Michael Putland/Getty

Autumn almanac: the inside cover of Pete Jolly's alluring *Seasons* LP.

FILE UNDER...

Here's Pete with the weather

Spontaneous jazz for all seasons.
By Jim Irvin.

I N 1970, THE starkly beautiful image of a giant, autumnal aspen leaf hinted that Pete Jolly's *Seasons* ★★★★ (Future Days Recordings) might be different from his previous releases. Indeed, the record inside came as a surprise even to the people who made it.

Jolly (born Peter Ceragioli Jr), was a highly respected pianist who'd worked with Art Pepper, Gerry Mulligan and Chet Baker, and been reasonably prolific under his own banner with a string of albums for RCA and CBS – starting in 1955 when he was 23. Musician and label boss Herb Alpert spotted him at Sherry's, a nightclub on Sunset Boulevard, and, deeply impressed by his sensitive playing, produced and endorsed Jolly's 1968 debut for A&M, a collection of standards, which went largely unnoticed, as did its follow-up in 1969. When time came for a third roll of the dice, Alpert opted to shake things up.

Wrecking Crew bass stalwart Chuck Berghofer (credits include These Boots Are Made For Walking) worked with Jolly for 40 years: "[*Seasons*] was totally different from anything else we did, which was straight-ahead jazz. Pete did it because that's what Herb wanted to do." The first innovation was to employ keyboards other than Jolly's usual instrument – Wurlitzer electric piano (heavily tremeloed on the album's opening solo moment, Leaves), Sanovox organ, accordions (Jolly had been a child accordion prodigy) and Hammond B-3 – and a tight group of hip players in percussionists Milt Holland and Emil Richards,

drummer Paul Humphrey (John Coltrane, Supremes), guitarist John Pisano (Sergio Mendes, Ken Nordine).

However, the main departure was entering the studio with hardly any material. The title track was a melody by esteemed sunshine-pop composer and engineer Roger Nichols, and there's a concessionary jog through Rodgers & Hammerstein's Younger Than Springtime, presumably because of its title, which feels like a warm-up, but instead of further tilts at seasonal standards, Pete and co improvised throughout a single four-hour session and edited the results down to half an hour of sweet music. "He'd start playing, and we'd just follow him," Berghofer told liner writer Dave Segal. "He was so easy to play with. His time was so great. I remember a trio playing the first time through, and then they added stuff to it."

Standouts? The buzzy high-speed Bees, played on what sounds like Wurlitzer through a fuzz pedal for a synth-like effect, the trippy accordion on Autumn Festival and the dubby, narcotic Springs. But *Seasons* functions best taken as a whole, a mellow, mood-altering suite of attractive reveries, shifting like the weather, climaxing with a refreshing blast of brass behind penultimate track The Indian's Summer.

"There was nobody like him, and I've played with many pianists," Berghofer says. "He could've been much more popular if he had [promoted] himself at all. He played and went home. And when we weren't working or had time off, he never touched the piano. Yet he could sit down and play after being off for three weeks."

Alpert too recalled Jolly as "an extreme introvert" who let his music do the talking, and when this inventive, atmospheric set also failed to connect, Jolly moved on with no hard feelings. He later cropped up recreating Bud Powell's performances with Charlie Parker for Clint Eastwood's Bird biopic. He died in 2004.

Seasons quickly went out of print and has remained so until now on vinyl – there was a limited CD reissue in 2007 – but in the intervening years has grown in stature thanks, inevitably, to use as samples (Jay Dee, Cypress Hill), but also because its spare, relaxed, subtly virtuoso textures have come back around, making sense to, say, fans of both Airs and both Azymuths, light jazz as transparent and alluring as that cover image.

Original copies now change hands for impressive sums. This new edition in clear amber or green vinyl with deluxe packaging is superbly done.

seasons.pete jolly

"A mellow, mood-altering suite of attractive reveries, shifting like the weather..."

Academy Events present

by arrangement with THE MAGNIFICENT AGENCY presents
academyevents

ALABAMA 3

A celebration of
EXILE ON COLDHARBOUR LANE
& LA PESTE
plus the greatest hits

2024

SAT 07 DECEMBER
MANCHESTER O₂ RITZ

FRI 13 DECEMBER
BRISTOL O₂ ACADEMY

SAT 14 DECEMBER
LONDON O₂ FORUM
KENTISH TOWN

alabama3.co.uk

academyevents
& friends by arrangement with NEIL O'BRIEN ENTERTAINMENT presents

THOMAS · DOLBY

PLUS SPECIAL GUEST
MARTIN McALOON
(PERFORMING THE SONGS OF PREFAB SPROUT)

2024

WED 14th AUG GLASGOW SAINT LUKE'S
FRI 16th AUG NEWCASTLE O₂ CITY HALL
SAT 17th AUG MANCHESTER O₂ RITZ
SUN 18th AUG WOLVERHAMPTON WULFRUN HALL
WED 21st AUG BRIGHTON CONCORDE 2
THU 22nd AUG LONDON O₂ SHEPHERD'S BUSH EMPIRE

academyevents & PINK DOT
by arrangement with SPIDER TOURING present

FIRST EVER CO-HEADLINE TOUR

EMF
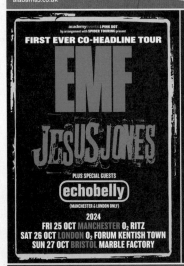

JESUSJONES

PLUS SPECIAL GUESTS
echobelly
(MANCHESTER & LONDON ONLY)

2024
FRI 25 OCT MANCHESTER O₂ RITZ
SAT 26 OCT LONDON O₂ FORUM KENTISH TOWN
SUN 27 OCT BRISTOL MARBLE FACTORY

academyevents
in association with SPIDER TOURING present

THE WEDDING PRESENT

BIZARRO **35th ANNIVERSARY**
Performing the album in its entirety
plus a selection of their greatest hits

FRIDAY 4th OCTOBER 2024
LONDON O₂ SHEPHERD'S BUSH EMPIRE

SATURDAY 5th OCTOBER 2024
LEEDS O₂ ACADEMY

theweddingpresent.co.uk

academyevents presents

INDIE TIL I DIE ...

The Enemy
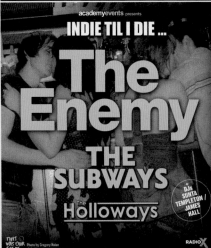

THE SUBWAYS

The **Holloways**

DJs SUNTA TEMPLETON / JAMES HALL

RADIO X

OCTOBER 2024

FRI 04
EDINBURGH
O₂ ACADEMY

SAT 05
GLASGOW
O₂ ACADEMY

FRI 11
NEWCASTLE
O₂ CITY HALL

SAT 12
MANCHESTER
O₂ VICTORIA WAREHOUSE

FRI 18
BIRMINGHAM
O₂ ACADEMY

SAT 19
LONDON
O₂ ACADEMY BRIXTON

THIS WAS OUR SCENE. Photo by Gregory Nolan visit thiswasourscene.com

academyevents & friends presents

ALTERED IMAGES
BITE
B A C K

PERFORMING THE ALBUM
IN ITS ENTIRETY
PLUS A GREATEST HITS SET

2024

SAT 19 OCT
BRIGHTON CONCORDE 2

SUN 20 OCT
BRISTOL O₂ ACADEMY

TUE 22 OCT
GLASGOW ST LUKE'S

WED 23 OCT
LIVERPOOL O₂ ACADEMY2

FRI 25 OCT
EXETER PHOENIX

SAT 26 OCT
STROUD SUBSCRIPTION ROOMS

MON 28 OCT
CAMBRIDGE JUNCTION

TUE 29 OCT
BIRMINGHAM O₂ ACADEMY2

WED 30 OCT
LEEDS BRUDENELL SOCIAL CLUB

FRI 01 NOV
HOLMFIRTH PICTUREDROME

academyevents
by arrangement with CIRCLE SKY presents

UK TOUR 2024

LOVE
WITH **JOHNNY ECHOLS**

PERFORMING DEEP CUTS
AND HIGHLIGHTS FROM THE ALBUMS
LOVE, DA CAPO, FOREVER CHANGES
AND FOUR SAIL

SATURDAY 13th JULY
LIVERPOOL
O₂ ACADEMY2

SATURDAY 20th JULY
LONDON
O₂ SHEPHERD'S
BUSH EMPIRE

PERFORMING
FOREVER CHANGES
with
STRINGS & HORNS

academyevents presents

The Smyths

plus special guest
BILLY BLAGG

National Tour 2024/5

2024
Sat 06 Apr LEEDS O₂ ACADEMY
Sat 25 May BIRMINGHAM O₂ ACADEMY2
Sat 19 Oct LEICESTER O₂ ACADEMY
Fri 25 Oct SHEFFIELD O₂ ACADEMY
Sat 26 Oct LIVERPOOL O₂ ACADEMY
Fri 08 Nov BRISTOL O₂ ACADEMY
Sat 30 Nov MANCHESTER O₂ RITZ
Fri 20 Dec OXFORD O₂ ACADEMY2
Sat 21 Dec BOURNEMOUTH O₂ ACADEMY

2025
Fri 24 Jan NEWCASTLE O₂ CITY HALL

thesmyths.net

academyevents & FEELING GLOOMY presents

The Devout

Depeche mode tribute

2024
Fri 14 Jun Leicester O₂ Academy2
Sat 15 Jun Liverpool O₂ Academy2
Fri 05 Jul Bournemouth O₂ Academy
Fri 12 Jul Bristol O₂ Academy
Fri 26 Jul Birmingham O₂ Academy3
Sat 31 Aug London O₂ Academy Islington

feelinggloomy.com

academyevents
by arrangement with NEIL O'BRIEN ENTERTAINMENT presents

EMILY WOLFE
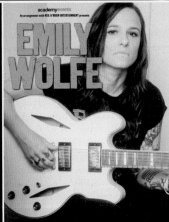

Wed 11th September 2024
O₂ Academy2 Islington, London

TICKETMASTER.CO.UK

Tripping the light fantastic: (from right) Pat Kilroy, Susan Graubard (now Archuletta) and Jeffrey Stewart as The New Age in 1967.

Paul Kagan

CREDITS

Tracks: The Magic Carpet/Roberta's Blues/Cancereal/A Day At The Beach/The Pipes Of Pan/Mississippi Blues/Vibrations/Light Of Day/The Fortune Teller/Canned Heat/The River/Star Dance

Personnel: Pat Kilroy (vocals, bass, guitar, finger cymbals, Jew's harp, glockenspiel); Eric Katz (blues harp); Jim Welch (congas); Susan Graubard (flute, glockenspiel); Stefan Grossman (guitar); Marc Silber (guitar, bass); Bob Amacker (tabla).

Producers: Peter K. Siegel, Jac Holzman (production supervisor)

Released: 1966

Recorded: unknown studio, New York

Current availability: streaming services

Dawn Of Perception

Retrieved from music's vault of the forgotten and slept-on, acid folk's ground zero?

Pat Kilroy
Light Of Day

ELEKTRA, 1966

"HE IS YOUNG, vigorous and wildly experimental," read Gramophone's review of Pat Kilroy's quietly visionary debut LP, perhaps the deepest-set gem in the Elektra catalogue. "I expect we shall hear from him again."

It was not to be the case. Having reacted swearily to the suggestion that the Elektra label might bring in an arranger to decorate a version of Joe Valino's Garden Of Eden planned for a putative second solo album, the enigmatic Kilroy returned to his native California to pursue an even more extreme East-West fusion with The New Age. Their debut album for Warner Bros was all but completed when he discovered that late-stage Hodgkin's lymphoma was the reason behind his constant exhaustion and the mysterious lumps in his body. He died on Christmas Day 1967, aged just 24.

"I was so sorry when he died, and so young," says Susan Archuletta, who as Susan Graubard was Kilroy's musical foil and sometime girlfriend. "We didn't really know anything about cancer in those days. Or illness. We were living on brown rice and veg. What could go wrong?"

Such boundless optimism courses through the one LP Kilroy managed to finish, compromised as Light Of Day is. When he first met the singer, producer Peter K Siegel was sold on Kilroy's multi-octave vocal range and ability to belt out blues standards. He was less enamoured of the interests in esoteric philosophy and Eastern musical scales that made Kilroy's signature tunes – Cancereal, Vibrations, Star Dance and Light Of Day's ecstatic title track – a forgotten prototype for what would come to be known as acid folk.

Archuletta first saw Kilroy singing Child ballads while she was a student at UC Berkeley, then ran into him by accident while he was a chef at the proto-New Age commune in Big Sur now known as the Esalen Institute. Kilroy was struck by her taste for Balinese, Japanese and Middle Eastern music, and – despite barely knowing her – took her to New York in early 1966 to accompany him and tabla player Bob Amacker on Light Of Day.

Unschooled in the kind of loose, improvisational process that forged Kilroy's songs, the classically trained Archuletta needed a degree of chemical assistance to get into their groove ("they gave me a tiny little dose of LSD," she tells MOJO).

After a first recording session for the album, Kilroy and Archuletta crossed the Atlantic in search of traditional music

and unusual instruments. They landed in Iceland, had what Archuletta calls "a rather unsuccessful" meeting with Bert Jansch in London, and then visited Kilroy's ancestral homelands (Ireland and Spain) before venturing into north Africa. All of those elements (plus the glockenspiel they picked up in London) fed into the songs that they brought back to New York.

Siegel, though, got cold feet, insisting that Kilroy record some of his material with an electric blues band, the muscular sound giving tales of spiritual self-discovery like A Day At The Beach and The Pipes Of Pan an oddly leathery heft.

Left to their own devices, Kilroy, Archuletta and Amacker wove rainbows. Archuletta's flute soars through The Magic Carpet as Kilroy accepts an invitation "to float through life's wonder in new peaceful life." Cancereal – a nod to the trio's shared star sign – is a loosely structured ramble, Kilroy singing about being "guided by the light of wonder… to the sea of the unknown." Archuletta's flute and London glockenspiel decorate the skeletal Star Dance while Kilroy's The Fortune Teller yearns for a way out of time: "I'm on the crossroads of tomorrow and yesterday and I want to stop dying and start living today."

The title track is the summit of their achievements, Kilroy foreshadowing the Incredible String Band and John Martyn as he wanders into primordial darkness, certain in his expectation of a new spiritual dawn. "More and more friends are starting to feel a light around that's shining through," he sings, his voice spiralling upwards. "And a voice within that's shouting – shouting to you, saying it's true."

Kilroy was hearing that call from somewhere, even if those around him were not quite sure what the message was. Elektra boss Jac Holzman would damn him with faint praise later, saying Kilroy was "heading in a direction that to some extent I would say Tim Buckley perfected." Kilroy had a similar vocal range, maybe, but his questing spirit and the uncanny arrangements Archuletta helped to create on Light Of Day and with The New Age set a unique course. Their back catalogue is small and frustrating – Light Of Day is strung between two worlds, while The New Age recordings, released in 2006 as All Around, are tantalisingly incomplete. Yet they remain a one-off.

"We were just constantly growing and evolving as musicians," says Archuletta, who also played with Robbie Basho, Mighty Baby and The Habibiyya, and later endured the same British Sufi commune as Richard and Linda Thompson. "I really miss Patrick as a music partner. He was brilliant, a really beautiful singer, I mean, just amazing. I've never met anyone else like him."

Jim Wirth

> "They gave me a tiny little dose of LSD…"
> **SUSAN ARCHULETTA**

BUY • SELL • TRADE

www.reckless.co.uk
recklessrecordsuk@gmail.com
Tel: 020 7437 4271

RECKLESS RECORDS

EST. 1983

Lots of fresh goodies in store every day!
Second-hand and new!
All types of music!

30 Berwick Street
Soho, London
W1F 8RH
10am–7pm, 7 days a week

VINYL • CDs • RARITIES

REMEMBER THAT GREAT FEELING?

Get back on board with your
first four issues for just £2*
when you subscribe to MCN!

SPRING BACK INTO BIKING ACTION NOW WITH MCN

- Gear up & go with the right kit
- Bike reviews to help with your new spring purchase
- All the advice you need to enhance your ride
- Be inspired by our route guides for your next adventure
- Why not do it yourself with our essential bike maintenance tips?
- ✔ Free UK delivery every week to your door
- ✔ Save on shop prices
- ✔ Choose digital access to read on-the-go, plus unlock our past issues archive and access rewards

ORDER NOW TO REAP THE REWARDS!
greatmagazines.co.uk/mcn-offer
Or call 01858 438 884
TERMS AND CONDITIONS APPLY. SEE ONLINE FOR FULL DETAILS

MCN

Love to the people: Curtis Mayfield, the definitive heart and soul man, in 1973.

10 Curtis Mayfield
New World Order
WARNER BROS, 1996

You say: "A heartbreaking listen but the genius is still audible and I love the Organised Noize production." **Martin Baylis, via mojo4music.com**

Paralysed from the neck down, Mayfield carried on writing, singing by lying down and letting gravity press down on his chest and lungs. Recorded line-by-line, assisted by Roger Troutman and TLC/Outkast production team Organized Noize, and with guest Aretha Franklin (on Back To Living Again, crying out "Right on, go ahead Mayfield"), *New World Order* is too long at 60 minutes but the album's highlights are many and the title track, Back To Living Again, Just A Little Bit Of Love and the astonishing Here But I'm Gone (written from the perspective of an ageing crack addict) all possess a laid-back Atlanta groove that has aged exceptionally well.

4 Curtis Mayfield
Back To The World
CURTOM, 1973

You say: "Curtis's answer to *What's Going On,* a layered and thoughtful album that rewards repeated listening." **@EddieRobson via X**

Recording with a new band after bidding farewell to arranger Johnny Pate and guitarist Craig McMullen, deep in a well of paranoia following his failure to win a Grammy for *Super Fly*, *Back To The World* is Mayfield's anti-Vietnam LP. Touring army bases he'd hear the phrase spoken by soldiers returning home and wrote this semi-concept LP about a veteran faced with no job, no woman, no money. Low key, bitter, melancholy, it's also a lean, attenuated album, closer to the high-frequency sibilancies of disco than funk. But it's also a subtly seductive sound, with Phil Upchurch's chicken-scratch guitar and Rich Tufo's melancholic strings all swirling under the surface of Mayfield's forlorn falsetto.

Curtis Mayfield

Taking nothing less than the supreme best. By Andrew Male.

IT'S FAIR to say that in 2024 Curtis Mayfield is still underrated. The Chicago-born singer-songwriter, producer, guitarist and record label boss died back in 1999, aged just 57, after having spent a whole decade as a quadriplegic, paralysed from the neck down after a stage lighting rig fell on him at an outdoor concert in Brooklyn in August 1990. That decade-long slide into silence may have had something to do with it, but even within rock and soul literature he's never mentioned in the same breath as Stevie Wonder, Al Green, Sly Stone, Aretha Franklin, James Brown or Marvin Gaye, though he arguably achieved more than all of them.

Raised in poverty, a high-school drop-out and teenage gospel singer in his grandmother's church, Mayfield formed The Impressions with high-school friend Jerry Butler in 1956, aged just 14. Blending soul melodies with gospel harmonies, politically conscious lyrics, and a distinctive, self-taught rhythm-guitar style (influenced by Andrés Segovia) that would come to influence Jimi Hendrix, The Impressions had a string of Top 20 US chart hits before Mayfield left the group in 1969 to go solo and concentrate on his just-launched record label, Curtom. As songwriter, composer, producer, A&R man, and CEO, Mayfield created a powerful soul stable at Curtom, re-

leasing a string of great albums, many co-written and produced by himself. In fact, an alternate How To Buy could be compiled solely from LPs Mayfield produced and co-wrote during that time, including Gladys Knight & The Pips' *Claudine*, Aretha Franklin's *Sparkle*, The Staple Singers' *Let's Do It Again*, Baby Huey's *The Living Legend*. But with this How To Buy, we've decided to concentrate on the albums that best expressed his individual talents and encapsulated Mayfield's genius, albums that expressed the hope and pain, the pride and prejudice of African-American life and did so with a defiant, unifying power but also a rare poetic vulnerability. In concentrating on those long-players we've ignored best-ofs. That's partly because streaming has done away with the need for a standard best-of, but also because there is still so much in the Mayfield vaults that is in need of a definitive archive box set. He's more than deserving of the gesture. For, more than Stevie Wonder, more than Marvin Gaye, Al Green, Aretha Franklin, Sly Stone or James Brown, the music of Curtis Mayfield captures the duality of the Black American experience; the highs, the lows, the euphoria and the depression. A vision of the world, as he sang on Right On For The Darkness, "that put its heavy weight on me".

> "The music of Curtis Mayfield captures the duality of the Black American experience."

Alamy, Levy/Dalle/eyevine

CAST YOUR VOTES...

This month you chose your Top 10 Curtis Mayfield LPs. Next month we want your Durutti Column Top 10. Send your selections via X, Facebook, Instagram or e-mail to mojo@bauermedia.co.uk with the subject 'How To Buy The Durutti Column' and we'll print the best comments.

9 The Impressions
Keep On Pushing
ABC-PARAMOUNT, 1964

You say: "Was there a more beautiful vocal trio than Mayfield, Cash and Gooden? Just heavenly." Carey Lake, via e-mail

One of the great soul albums of the early 1960s. Mayfield wrote the gospel-soul title track "to help motivate the people" after seeing the divisions in the Civil Rights movement, but what astonishes is how emotionally coherent the entire album is. That's largely down to the beautifully arranged vocal harmonies from Fred Cash and Sam Gooden but also the standard of the other tracks, from the haunting torch song I've Been Trying and the gospel-march of Amen, to soul confessional I Made A Mistake and declamatory call-and-response floor-filler I Love You (Yeah). Also, it's one of the great early showcases for Mayfield's exceptional (and hugely influential) open F# guitar style.

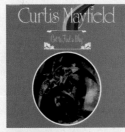

8 Curtis Mayfield
Got To Find A Way
CURTOM, 1974

You say: "His most overlooked album, IMO and the one I thrust on friends who only know him for *Super Fly*." Ian Benson, via mojo4music.com

In 1974 Mayfield made three great studio albums: *Sweet Exorcist*, the film soundtrack *Claudine* (cut with Gladys Knight & The Pips), and *Got To Find A Way*. Overworked, exhausted, feeling that the mood of the country had changed, these LPs are more personal than political. *Got To Find A Way* is arguably his most emotionally complex, weighted with disillusionment where songs of seductive eroticism sit next to despairing heartbreakers (So You Don't Love Me), Impressions gospel soul (A Prayer) is now imbued with weariness, and the sole political song (Cannot Find A Way) is a political songwriter admitting defeat. The biggest flop of his career to that point.

7 The Impressions
The Young Mods' Forgotten Story
CURTOM, 1969

You say: "A perfect album, sleeve, title, contents. My Deceiving Heart is his most beautiful performance. It's glorious." Natural Conker, @bookworm_north via X

In 1968 Mayfield abandoned The Impressions' dual vocal style and wrote a song from the heart that addressed the deaths of Martin Luther King and Robert Kennedy. This Is My Country changed the direction of the group forever, allied Mayfield with Black Power and informed two great records, *This Is My Country* and 1969's *Young Mods...* Recorded in the wake of the student protests at the 1968 Chicago Democratic National Convention, *Mods* is the most focused of the two and its cover, Mayfield modelling his long, leather German overcoat, is a statement of stylish defiance in and of itself.

6 Curtis Mayfield
Curtis
CURTOM, 1970

You say: "The pivotal album between The Impressions and his stellar solo career. Sounds like a greatest hits album." Judah Warsky, @JudahWar via X

Midway through recording The Impressions' thirteenth studio LP *Check Out Your Mind!*, Mayfield announced he was quitting. Yet while the growling eight-minute apocalyptic acid-funk of (Don't Worry) If There's A Hell Below, We're All Going To Go and the exultant positivity of the nine-minute Move On Up signalled a more defiantly political songwriter, much of this solo debut is low-key psychedelic soul, still rooted in the sorrowful sound of late-era Impressions. That's not to say The Other Side Of Town's string-laden ghetto melancholy, and We The People...'s questions of self-identity aren't exquisite exercises, but there would be stronger solo Curtis albums to come.

5 Curtis Mayfield
Roots
CURTOM, 1971

You say: "He really finds a different voice with this album, and the music is just sublime. Deeply contemplative." Johnny Mains, @ohsinnerman via X

Working with a tight, road-hardened band, Mayfield's second solo album is the sound of a naturally reflective artist reinvigorated. Beginning with the dancefloor sensuality of Get Down, *Roots* is, for the most part, one of his most hopeful solo LPs, best encapsulated in the infectious anti-war anthem We Got To Have Peace and the epic Black Power groove Beautiful Brother Of Mine. Of course, it wouldn't be a Mayfield album without a touch of dark introspection, and he nails it in the dystopian groove of Underground, and Keep On Keeping On which looks at black society in 1971 and says: "Many think that we have blown it/But... there's still a lot of love among us."

3 Curtis Mayfield
Super Fly
CURTOM, 1972

You say: "The film would have been immeasurably reduced without this marriage of lyrical heaviness and soaring funky orchestral tightness." @boscobel19751 via X

In late 1971, when Curtis was sent the script for Gordon Parks Jr's urban noir Super Fly, the term 'blaxploitation' was still in its infancy. Today, it's clear Mayfield's quality control was higher than Parks'. With Johnny Pate, Mayfield crafted a masterpiece that invests this low-budget street thriller with an almost auteurist narrative, each of his driving two-chord falsetto raps (Pusherman; Superfly; Freddie's Dead; Little Child...) giving the film's two-dimensional characters much-needed depth and humanity. And Pate's dazzlingly intricate arrangements, cut with a live orchestra, invest Mayfield's street tales with an eerie, kaleidoscopic richness.

2 Curtis Mayfield
Curtis/Live!
CURTOM, 1971

You say: "You're actually *there* in The Bitter End... unlike some live LPs, the audience reactions actually enhances the listening experience." @Henrypriestman via X

Recorded during a bitterly cold January in 1971, in New York's cramped Bitter End, *Curtis/Live!* is a classic act of Mayfield mercurialness, the unveiling of a new band for their first ever dates documented on a double LP. Comprised solely of guitarist Craig McMullen, bassist Joseph Scott, drummer Tyrone McCullen and percussionist 'Master' Henry Gibson, this might be one of the greatest live albums ever released, not for its power but for its pared-down intimacy. Witness the way Mayfield and band subtly transform the Carpenters' We've Only Just Begun into an inclusive Black Power anthem before sweetly segueing into The Impressions' People Get Ready. Perfection.

1 Curtis Mayfield
There's No Place Like America Today
CURTOM, 1975

You say: "A funereal, seven-song state-of-the-union blues. Perfect." James Caig, @jamescaig via X

According to his son Todd's exemplary Curtis biography/memoir Traveling Soul, There's No Place... was written in Atlanta in 1975 during two weeks of depression. "It was a long way from *Super Fly*," said Curtis himself, "a hard look at some of the things that sour our life experience." A concept album about the parlous state of modern America and Mayfield's own fragile mental health, *TNPLAT* is an understated masterpiece. Arrangements are chilly and sparse, rhythms slow and laid back, with Mayfield's falsetto intimate and confessional. We get pulled in to these slowly unfolding, long-form tales of murder (Billy Jack), depression (When Seasons Change; Blue Monday People), romance (So In Love), prayer (Jesus), paranoia (Hard Times) and poverty (Love To The People). Suffused in vulnerability and defeat, it might also be his most confident album, utterly certain of its lyrical message and its sedate, slow-burn power.

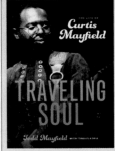

NOW DIG THIS

For an overview of Mayfield's '60s writing and production work, track down *Curtis Mayfield's Chicago Soul* (Okeh, 1995). For his work at Curtom, the 3-CD *The Curtom Story – We're A Winner*, is essential. As for Mayfield albums that didn't make the cut, there are too many but they should include 1974's *Sweet Exorcist*, raw-edged 1977 soundtrack *Short Eyes*, and 1980's gorgeous Philly-style soul-disco outing *Something To Believe In*. Also, Mayfield's influence on Jamaican music gets a showcase with the vital Trojan Records compilation, *I'm So Proud (A Jamaican Tribute To Curtis Mayfield)*. We're still waiting for the definitive documentary on Mayfield, while the only biography that does the great man justice is Traveling Soul (Chicago Review Press, 2018) written by his son, Todd Mayfield with Travis Atria.

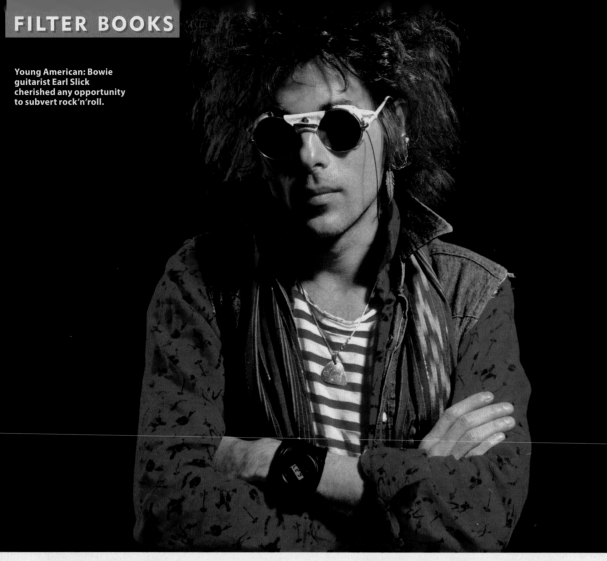

Young American: Bowie guitarist Earl Slick cherished any opportunity to subvert rock'n'roll.

WHAT WE'VE LEARNT

● Slick met Bowie via ex-Julliard student Michael Kamen. Taking the guitarist under his wing, Kamen sent him to audition for Dr. John, had him roadie for his band before inviting him to join – alongside future Bowie associate David Sanborn. Early in 1974, Kamen told Slick, "I've got an audition for you with something that's pretty serious…"

● Slick, born Frank Madeloni, acquired his nickname by virtue of his Brooklyn accent. Jack O'Neill, frontman for Slick's first serious band Beau Jack, misheard the guitarist commenting on an oil slick that had hit New York Harbour. "It's oil slick, not earl slick!" he chided.

● Backstage during the early part of the *Diamond Dogs* tour, new boy Slick and Bowie would discuss their mutual love for R&B and soul. One time, Slick enthused about Eddie Floyd's Knock On Wood. By the end of the first leg of the tour, in Philadelphia, July 1974, Knock On Wood was introduced into the set.

● Stay began as a reworked version of John, I'm Only Dancing. "[David] asked me to come up with a riff and it turned out to be a total monster."

My name is Earl

Breezy memoir from Bowie's key guitarist. By Mark Paytress.

Guitar: Playing With David Bowie, John Lennon And Rock And Roll's Greatest Heroes

★★★

Earl Slick with Jeff Slate

PENGUIN MICHAEL JOSEPH, £25

A STRUGGLING YOUNG guitarist gets the nod in 1974 to attend a big-name audition. He is met by an inscrutable young PA named Coco, invited into a darkened studio and asked to play along to several backing tracks.

Twenty minutes later, in walks a skinny, pale figure, "dressed the way an English rock star might think a Harlem pimp would dress". It's David Bowie, in need of a guitarist for his first touring band since the Spiders.

The next day, 22-year-old Earl Slick is invited to Bowie's hotel suite and given the go-ahead. What he hadn't expected was a makeover: a hairdresser removed his long locks, a stylist put him in a 1940s-style suit. Slick, whose ideal was Keith Richards, felt ashamed. Musically, though, he was a great fit. Five tours, five studio albums and two live albums pay testament to his importance in the Bowie universe. Between 1974 and his work on *The Next Day* (2013), Slick was called back half a dozen times – usually by Coco or the management, rarely by Bowie. He was never officially dropped; it's just that things would go silent for a few years.

Understandably, as his breezy, anecdotal memoir confirms, this played havoc with Slick's various attempts to ignite his own career. Neither writer nor frontman, Slick's forte was as a flash, fearless sideman who played loud rock'n'roll and cherished any opportunity to subvert it. That was Bowie all over.

Initially, Slick was regarded as a bridge between the Mick Ronson era and Bowie's incoming Americanised sound. He then devised intros for Young Americans and Golden Years and played at the Bowie/Lennon session. But the pair struck gold while working on *Station To Station*, "one of the true highlights of my career," Slick writes. "David pulled shit out of me that I didn't even know was there."

The title track marked a memorable moment in the pair's working relationship. "We spent more time on that solo than I've ever done on any record in my life," Slick recalls. "We were both in a cocaine haze, so we'd just keep working until we were done," sometimes up to 24 hours later.

After an interlude that included working on John and Yoko's *Double Fantasy* – a more orderly affair with breaks for fine sushi – Slick got the call for Bowie's 1983 Serious Moonlight tour.

After that, his personal life darkened with addiction, a car crash and hit rock bottom in 1988. By 1992 he was selling timeshares and declining offers of work from Prince, Joe Cocker and David Coverdale. Things were different the day Bowie called, just before Christmas 1999. He wanted his old stage foil to join his new band for a mini tour the following June. "David was a lot softer," Slick recalls. "He wasn't as intense. Sobriety will do that."

Later, Slick witnessed Bowie's collapse during the *Reality* tour. He was also present at sessions for 2013's *The Next Day*. During a playback of (You Will) Set The World On Fire, Bowie exclaimed: "Man, that would be great live!" Slick, not always privy to Bowie's innermost thoughts, knew David was never going out again. "I could see it in his eyes."

> "Slick's forte was as a flash, fearless sideman who played loud rock'n'roll…"

Getty/John Kisch Archive

CRATEDIGGERS ASSEMBLE!

THE MOJO RECORD CLUB PODCAST

Join ANDREW MALE and his famous guests as they hunt down unheralded gems, reconsider classic albums and bring you the very best new music. Listen now to episodes starring R.E.M., THE WATERBOYS, IDLES, TOYAH WILLCOX & ROBERT FRIPP, JIM O'ROURKE, RICKIE LEE JONES, SONIC YOUTH, DEXYS, THE CORAL, NATALIE MERCHANT and many more.

AVAILABLE ON APPLE, SPOTIFY, PLANET RADIO, AND ALL YOUR REGULAR PODCAST PLACES.

SCAN ME
TO LISTEN

MOJO's definitive companion
Depeche Mode's albums, songs,
...s and books. Available Now!

MOJO THE COLLECTORS' SERIES

New!

Depeche
Mode Essentials

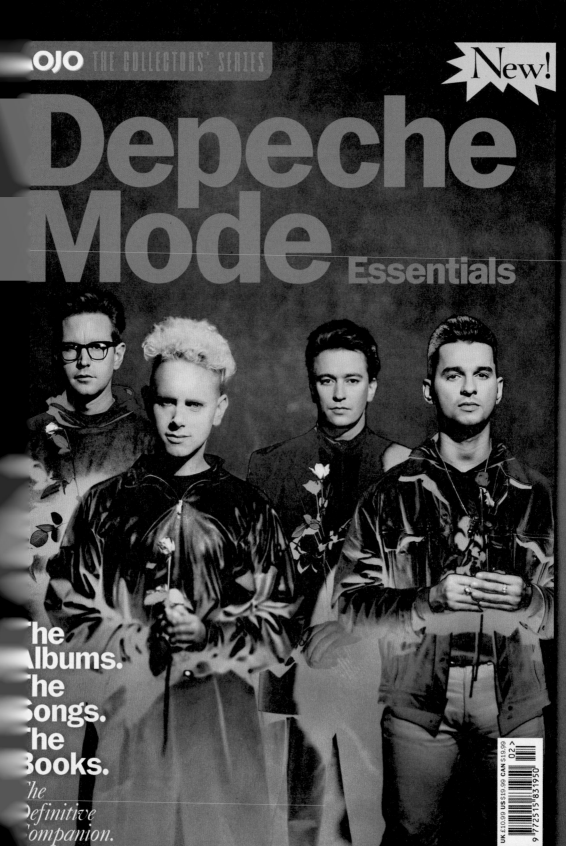

The
Albums.
The
Songs.
The
Books.

The
Definitive
Companion.

UK £10.99   US $19.99   CAN $19.99

02

9 772515 831950

Destiny Stopped Screaming: The Life And Times Of Adrian Borland

★★★★

Simon Heavisides

STICHTING OPPOSITE DIRECTION. £23

Assiduously researched biography of The Sound's frontman.

Heavisides' book is compelling from the first page as he combines his own interviews with Borland and his friends and family, with press cuttings and lyrics to build a multifaceted picture of the singer and guitarist who died by suicide in 1999. Crucially, it's a celebration of Borland's talent, and charts The Sound's journey from their 1979 formation through the '80s when they were signed and dropped by WEA and always operated in the shadows of U2 and the Bunnymen. The author chronicles Borland's deteriorating mental state with perception and sensitivity, noting how difficult it was to fully understand what was going on then or even with hindsight. But even as a troubled solo artist Borland had a near obsessive creative drive. He told The Limit magazine in 1998: "It's terrible to walk around with 40 songs in my mind; sooner or later my head explodes if I don't record them."

Mike Barnes

Neu Klang: The Definitive History Of Krautrock

★★★

Christoph Dallach

FABER. £25

Oral history of Germany's Kosmische Musik.

At one point here, Amon Düül II's Renate Knaup finds members of the Baader-Meinhof terrorist group sleeping unbidden in her communal home. Furious, she sends them packing. Compiled by German journalist Dallach, this first-person narrative is most remarkable when it moves beyond music. Can's Irmin Schmidt and Hans-Joachim Roedelius of Cluster and Harmonia were born in the 1930s, growing up in Nazi Germany. They and others speak in detail of the darkness that contaminated their childhood. It's laudable that Dallach builds the book on his own interviews, but this means only Karl Bartos represents Kraftwerk, while a 30-page section solely on the record industry figure Rolf-Ulrich Kaiser seems too marginal even for such wonderfully cult terrain. Overall, though, with Can's Schmidt dismissing the "abysmally stupid" Andreas Baader along the way, this is a substantial and valuable adjunct to the growing Krautrock bibliography.

Roy Wilkinson

Dream Machines: Electronic Music From Doctor Who To Acid House

★★★★

Matthew Collin

OMNIBUS PRESS. £25

First-hand testimonies pepper insightful, no-stone-unturned history of UK electronic music.

In Dream Machines, Altered State and Rave On author Matthew Collin meticulously traces British electronic music's back history via Daphne Oram and the BBC Radiophonic Workshop through Joe Meek, The Beatles, Pink Floyd, Bowie and Hawkwind, its many insights backed up by interviews with movers and shakers. The most illuminating chapters are on the least reported genres (electro, early UK hip-hop, hi-NRG, noise, power electronics), Collin's even-handed approach giving equal weight to cassette culture outliers such as Nocturnal Emissions and Muslimgauze as more obvious names. Contextualised via the clubs and drugs of the time, he repeatedly shows how technology – or its limitations – is transformative in the right hands, as a trail of unfancied outsiders turn mainstream game-changers. The book ends as the '90s begin, but the diverse culture it begets surely begs a second volume.

Andy Cowan

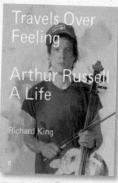

Travels Over Feeling: Arthur Russell, A Life

★★★★

Richard King

FABER. £30

The immense archive of a pioneering polyglot opens wide to more mystery.

"Mortality plays funny tricks," multi-instrumentalist and composer Peter Gordon opines late in this loving attempt to untangle the creative drive and tragic end of Arthur Russell, one of the late 20th century's most borderless musical minds. Gordon is talking about the belief Russell was predestined to be famous, that his concurrent forays into songcraft, disco, and experimental composition would make him a star. But he only came to widespread attention after his death from Aids in April 1992, less a star than an air of inspiration. King diligently explored Russell's gargantuan archive, stitching poignant ephemera – love letters and wistful postcards, working scores and candid photos – alongside an oral history built from conversations with Russell's collaborators and confidants. Russell's dogged work ethic and singular focus drift into view, but what's most astonishing is how he remained a mystery even to those who knew him best, his mind always churning through ideas for what came next.

Grayson Haver Currin

Chopping Wood: Thoughts & Stories Of A Legendary American Folksinger

★★★★

Pete Seeger with David Bernz

JAWBONE PRESS. £16.95

Reminiscences from the father of the folk boom.

Few have earned the title "legend" as deservedly as the late Pete Seeger. Songs he popularised include We Shall Overcome, Where Have All The Flowers Gone, Guantanamera and If I Had A Hammer. He courageously refused to name names when subpoenaed by a congressional committee rooting out communists, which he admits he was for a time. He inspired generations of singer-songwriters, notably Dylan, Baez and Springsteen. This inspiring book collects century-long memories, divided into categories: Woody Guthrie, banjo, politics, philosophy and more, and includes sketches, lyrics and recollections by Steve Earle and others. Revelations include his take on Newport '65's skirmish: never a purist, he didn't object to Dylan's electric guitar – Seeger simply worried the volume would keep his own elderly father from hearing young Bob's lyrics. His lifelong worldview maintained the still-topical beliefs that small eclipses big and that the arts can prevent conflict.

Michael Simmons

A Dysfunctional Success: The Wreckless Eric Manual

★★★★

Eric Goulden

VENTIL VERLAG. £22

Stiff oddball's Whole Wild World of pain.

Eric Goulden entered into something like pop legend when he dropped a home recording of his Kevin Ayers-inspired signature tune Whole Wild World into Stiff Records' London office with the words, "I'm one of those cunts that brings tapes into record companies." Shame-faced and clear-sighted, his grisly memoir – first published in 2003 – details his transformation from hard-drinking art school graduate and ex-banana grader into what NME called "a belligerent alcoholic dwarf". A Dysfunctional Success blacks out for the worst of Wreckless Eric's Stiff years, but goes in deep and hard on the period of "serious depressive drinking" that followed in the early 1980s, as Goulden struggled to keep afloat with Medway-based bands The Captains Of Industry and The Len Bright Combo. "I wanted to write about what happens when the firework fizzles out," explains the resilient Goulden in a new introduction. A suitably sobering account.

Jim Wirth

Cello-man: Arthur Russell – one of the late 20th century's most borderless musical minds.

Tom Lee/Arthur Russell Estate

Getty, Michael Putland

THE LEGACY

The Album:
Cockney Rebel:
The Psychomodo
(EMI, 1974)
The Sound: Make
Me Smile will
forever be Harley's
calling card, but *The
Psychomodo* album
better encapsulates
his gifts. It's more
innovative, dramatic,
lavish and playful
(even knowingly
preposterous at
times), a bejewelled
glam rock universe
unto itself which
climaxes with
ecstatic finale
Tumbling Down,
Harley's very own
Hey Jude.

**Rebel with a cause:
Steve Harley in
1976.**

Behind The Smile

Cockney Rebel's Steve Harley
took his final bow on March 17.

INITIALLY, STEVE HARLEY was known for his
assurance, self-possession and drive as well
as his accomplishments as a songwriter. In
his first Melody Maker interview, he claimed,
"There's a buzz in Cockney Rebel saying we're
on the brink of being big, being leaders... a
musical force that others will follow."

But like Marc Bolan, Harley was inspired
not only by rampant self-belief and a wild,
onomatopoeic style of wordplay but what he
envisaged as a new sound for a new age. Born
Stephen Nice in Deptford, south London, on
February 27, 1951, Harley endured childhood
polio and frequent hospitalisation, which he
says only strengthened his
resolve to succeed, and gave
him ample time to lose
himself in music and poetry.
He later worked as a journalist
on local newspapers, but
music took hold, first as
co-singer and rhythm
guitarist for folk-rockers Odin
before Cockney Rebel,
formed with Odin violinist
John-Paul Crocker.

> **"He
> envisaged
> a new
> sound for a
> new age."**

Harley conceived Cockney Rebel
as an electric guitar-free zone, led
instead by Crocker's violin and
Milton Reame-James's electric
piano alongside his own stylised
camp delivery; a modern-day
version of Harley's beloved Weimar
cabaret scene, which chimed
perfectly with glam rock. It was
Europe that first succumbed; 1973's
debut single Sebastian – an OTT
seven-minute epic complete with orchestra
and choir – was a huge hit in the Lowlands,
but flatlined at home; likewise Cockney
Rebel's debut album *The Human Menagerie*.

1974 changed all that. Trimmed-down
singles Judy Teen and Mr Soft went Top 5 and
10 respectively, followed by
Top 10 album *The Psychomodo*.
When Harley refused his
bandmates' demands for a
share of the songwriting,
though, all except drummer
Stuart Elliott walked.
Undeterred, Harley formed a
new Rebel within weeks, and
wrote Make Me Smile (Come
Up And See Me) about the
mutiny, complete with guitar

solo. Revenge was sweet when the
single leapt to Number 1 in the UK
and across Europe.

Another Top 5 hit, Cockney
Rebel's third album *The Best Years Of
Our Lives* was well named. Harley
only ever breached the Top 10 again
with Rebel's cover of The Beatles'
Here Comes The Sun in 1976 and,
after going solo, the title song from
Andrew Lloyd Webber's The
Phantom Of The Opera in 1986,
co-sung with Sara Brightman.
His self-confidence shattered,
Harley admitted to a drug phase
("the bulk of my success went up my nose,"
he said, not forgetting 300 acid trips), and
though he starred as 16th century playwright
Christopher Marlowe in the musical drama
Marlowe, Harley's new career stalled when
Michael Crawford replaced him at the
last minute in The Phantom Of The Opera's
stage version.

Only releasing music sporadically
thereafter, Harley found other guises:
house-husband dad, racehorse owner, BBC
Radio 2 Sounds Of The '70s presenter and
regular touring performer, bolstered by Make
Me Smile's ongoing success, whilst his
interviews took on a relaxed demeanour.
"I know who I am now and I like it," he said.
"I'm not worried any more."

Martin Aston

Karl Wallinger

World Party chief and Waterboy.
BORN 1957

"I'M PERCEIVED as quite serious," Karl Wallinger once said, but the green politics central to World Party's 1990 masterpiece *Goodbye Jumbo* didn't preclude joyful music, and Wallinger's zany, Goons-via-The-Fabs sense of humour was his default. Noting his one-man-band skills, Q called him "the new Prince", while his 1997 ballad She's The One permeated deep after a UK Number 1 cover by Robbie Williams. "That song wrote itself," Wallinger told this writer. "I tried to make it as long-zoom as possible. She didn't even have a name."

Born Karl Edmond De Vere Wallinger in Prestatyn, north Wales, he studied piano and oboe at Surrey public school Charterhouse ("awful, elitist people") before escaping to London. He became MD of The Rocky Horror Picture Show, worked at ATV Music Publishing, and briefly played with future members of The Alarm before joining The Waterboys on keyboards in 1983. Wallinger made incisive contributions to 1984's *A Pagan Place* and 1985's *This Is The Sea*, but formed World Party (initially a one-man operation) in 1986 after scoring a solo deal with Ensign. Prince's manager Steve Fargnoli handled Wallinger, and *Goodbye Jumbo* follow-up *Bang!* peaked at UK Number 2 in July 1993. Top 20 hit Is It Like Today? tapped Bertrand Russell's philosophy, but off-camera,

Wallinger still made merry, hence Lennon-esque pastiche I'm Only Dozing. The 2001 brain aneurysm he suffered while holidaying with his family left him unable to work until 2006, but courageously, Wallinger regained full capacity and began playing live again. "I'd love a return to form like Dylan's *Oh Mercy*," he told this writer in 2012, while, interviewed for MOJO in 2021, he claimed to be "quite far advanced with a new album."

It wasn't to be. Wallinger died at his home in Hastings on March 10. The Waterboys' Mike Scott paid tribute, calling him, "one of the finest musicians I've ever known."

James McNair

Jimmy Hastings

Canterbury reedsman.
BORN 1938

IN 1969, JIMMY Hastings played the mellifluous flute on the aptly-named Love Song With Flute on the debut album by Caravan, the Canterbury jazz-rockers led by his younger brother Pye. The group's "fifth member" and occasional live musician, he played on all their albums until 1976; within that same scene, he also contributed to Soft Machine's *Third* and *Fourth*, every album by National Health, and *The Rotters' Club* by Hatfield And The North. He also played with the BBC Radio Orchestra, accompanied singers including Aretha Franklin, Frank Sinatra and Tony Bennett, played in West End musicals, was Professor of Jazz Saxophone at the London College Of Music, and took part in Caravan reunions during the '90s. His session credits, meanwhile, included recordings for Bryan Ferry, Amy Winehouse, Ultramarine, The Bevis Frond, and, as part of Humphrey Lyttelton's group, Radiohead's 2001 album *Amnesiac*.

Ian Harrison

Gylan Kain

Fiery rap progenitor
BORN 1942

INSPIRED BY the thundering oratories of Pentecostal church services and Shakespeare, Gylan Kain's rhythmic recitals paved the way for hip-hop. The Harlem-born poet, playwright and actor founded East Village's Far East Theater in 1965 but divined a more direct route to black consciousness by mixing free verse with jazz via the Beats-inspired Last Poets. Kain split before 1970's self-titled LP to issue ballsy solo debut *The Blue Guerrilla*, his brimstone raps backed by a percussively bold mish-mash of free jazz, stormy blues and way-out funk, featuring teenage guitarist Nile Rodgers. Kain briefly reunited with ex-bandmates for 1971's *Right On!* soundtrack but pursued thespian ambitions either side of relocating to Amsterdam in 1984. Widely sampled (that's him on The

Well versed: poet, playwright and actor Gylan Kain.

Prodigy's Voodoo People and Dr Dre's The Chronic), Kain's theatrical flow resurfaced on 1997's *Feel This* (as Baby Kain) and on Dutch fusionists Electric Barbarian's *él* in 2004. He died from heart disease.

Andy Cowan

Vince Power

Impresario, music-lover
BORN 1947

FROM Kilmacthomas in County Waterford, Vince Power moved to London aged just 16. After founding a successful secondhand furniture business, in 1982 he opened Harlesden venue the Mean Fiddler, which specialised in country and Irish music. In the decades that followed, he ran London venues including the Forum, the Astoria, the Jazz Café, Subterania and Dingwalls. He also promoted festivals, modernising Reading in '89, and going on to organise events including Phoenix, the Sex Pistols' 1996 reunion, Tribal Gathering, Benicàssim, Madstock, Hop Farm and the Fleadh at Finsbury Park, though putting on Jerry Lee Lewis, Bob Dylan, Ray Charles and Van Morrison at Tramore Racecourse in 1993 left him with debts of millions (when Hop Farm collapsed in 2012, Power said he had to live on a canal boat). He also lent his talents to Glastonbury when it was in danger of losing its licence in the early '90s, accepted an honorary CBE for services to the music industry in 2006, and admitted that he wished he could have promoted Elvis. Among those paying tribute was Hang Wangford, who called Power, "a wonderful, wonderful man."

Ian Harrison

Worlds apart: Karl Wallinger was one of the finest musicians Mike Scott has ever known.

"Gylan Kain's rhythmic recitals paved the way for hip-hop."

Martyn Goodacre/Getty Images, Graham Quick/Shutterstock, Nick Cunard/Shutterstock, Gie Knaeps/Getty Images

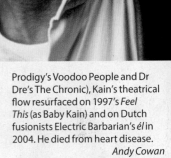

Power player: All By Myself writer/singer Eric Carmen in the mid '70s.

Eric Carmen
Classic pop hitmaker
BORN 1949

A PIONEERING and talented songwriter who drew inspiration from the '60s and parlayed it into an entire musical sub-genre, Ohio-born Eric Carmen was the man who arguably created 'powerpop'. If that category can seem ill-defined, the music he created with his '70s band the Raspberries and as a solo artist remains pure and near visionary.

That vision was evident from the start via the Raspberries' 1972 debut album, which bore a picture of an aggressively retro-looking black-clad quartet, a raspberry-scented scratch'n'sniff sticker, and one of the finest opening tracks of the era, the Carmen-penned Go All The Way. The song said it all: catchy, chorused vocals, fierce lead guitar riffing, and an exceptional melody drawing from The Beatles, The Beach Boys, The Who, and all who came before them.

There would be three more Raspberries albums, and such agreeably fab hits as I Wanna Be With You, Tonight, Ecstasy and the stunning, castanet-laden Overnight Sensation (Hit Record). Then in 1975 the band broke up. After being pursued by label exec Clive Davis, Carmen signed a solo deal with Arista and successfully went the soft-rock route. Out of the box, Carmen scored with two Rachmaninoff-inspired ballads – All

By Myself (a hit for Celine Dion in 1997) and Never Gonna Fall In Love Again – but after 1980's Tonight You're Mine, he'd fall off the label roster entirely.

Signed to Geffen Records, Carmen next found success with songs for movies, co-writing 1984's Almost Paradise, from Footloose, and in 1987, singing Hungry Eyes from Dirty Dancing. After 1988's US Number 3 Make Me Lose Control, his career momentum slowed. Like other once-celebrated artists, he'd later enjoy acclaim as part of Ringo Starr's All Starr Band, likely thrilled in the year 2000 to be accompanying the drummer whose group inspired him to pick up a guitar in the first place.
Dave DiMartino

Jim Beard
Dan keysman and more
BORN 1960

AGED 16, Pennsylvania-born Jim Beard was tutored by George Shearing, and later played in bar bands while studying jazz in Indiana. He moved to New York aged 25 to play with John McLaughlin's re-formed Mahavishnu Orchestra. In the next two decades Beard also began a long creative relationship with Wayne Shorter, joined the groups of John Scofield and Pat Metheny, wrote and produced widely, and

recorded solo LPs including the acclaimed Song Of The Sun, released on CTI in 1991. The year after sharing a Grammy for Randy and Michael Brecker's Some Skunk Funk in 2007, he joined Steely Dan as touring keyboardist, also appearing with Donald Fagen's live shows for The Nightfly and with the Fagen/Boz Scaggs/Michael McDonald live show The Dukes Of September. He also formed a duo with guitarist Jon Herington, taught internationally, and played sessions for names including Bob Berg, Madeleine Peyroux and Mike Stern.
Ian Harrison

Malcolm Holcombe
The roughest of diamonds
BORN 1955

HIS SONGWRITING was beloved of Steve Earle, John Prine, Shelby Lynne and Emmylou Harris, and although his records never took off, it was playing live where Malcolm Holcombe really gripped your soul. A mesmeric performer, he wove spells that turned any room into a remote wooded mountain shack. Born in Weaverville, North Carolina, his 1994 solo debut A Far Cry From Here scored him a contract with Geffen Records, but the planned album was shelved even as critics who'd received promo copies raved about it. Holcombe eventually released the record as A Hundred Lies two years later, remaining resolutely independent over another 16 albums. His sandpaper baritone

and soulful, bluesy country guitar were the blueprint for hordes of post-millennium, Americana-leaning singer-songwriters, but few matched his sustained intensity. A pure and true 'lifer' musician, Holcombe was still performing his online Shed Sessions, often hooked up to oxygen, just weeks before his death from cancer-related respiratory failure.
Andy Fyfe

Johnny Gentle
Fabs-connected pop crooner
BORN 1936

LIVERPOOL-BORN John Askew worked in carpentry and sang on cruise ships – his stage names included George Baker and Ricky Damone – before coming to the attention of British rock'n'roll impresario Larry Parnes after winning a talent show at the Streatham Locarno. He was duly re-christened Johnny Gentle and took his place alongside Marty Wilde, Billy Fury, Vince Eager, Dickie Pride and others in the Parnes stable. Though Johnny Gentle would not enjoy success with his '59 to '61 solo output, a share in immortality became his when The Silver Beetles served as his backing group on a Scottish tour in May 1960, and at a one-off gig in Wallasey soon after. The singer recalled John Lennon helping him finish his song I've Just Fallen For Someone, which he recorded as Darren Young in 1962. He later returned to joinery, appeared at Beatles cons, and published 1998 memoir First Ever Tour of his brush with The Beatles.
Ian Harrison

Johnny Gentle, AKA John Askew, was backed by The Silver Beetles in 1960.

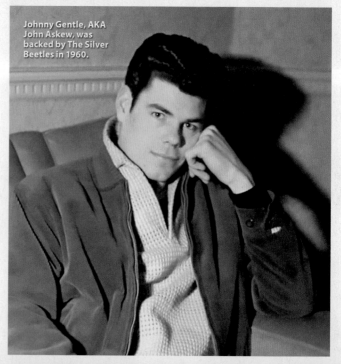

Koh Hasebe/Shinko Music/Getty Images, Erika Goldring/Getty Images, Sophie Le Roux/Dalle/Eyevine, Pictorial Press Ltd/Alamy Stock Photo

B.B. Seaton

Gaylads' singer, facilitator
BORN 1944

BEST KNOWN as leader of Jamaican hitmakers The Gaylads, B.B. Seaton made his contribution to reggae's development as an audition supervisor at Studio One, enabling Lee 'Scratch' Perry, The Melodians and The Heptones to begin their careers in the '60s. After writing songs for the Rhythm Aces, early that decade, Seaton and Delano Stewart began recording for Clement Dodd as Winston & Bibby; Seaton then fronted The Astronauts, and subsequently formed The Gaylads in 1963. Seaton also founded the independent Links label with Delroy Wilson, Ken Boothe and The Melodians in the late 1960s, but disputes ended the partnership. He went solo for 1973's Thin Line Between Love And Hate and, on

Virgin's Caroline subsidiary, '74's Dancing Shoes, and became an in-house producer at Treasure Isle, where he arranged for Justin Hinds and Claudette Miller, as well writing/producing 1975's early dub set, Gun Court Dub. He ultimately settled in northwest London.

David Katz

Pete Rodriguez

King Of The Boogaloo
BORN 1932

RAISED IN the Bronx to Puerto Rican parents, pianist and bandleader Pete Rodriguez formed his first large ensemble in the mid-'50s after serving in the US navy, playing the lounges and ballrooms of New York. He made his long-playing debut with the boleros, merengues and guajiras of 1964's At Last!, but the Latin/soul hybrid that would be called boogaloo was brewing, and Rodriguez did his bit to bring it to wider notice with 1965's The King Of The Boogaloo and 1967's I Like It Like That (A Mi Me Gusta Asi), whose title

As he liked it: (centre) Pete Rodriguez, Latin soul man supreme.

single was a classic of the genre and was covered by Latin super-band The Blackout All-Stars in 1994. He recorded into the '70s – 1970's team-up LP From Panama To New York saw Ruben Blades make his debut – and later paused

his retirement to appear alongside such fellow Latin heavyweights as Joe Bataan and Johnny Colon on-screen and on-stage for the 2014 Boogaloo documentary titled, inevitably, We Like It Like That.

Ian Harrison

THEY ALSO **SERVED**

GHANAIAN singer, guitarist and songwriter **GEORGE DARKO** (b.1951) played with **The Golden Stool Band** before moving to West Germany in the early '80s. A fan of The Beatles and Hendrix, he became a leading light of the burger-highlife crossover style created by immigrants: his first hit was 1983's infectious Ako Te Brofo. LPs including 1986's Moni Palava and 1988's Soronko followed before he returned to Ghana. Thanks to his Highlife Time getting a release on Charlie Gillett's Oval label, John Peel played him to listeners in 1984.

DRUMMER **JOHN BLUNT** (above, b.1947) joined Merseybeat outfit **The Searchers** after Chris Curtis left in February 1966. The Keith Moon-influenced Blunt brought a more accomplished style as, post-hits, the group attempted to move beyond Merseybeat, with modest success, hitting UK Number 31 in April '66 with Take It Or Leave It, a song gifted by Jagger and Richards. Blunt left in 1969, later working as a taxi driver and playing rock'n'roll in Croydon as **Johnny B. Goode**.

MULTI-INSTRUMENTALIST and singer **VINCENT**

BONHAM (b.1957) was a founder member of Detroit R&B group **Raydio**. The group released four US chart LPs between 1978 and 1981, latterly as **Ray Parker Jr. & Raydio**: the group also scored three US Top 10 singles, including '78's Jack And Jill, also a UK hit. In 2014, Bonham reactivated Raydio.

BASSIST **DENNIS SCHIAVON** (b.1961) played with **The Revillos** from 1981 until 1984, appearing on 1982's LP Attack! and adopting the alter ego Vince Santini. He later joined **The Pork Dukes** and worked with Hereford charity Music Pool.

KARAOKE PIONEER **SHIGEICHI NEGISHI** (below, b.1923) invented the earliest mechanism for revellers to sing over pre-recorded backing tracks. After a colleague at his Tokyo electronics firm commented on his questionable singing voice, he marketed his 'Sparko Box' from 1967 to 1975. The former Japanese POW did not patent his invention, however. He retired aged 70, and devoted his time to sculpture and Japanese basket weaving.

DRUMMER **BRIT TURNER**

(b.1967) co-founded Georgia country rockers **Blackberry Smoke**, alongside bassist brother Richard, in 2000. In 2015 they became the first independent artists to have a Number 1 album on the Billboard Country charts with their fourth LP Holding All The Roses. Turner was diagnosed with glioblastoma in 2022, but continued to play and appeared on the band's last album, Be Right Here, released in February.

MUSICIAN/ACTIVIST **COLA BOYY** (b. Matthew Urango, 1990) was a songwriter, performer and self-proclaimed "disabled disco innovator". Born in Oxnard, California with spina bifida, kyphosis and scoliosis, he was drawn to the city's punk scene and later joined experimental pop group **Sea Lions**. As a solo artist he released his sole LP Prosthetic Boombox in 2021, and collaborated with **The Avalanches**, Air's **Nicolas Godin**, and MGMT's **Andrew VanWyngarden**. He was also a disability and pro-migrant activist.

AUDIO ENGINEER **BOB HEIL** (b.1940) invented the Heil Talk Box in 1973, the voice-and-instrument modulating effects unit which was first used by Joe Walsh and was made famous by 1976's Frampton Comes Alive. Founding PA manufacturer

Heil Sound in Illinois in 1966, Heil also manufactured microphones and radio equipment, and was taken on tour by the Grateful Dead when their gear was confiscated in 1971.

BASSIST **T.M. STEVENS** (below, b.1951) joined the **Pretenders** for 1986's Get Close. He was also a member of **Steve Vai**'s band for 1993's Sex & Religion. Stevens also recorded solo, played sessions for names including **James Brown**, **Tina Turner** and **Joe Cocker**, and was the self-described originator of the 'heavy-metal-funk' style.

GUITARIST **PAUL NELSON** (b.unknown) was born in New York. As a member of the **Johnny Winter Band**, he shared a Best Blues Album Grammy for producing Winter's 2014 album Step Back. His session and touring credits included playing with **Eric Clapton**, **Buddy Guy** and **Dr. John**. He also played with Connecticut speed metallers **Liege Lord**, managed Johnny Winter, and released Badass Generation with his **Paul Nelson Band** in 2016.

PIANIST/COMPOSER **KEVIN TONEY** (b.1953) was a founder member of **The Blackbyrds**, the Washington DC jazz-funk group mentored and produced by

trumpeter **Donald Byrd**. Three of their albums went US gold, with 1975 single Walking In Rhythm selling over a million copies. George Duke produced the disco-fied Better Days before the group disbanded in 1980. Toney recorded 11 solo albums, including 2002's Strut, which soundtracked that year's Winter Olympics.

SINGER AND ACTOR **STEVE LAWRENCE** (b.1935) performed in a duo with **Eydie Gormé**, who he married in 1957, until 2009. Their hits included 1963 UK Top 3 I Want To Stay Here; they were also US TV and Las Vegas stalwarts. From 1952, Lawrence also had 11 solo US Top 30 hits, with Go Away Little Girl a Number 1 in 1963. He played booking agent Maury Sline in both Blues Brothers movies.

SINGER **GREG LEE** (b.1970) was a founder member of Los Angeles ska/reggae torchbearers **Hepcat** in 1989, appearing on their 1990 debut 45 Nigel and six LPs, with 1998's Right On Time causing the biggest stir. The group played three instalments of the Vans Warped Tour, and after several periods of inactivity, were gigging again.

Chris Catchpole, Jenny Bulley and Ian Harrison

Courtesy Munster Records, David Corio/Getty, Hiroko Yoda, Pictorial Press Ltd/Alamy Stock Photo, Gary Miller/Getty

MOJO THE COLLECTORS' SERIES

Music's legends.
MOJO's finest writers.
The full stories.
Available Now!

MOJO THE COLLECTORS' SERIES — MOD ICONS PART ONE
THE WHO
Maximum R&B! The Finest Writers. The Full Story.

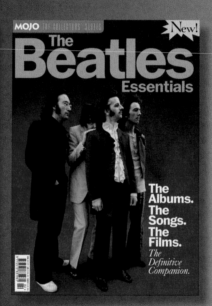

MOJO THE COLLECTORS' SERIES
New!
The Beatles Essentials
The Albums. The Songs. The Films.
The Definitive Companion.

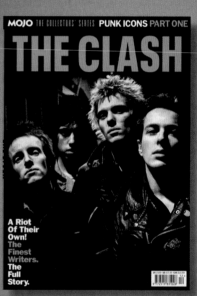

MOJO THE COLLECTORS' SERIES — PUNK ICONS PART ONE
THE CLASH
A Riot Of Their Own! The Finest Writers. The Full Story.

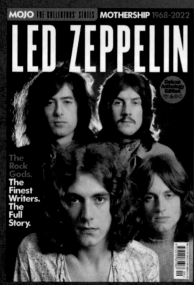

MOJO THE COLLECTORS' SERIES — MOTHERSHIP 1968-2022
LED ZEPPELIN
Deluxe Anthology Edition
The Rock Gods. The Finest Writers. The Full Story.

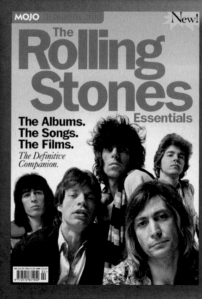

MOJO THE COLLECTORS' SERIES
New!
The Rolling Stones Essentials
The Albums. The Songs. The Films.
The Definitive Companion.

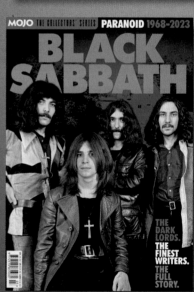

MOJO THE COLLECTORS' SERIES — PARANOID 1968-2023
BLACK SABBATH
The Dark Lords. The Finest Writers. The Full Story.

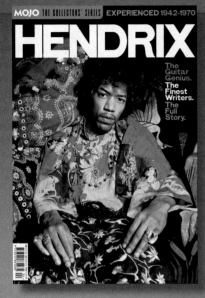

MOJO THE COLLECTORS' SERIES   EXPERIENCED 1942-1970

HENDRIX

The Guitar Genius. **The Finest Writers.** The Full Story.

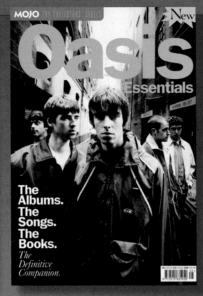

MOJO THE COLLECTORS' SERIES   New

Oasis
Essentials

The Albums. The Songs. The Books. *The Definitive Companion.*

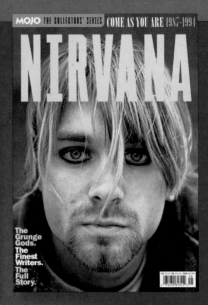

MOJO THE COLLECTORS' SERIES   COME AS YOU ARE 1987-1994

NIRVANA

The Grunge Gods. The Finest Writers. The Full Story.

MOJO THE COLLECTORS' SERIES   New!

Dylan
Essentials

The Albums. The Songs. The Films. *The Definitive Companion.*

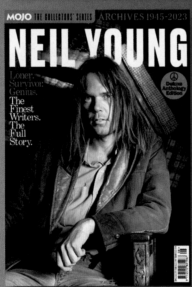

MOJO THE COLLECTORS' SERIES   ARCHIVES 1945-2023

NEIL YOUNG

Loner. Survivor. Genius. The Finest Writers. The Full Story.

Deluxe Anthology Edition

MOJO THE COLLECTORS' SERIES   THE COMPLETE WORKS

QUEEN

The Finest Writers. The Full Story. The Show Must Go On!

Golden Jubilee Special!

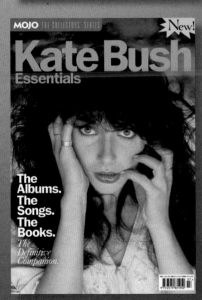

MOJO THE COLLECTORS' SERIES   New!

Kate Bush
Essentials

The Albums. The Songs. The Books. *The Definitive Companion.*

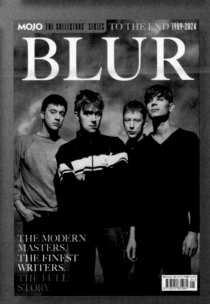

MOJO THE COLLECTORS' SERIES   TO THE END 1989-2024

BLUR

THE MODERN MASTERS. THE FINEST WRITERS. THE FULL STORY.

MOJO THE COLLECTORS' SERIES   New!

Depeche Mode ### Essentials

The Albums. The Songs. The Books. *The Definitive Companion.*

Buy online at greatmagazines.co.uk/mojocollectors

Eastern promise: (clockwise from above) Cheap Trick's Robin Zander on-stage at Nippon Budokan Hall, Tokyo, April 1978; dickie-bowed guitarist Rick Nielsen, 1979; the Tricksters (clockwise from top left) Nielsen, Zander, Bun E. Carlos and Tom Petersson salute Japan.

MAY 1979...
Cheap Trick At
Budokan triumphs

MAY 12 A live album recorded at Tokyo's 14,500-capacity Nippon Budokan Hall had just entered the American Top 100, and would enter the UK Top 10 a week later. This was a special promotional weekend, and British buyers were able to pick up the double set for £5.99 rather than £7.49. But enough about the re-arranged hits collection *Bob Dylan At Budokan*. In the US album charts, Cheap Trick's *At Budokan* had just breached the Top 10, where it would peak at Number 4 and go on to sell more than three million copies.

It had a circuitous route to release. From Rockford, Illinois and not without eccentricity, Cheap Trick were hard-touring pop-rockers who debuted on vinyl in 1977. The highest placing they'd achieved in America was Number 48 for 1978's *Heaven Tonight*, but in Japan, greater sales and adoration – they'd even joined Queen and Kiss as stars of Japanese cartoon strips – were theirs.

Accordingly, in April 1978, the group flew to Japan for a sold-out six-date tour and as much promo as they could handle. To Trouser Press, drummer Bun E Carlos later likened

their response to, "a déjà vu of A Hard Day's Night", while local commentators dubbed their reception 'Trickmania'. Sensing hysteria, Newsday reported that "during one confrontation between 400 Cheap Trick fans, the band and three bodyguards, lead singer Robin Zander was stabbed in the back of the head by a scissor-wielding girl who wanted a lock of his blond hair." Furthermore, guitarist Rick Nielsen was presented with a haul of locally built guitars, one inlaid with the words 'YOU KNOW YOU LIKE IT'.

The gigs went down a storm. The second Budokan show aired on Japanese TV in July,

> ## "Playing long songs is mostly a waste of time."
> TOM PETERSSON

allowing the jubilance to translate even more. With Zander all in white, and baseball-capped, dickie-bowed Rick Nielsen a riffing goofball, songs such as Big Eyes and I Want You To Want Me (later a Top 10 US hit single in its Budokan form) were fat-free and urgent, rocking hard with an eye forever on the power of pop. Unreleased songs Lookout and Need Your Love, and a version of Fats Domino's Ain't That A Shame, further sweetened the pot for Japanese fans. "Playing long songs is mostly a waste of time," bassist Tom Petersson reflected to NME. "Who wants to hear tedious instrumental passages?"

Plans were then drawn for a Japan-only live album to be released that October. Parts of Budokan shows from April 28 and 30 turned out rough – "when we heard the tapes of the concert we thought it sounded hideous," Nielsen told the LA Weekly – and mixing supervisor Jack Douglas later said that recordings from an Osaka gig on April 27 were interpolated. As well as mixing audience screams as low as possible, discreet audio polishing and restoration took place at New York's Record Plant. Like a Japan-only advert by a western celebrity – think Sylvester Stallone endorsing Itoham processed meat; or Roger Moore's wacky TV spots for Lark

Getty (8)

cigarettes – it wasn't like anyone was going to check.

Then, buoyed by US radio play, it began to sell in big numbers on import. And so *At Budokan* was granted an American release in February '79: it also peaked at 29 in the UK, where it was released as *At The Budokan*, with 10,000 copies pressed on what was questionably dubbed 'Kamikaze Yellow' translucent vinyl.

The band were wrong-footed by *At Budokan*'s success, with Petersson later telling Sounds, "it kept going up and up… it's like, Wait a minute! It's almost like a joke, come on, they gotta be kidding…" They even had to let already-recorded new album *Dream Police* wait eight months while they let the success of *At Budokan* play itself out. In September, *Dream Police* peaked at US Number 6, their highest album chart placing.

Bun E Carlos has now retired, but Cheap Trick remain a working band. Inducted into the Rock and Roll Hall of Fame in 2016, they tour the UK in November supporting Journey. The Budokan is also still open for business, and thanks to its rich acoustics and always-appreciative crowds, it remains a popular venue for recording live LPs. Blur, Eric Clapton and Chic are among those who did just that, but there's one band who are synonymous with the storied venue, as Cheap Trick follow-ups *Budokan II* (1994), *At Budokan: The Complete Concert* (1998) and 30th anniversary four-disc set *Budokan!* (2008) confirmed. "We were tailor-made for Japan," reflected Nielsen in 2008. "We just didn't know it."

Ian Harrison

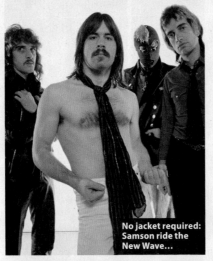

No jacket required: Samson ride the New Wave…

NWOBHM is born

MAY 19 Sounds reports on a May 8 gig at Camden's Music Machine promoted by metal DJ Neal Kay, when Angel Witch, Iron Maiden and Samson all play. Writer Geoff Barton notes that Angel Witch wear cheese cloth and loons and play Black Sabbath's Paranoid, Iron Maiden's Dave Murray clangs his guitar with a crowd-member's home-made cardboard flying V, and argues that Samson's use of stage pyrotechnics is better than Kiss (he's also struck by masked drummer Thunderstick). While admitting to certain reservations about the bands, he's impressed, and the intro to the write-up features the first use of the phrase 'The New Wave of British Heavy Metal.' The wording was later credited to Sounds editor Alan Lewis.

ALSO ON!

STRUMMER AS PM!
5 As a general election looms, The Clash's Joe Strummer (above) beats Tom Robinson and Siouxsie Sioux as the NME readers' choice for Prime Minister. As leader of the Riot Party, he promises to legalise graffiti and ganja, proposes Lemmy as Minister of Health, and says Margaret Thatcher will be deported to Uganda.

SQUARES FREAK!
7 US TV game show The Hollywood Squares has an all-music special: contestants include Chaka Khan, Todd Rundgren, the Commodores, Kiki Dee, KC of The Sunshine Band and Pete Way from UFO.

HELLO, CURE
8 The Cure's debut LP *Three Imaginary Boys* is released. Tour dates this month include Northwich Memorial Hall (17), Birmingham Barbarella's (22) and Sheffield's The Limit (29).

RIP LESTER FLATT
11 Bluegrass guitar and mandolin great Lester Flatt dies of heart failure in Nashville aged 64. Rising to fame with Bill Monroe's band in the '40s, he later played in a duo with Earl Scruggs and the Foggy Mountain Boys.

BOWIE SWINGS
18 David Bowie's 13th album *Lodger* is released. With 45 Boys Keep Swinging in the Top 10, the LP debuts at 5. This month Bowie also shoots videos with David Mallet for Boys Keep Swinging, Look Back In Anger and D.J., and parties at NY's Studio 54.

TOP TEN

SWITZERLAND SINGLES MAY 1

1 HEART OF GLASS BLONDIE CHRYSALIS

2 HOORAY! HOORAY! IT'S A HOLI-HOLIDAY BONEY M HANSA

3 DSCHINGIS KHAN DSCHINGIS KHAN JUPITER

4 TRAGEDY BEE GEES RSO

5 ONE WAY TICKET ERUPTION HANSA

6 CHIQUITITA ABBA POLYDOR

7 SANDOKAN OLIVER ONIONS RCA VICTOR

8 IN THE NAVY VILLAGE PEOPLE BARCLAY

9 BORN TO BE ALIVE PATRICK HERNANDEZ AQUARIUS

10 YMCA VILLAGE PEOPLE BARCLAY

No return: Eruption on a One Way Ticket at 5.

All Mod cons: (above) The Who's Roger Daltrey at the Rainbow, May 2, '79; (right) scene revivalists Secret Affair.

THE WHO COME BACK

MAY 2 The Who play their first concert since Keith Moon's death, at London's Rainbow Theatre, with ex-Faces drummer Kenney Jones. "The Who is the best drug in the world," Pete Townshend tells Melody Maker of the gig. "I felt weird but it was great." Later in the month, Who movies Quadrophenia and The Kids Are Alright are premiered at the Cannes Film Festival. There's also Mod revival activity: on May 7, bands including Secret Affair, Squire and The Mods are recorded for the *Mods Mayday '79* LP at the Bridge House, Canning Town, while a bash in Bishop's Stortford on May 26 features Purple Hearts. "It's a shame they can't find their own thing," muses Townshend.

AD ARCHIVE 1979

Is this how the Tories would look at Youth Unemployment?

VOTE LABOUR on Thursday.

The Labour Party say DO NOT vote for Margaret Thatcher's Conservatives in the May 3 UK general election. If only they'd known, etc.

When have two bands shared a name?

Let us answer your music-related queries and put musical dilemmas to rest.

I found a Sham 69 LP on Spotify called *To The Ends Of The Earth*, which isn't by the current Jimmy Pursey-led Sham, but another with latterday frontman Tim V singing. What other band names have been used by different line-ups at the same time?

Alan Lloyd, via e-mail

MOJO says: If it's not a case of plain old name-lifting by strangers – see the fake Frankie Goes To Hollywood from Alabama, or the Norwegian Popol Vuh, which was apparently an honest mistake – distinct yet connected groups using the same name is rare but does happen. Faust existed in two formations for years, one led by Werner 'Zappi' Diermaier and Jean-Hervé Péron, and another by Hans Joachim Irmler (and now it seems Zappi has his own Faust). There were also two bands called The Sweet in the 2010s, led by Andy Scott (for Europe) and Steve Priest (for North America). While they waited for a judgment from our learned friends, for a time there were two bands called Queensrÿche, who both released LPs in 2013. The '…featuring…' option is an effective legal salve in off-shoots for groups including Yes, UB40, Asia and Starship. It's also worth reflecting on the two Sonny Boy Williamsons, how Tom Petty and Johnny Thunders were both backed by groups called The Heartbreakers, and the strange case of identical twins Jay and Michael Aston's band Gene Loves Jezebel. A post-split court case concluded that Jay's band can be Gene Loves Jezebel in Britain and Jay Aston's Gene Loves Jezebel in the US, while Michael's band is Gene Loves Jezebel in the US and Michael Aston's Gene Loves Jezebel in the UK. Got that? Feel free to tell us your favourites!

A PUN TOO FAR

A fellow listener told me they'd never realised that Sandie Shaw was meant to suggest a sandy shore, which until that moment, I had never realised either. What are the other too-good-to-notice punning names of musical history?

Nick Draper, via e-mail

MOJO says: Sandie Shaw/sandy shore is a great example of not seeing something that should be obvious. Other handles which straddle meaning in this way, many of which seem to be from the punk *oeuvre*, include Adam Ant (adamant), Ari Up (hurry up, Cockney-style), Rezillos' Fay Fife ("fae Fife" in the local vernacular), Boomtown Rat Pete Briquette (after the peat kindling), Perry Farrell ("peripheral") and Pat Smear (pap smear). And does everyone see what's happening with Lipps.Inc, the Electric Light Orchestra and Rose Royce? Please send us examples of the form. For now we'll leave it with the bassist from the Dwarves – HeWhoCannotBeNamed.

WAYWARD LP TITLE SONGS REVISITED

Re: Which LPs don't include their title track? (Ask MOJO 365) We've had a torrent of suggestions. Album title songs only released on single formats include Emerson, Lake & Palmer's Brain Salad Surgery, Ride's Going Blank Again, Tears For Fears' Songs From The Big Chair, The Teardrop Explodes' Kilimanjaro, and Guided

By Voices' Bee Thousand and Alien Lanes, which are both on 1993 EP The Grand Hour. Title songs that appeared on different albums number Julian Cope's World Shut Your Mouth (an LP in '84, a song on *Saint Julian* in 1986), Gomez's Bring It On (an LP title in '98, on 1999's *Liquid Skin*), Ultravox's Systems Of Romance (an album in '78, on John Foxx's '81 solo album *The Garden*), and Pete Townshend's Face Dances (title of The Who's 1981 LP, which appeared on Pete's '82 solo record *All The Best Cowboys Have Chinese Eyes*). Thanks to contributing readers Jono Roseveare, Rob Kirby, Tom Clayton, William Allen, Adie Turner and Si Farrier.

HELP MOJO

The Beatles were scheduled to appear on Sunday Night At The London Palladium. The headlining act always appeared at the end of the show. But this time, the curtains opened at the beginning, and there were the four of them – though all in shadow. The audience went mental. Then the lights came up and it was the host (I think, Norman Vaughan) and three stagehands all holding broomsticks as guitars. Hilarious. I remember it distinctly, but I've never seen it mentioned in any of the countless books I've read about the Fab Four. Does anybody else recall this, or did I just dream it?

James O'Brien, via e-mail

Double trouble: Faust's Jean-Hervé Péron in 1996; Sandie Shaw likes to be beside the sandy shore; Emerson, Lake & Palmer's *Brain Salad Surgery* LP did not include the title song; curtain-raiser: comedian Norman Vaughan, with his wife, opened for the Fabs.

CONTACT MOJO

Have you got a challenging musical question for the MOJO Brains Trust? E-mail askmojo@bauermedia.co.uk and we'll help untangle your trickiest puzzles.

Getty (3)

Shades Of The King

Win! Renauld luxury sunglasses with a real piece of **Elvis.**

A FAMOUS ELVIS quote runs as follows: "My fans want my shirt. They can have my shirt. They put it on my back." The chance to own a piece of Elvis's shirt comes with a new range of luxury sunglasses from revived '60s label Renauld. The Elvis 'Tupelo special', worth a cool £695, contains an actual piece of one of Elvis's shirts, housed within the lens. This patented and radical Renauld precision lens engineering seamlessly integrates a wafer-thin, transparent and vacuum-sealed compartment into the aerodynamic shape of the lens. That compartment forever encapsulates part of Elvis's actual wardrobe. Each sunglass arrives with a Renauld and Graceland certificate of authenticity.

We have one pair to give away to a lucky reader with a stylish summer to look forward to. How to enter: take the letters from each coloured square below and rearrange them to form the name of a musician. Visit www.mojo4music.com/crossword and fill out the form, along with your answer, in the provided field. Entry is free and closes at midnight on **June 2, 2024.** Winners are selected at random. For the rules of the quiz, see www.mojo4music.com.

For more info visit: www.renauld.co.uk

ANSWERS

MOJO 365

Across: 1 Lionel Richie, 8 Sue, 9 Shipbuilding, 11 Strategy, 13 Satisfaction, 18 OP, 20 Gardens, 21 Scaramouche, 23 We, 24 Cud, 25 School's Out, 27 Eagles, 28 Edison, 29 Yeah, 31 Onion, 33 Om, 34 Evil, 36 Acid, 37 Now, 39 Camel, 41 Byford, 43 Tower, 44 AC, 45 Jawbone, 46 Ash, 47 Oh Well, 50 Aslan, 51 Juno, 52 Prick, 54 Dio, 55 O My Soul, 57 Smooth, 58 Adverts, 60 Abacab, 61 Is, 62 Yod, 64 Pye, 65 Eponymous, 66 Junk.

Down: 1 Lost And Found, 2 Oliver Nelson, 3 Embryo, 4 Rails, 5 Cadet, 6 Inn, 7 Buzzcocks, 10 Gift Of Love, 12 Trance, 14 Adam, 15 I'm A Man, 16 Ice Cream For Crow, 17 Noddy Holder, 19 Pseudo, 22 Woe, 26 Timmy Thomas, 27 Eon, 30 Mantrap, 31 Oil Well, 32 Norah Jones, 35 LC, 38 Brel, 40 Grandaddy, 42 Warp, 47 Ono, 48 Ecstasy, 49 Laura, 53 Rambo, 56 Chakk, 57 Says, 59 Top, 61 In, 63 DJ.

Anagram: Syd Barrett

Winner: Ron Unwin wins a Lenco LS-600WA record deck with built-in amplifier and Bluetooth.

ACROSS

1 See photoclue A (6,5)
7 Underworld's Batman & Robin complainant (6)
10 First UK punk 45, by The Damned? (3,4)
11 Noah House Of Dread cover Tony Hatch and Jackie Trent's Aussie soap theme (10)
12 X's John --- (3)
14 For dessert, Dick Cuthell's group (6)
16 After the Talking stopped, Tina, Chris and Jerry were The ----- (5)
17 See photoclue B (8)
18 Corinne Bailey, Jesse or Mark (3)
19 London culture centre where the C86 crowd played (3)
20 See 44 across (6)
21 Ryan, Oleta or Craig (5)
22 Sting's 1985 song of Cold War apprehension (7)
24 Blur tune with a Bowie/Eno co-writing credit (1,1,1)
25 UK music copyright collective (1,1,1)
26 Kula Shaker's debut hit (6)
27 Dance favoured by Fleetwood Mac (5)
28 Wayne Shorter, and so on, in 1980 (8)
30 Note well this Natasha Bedingfield album (1,1)
32 *Hearken To The Witches* ---- (Dave & Toni Arthur) (4)
34 Black Dog Productions snap in '93 (5)
35 Wolfmother's was *Cosmic* (3)
37 Ex-Fall members' escape vehicle (3)
38 They went through the desert on A Horse With No Name (7)
41 The Wu-Tang Clan's Abbot (3)
43 Nick Cave's song of Elvis's birth (6)
44 and 20 across New York club (8,6)
46 Wishbone Ash's biggest LP (5)
47 All Tomorrow's Parties festival's label (4)
49 Polvo's last '90s LP (6)
50 1989 New Order live film (7)
52 ------ Sportivo, Dutch new wavers (6)
53 The Beautiful South's was Perfect (3)
55 Van Morrison, Laura Brannigan and U2 all had songs of this title (6)
56 Jello Biafra teams up with Ministry (4)
57 Jenny Fabian's cult rock book (7)
58 Elliott Smith's penultimate LP (2)
59 Tony Allen meets Moritz von Oswald in 2007 (3)
60 Belgian Middle East/psych outfit ---------- Drive (10)
62 Laibach seek European security in '94 (4)
64 Pluto Shervington's 1976 UK hit (3)
65 Judas Priest's prophetic concept LP (11)

DOWN

1 Blue Öyster Cult reflect on death (4,4,3,6)
2 Fabs song for Jeremy Hillary Boob? (7,3)
3 Kate Bush's hastily recorded second (9)
4 See photoclue C (5,5)
5 Throbbing Gristle/Psychic TV provocateur (7,1,7)
6 Multi-instrumentalist who played with Randy Newman, Leonard Cohen etc (4,6)
7 Alan Hawkshaw's band who recorded The Champ (7)
8 Smashing Pumpkins' fanbase-dividing work of 1998 (5)
9 Billy MacKenzie and Steve Aungle, with no time for Brexit (11)
13 The Last Poets' song of jazz giants and heroin (1,1)
15 NY anarcho-punks who debuted with *Youth Anthems For The New Order* (6,5)
23 Much-missed Small Faces/Humble Pie/Packet Of Three singer and guitarist (5,8)
29 Pink Floyd's early alias (3,3)
31 Happy Mondays' maracas player (3)
33 Roxy/Crimson prog superband (1,1)
36 Bringers of Oops Upside Your Head (3,4)
39 AKA James Newell Osterberg (4,3)
40 Insult used by Sebadoh (7)
41 Elvis movie featuring Little Egypt (10)
42 Lee Perry's were in Moonlight (10)
45 John Mayer's song for The Bucket List movie (3)
48 Peter Gabriel was Rated -- (1,1)
49 The Exploited on police matters (1,1,1)
51 Michigan's Queen Of Pop (7)
54 Pet Shop Boys EP featuring Give Stupidity A Chance (10)
58 Lord Rockingham's magic number (2)
60 Jim Diamond's learned duo (2,1)
61 Trent Reznor's industrial rockers (1,1,1)
63 John Dwyer's unruly outfit (3)

Getty (2), Wilko Wilkinson

Superpower trio: The Crucial Three's vital sparks (from left) Julian Cope, Pete Wylie, Ian McCulloch; (below) Wylie today.

Pete Wylie and The Crucial Three

It began when the singers of three legendary Liverpool bands collided at a Clash gig. But six weeks later, it fizzled.

HELLO MAY 1977

It was in the summer of '77, which sounds like a folk song. I was mates with Ian McCulloch, and on October 1, 1976 [Liverpool punk crucible] Eric's opened. We became regulars. That was the key, really.

The night The Clash played [May 5, 1977], I got right down to the front and the guy next to me starts doing this weird back and forth dance, and after 40 seconds I said, "Stop dancing like that or I'll twat yer." That was Julian Cope, who says, "Why don't we form a band instead?" We're all buzzing and sweating. I had no idea who he was, he was at teacher training college, but there was a lot of that going on. At the end of the gig, I introduced Mac – it was his 18th birthday, a night of significance anyway.

The name came from a mate from school who was studying economics, who said, "We've got to learn these three things, they're the crucial three." We rehearsed in my mother's house first, on Sonning Road, Liverpool L4 9RJ. My mate Spenner became the drummer, on a straight back chair played with a pair of knitting needles. Julian had a bass and I had my little cheap electric. Mac had some very solid song ideas – one was called I'm Bloody Sure You're On Dope, which was on E and F, a bit Lou Reed. (Sings) "I'm bloody sure you're on dope/All I know is I can't cope." Another one I wrote the music for

was called the Salomine Shuffle, which was kind of Doors-y, and Spacehopper, which is different to the version Julian did later. Spenner had one as well, LAMMAFOM, which was 'Look at me making a fool of myself'. Mac never sang, he just kind of hunched over while we played. We took it on trust that he was preparing his performance in his head, shall we say. It wasn't a great master plan, but it was pretty good, you know. It was more than fine. It was great and we were a band. We were The Crucial Three.

GOODBYE JUNE 1977

There was nearly another member of The Crucial Three. I said, "There's this postman called Colin who plays guitar…", and Julian said "no, no, no", and he went over and just told him, "We're forming a band and you won't be in it." I was astonished. Julian was middle-class, he had a confidence about him. Pretty soon we realised that his ideas and ours weren't the same.

We had a last rehearsal in my mum's. Julian had this Fender bass copy, he's painted it industrial grey and stencilled a lyric he'd written on it which said, roughly – this was the clincher – "and the apathy that's spreading through our country's furthest shores." Me and Mac both looked at each

other and went, "Uh-oh". That was what made us kind of say, "stop". It's also about us being that petty in a way. I think it just wore off and we let it fizzle out. It didn't bother us. This is punk rock time, where everything was exciting all the time! You just got on with other things.

I never worked with Mac again but I worked with Julian, we formed the Mystery Girls with Pete Burns, and The Nova Mob. I loved the [Cope-fronted] Teardrop Explodes and early [McCulloch-fronted] Bunnymen, and they formed more of an alliance. Then I was in Wah! Heat, and we all became somebody else.

Our problems came when, because [in the press] we were just mouths on a stick, coming up with some sarcasm, some quip about each other, and we all ended up taking them to heart. I felt hurt and I identified it as anger. One of the aspects of my ADHD is called RSD – not Record Store Day – which is Rejection Sensitivity Dysphoria, which is basically a disproportionate reaction to a perceived slight. For years and years me and Julian never spoke, but I became friends with his wife Dorian on Twitter, and now she's a conduit, you know?

We were all different personalities but we fit together in a weird way. Now more than ever, I fundamentally love them. It used to drive me a little bit mad when they said The Crucial Three wasn't ever a real thing. But it was. I could play you the songs now. We never played live, no. Could we? I'm ready now!

As told to Ian Harrison

Teach Yself Wah! – A Best Of Pete Wylie & The Mighty Wah! is out now on Chrysalis Records.

"One song was called I'm Bloody Sure You're On Dope."
PETE WYLIE

© Paul Ripley, Camera Press/Paul Slattery (2), Getty Images/Kevin Cummins